The Philosophy of Social Evolution

From mitochondria to meerkats, the natural world is full of spectacular examples of social behaviour. In the early 1960s Bill Hamilton changed the way we think about how such behaviour evolves. He introduced three key innovations—now known as *Hamilton's rule, kin selection,* and *inclusive fitness*—which have been highly influential, yet remain the subject of fierce controversy.

Hamilton's pioneering work kick-started a research program now known as social evolution theory. This is a book about the conceptual foundations and future prospects of that program. Part I, 'Foundations', provides an organizing framework for social evolution research based on Hamilton's ideas. The framework clarifies the explanatory roles of Hamilton's rule, kin selection and inclusive fitness, acknowledging their limitations while defending their enduring value. Part II, 'Extensions', shows how these ideas can be applied to cooperation in micro-organisms, cooperation among the cells of a multicellular organism, and culturally evolved cooperation in the earliest human societies. Birch argues that real progress can be made in understanding microbial evolution, evolutionary transitions, and human evolution by viewing them through the lens of Hamilton's ideas, provided those ideas are interpreted with care and adapted where necessary.

The Philosophy of Social Evolution places social evolution theory on firm conceptual foundations and sets out exciting new directions for further work.

Jonathan Birch is an Associate Professor in the Department of Philosophy, Logic and Scientific Method at the London School of Economics and Political Science, specializing in the philosophy of evolutionary biology. His research mainly concerns the evolution of social behaviour, with a particular focus on the work of W. D. Hamilton. He has published widely on various topics in the philosophy of the life sciences, in journals such as *The American Naturalist, Current Biology, Biological Reviews, Philosophy of Science* and *The British Journal for the Philosophy of Science.*

The Philosophy of
Social Evolution

Jonathan Birch

OXFORD
UNIVERSITY PRESS

Great Clarendon Street, Oxford, OX2 6DP,
United Kingdom

Oxford University Press is a department of the University of Oxford.
It furthers the University's objective of excellence in research, scholarship,
and education by publishing worldwide. Oxford is a registered trade mark of
Oxford University Press in the UK and in certain other countries

First Edition published in 2017
First published in paperback 2019

Published in the United States of America by Oxford University Press
198 Madison Avenue, New York, NY 10016, United States of America

British Library Cataloguing in Publication Data
Data available

Library of Congress Cataloging in Publication Data
Data available

ISBN 978-0-19-873305-8 (Hbk.)
ISBN 978-0-19-885168-4 (Pbk.)

For Caroline

Contents

Part II. Extensions

Acknowledgements

I thank all the audiences at seminars where I have presented parts of this material, all the readers who have sent me comments and questions, and all my present and former colleagues at the London School of Economics and Political Science (LSE) and the University of Cambridge. I especially thank Tim Lewens for his support over many years.

I am very grateful to Caroline Birch, Andrew Buskell, Ellen Clarke, Steve Frank, Peter Godfrey-Smith, Heikki Helanterä, James Marshall, Samir Okasha, Hannah Rubin, Tobias Uller, two anonymous readers for Oxford University Press (OUP), and reading groups at UC Irvine and the Australian National University (ANU) for their comments on a draft manuscript. They really helped to shape my thinking as I prepared the final version. I am also grateful to Peter Momtchiloff and his colleagues at OUP, Clement Raj and his colleagues at SPi Global, Christine Boylan, Kathleen Gill, and Fiona Tatham for turning the manuscript into a book.

The book incorporates some material from my own journal articles, and I thank the publishers for permitting the re-use of that material. The articles are 'Gene Mobility and the Concept of Relatedness' (*Biology and Philosophy* 29(4), 2014); 'Hamilton's Two Conceptions of Social Fitness' (*Philosophy of Science* 83(5), 2016); and 'Kin Selection, Group Selection and the Varieties of Population Structure' (*The British Journal for the Philosophy of Science*, in press).

The writing of this book was generously supported by a Philip Leverhulme Prize from the Leverhulme Trust, and by visiting fellowships at UC Irvine and ANU. I also gratefully acknowledge the support I've received over the years from the LSE, the Arts and Humanities Research Council, and Christ's College, Cambridge.

Most of all, I thank my wife Caroline, my parents Peter and Marie, and my sister Rosie for their love and encouragement.

Jonathan Birch

LSE
July 2017

List of Figures and Boxes

Figures

Boxes

Jumping into the River...

In what circumstances does natural selection favour self-sacrifice? As legend has it, the best known answer to this question was first spoken in a London pub, the Orange Tree, that once stood at the corner of Gower Street and Euston Road. One unspecified night in the 1950s, after 'calculating on the back of an envelope for some minutes', the UCL geneticist J. B. S. Haldane remarked to one of his graduate students, John Maynard Smith, that 'he was prepared to lay down his life for eight cousins or two brothers' (Maynard Smith, 1975).

If the story is true, Haldane had latched on to a profound insight about the evolution of cooperation.[1] He had seen that genetically related organisms may, in certain circumstances, have an evolutionary incentive to help one another. He had also seen that the incentive comes in degrees, and that the size of the incentive depends on the closeness of the helper's genetic relationship to the potential beneficiary. Haldane may not have been the first to see these things—R. A. Fisher has a good claim to that accolade—but he may have been the first to glimpse their potential explanatory power.[2] In a 1955 article, he illustrated these ideas with a vivid example:

---

[1] Hamilton vigorously disputed Maynard Smith's account, but eventually came to accept it; see Segerstrale (2013, Chs. 12, 14, and 15). There is no conclusive proof of Haldane's pub quip, although it makes for a lovely story.

[2] In a discussion of why some insects have evolved to be distasteful to predators, Fisher (1930, Ch. 7) observed that, although the trait is unlikely to benefit an eaten individual, it may benefit its siblings; and he writes that 'the selective potency of the avoidance of brothers will of course be only half as great as if the individual itself were protected'. Hamilton, who had read Fisher's book closely as an undergraduate, noted this, along with Haldane's (1955) paper, as an early precursor of his own theory (Hamilton, 1964). In a sense, the whole theory can be seen as a careful unpacking of Fisher's 'of course'. Sometimes the notion of kin selection is projected back even further—on to Darwin—but I regard this as rather tenuous (for reasons set out by Ratnieks and Helanterä 2009 and Ratnieks et al. 2011).

Let us suppose that you carry a rare gene which affects your behaviour so that you jump into a river and save a child, but you have one chance in ten of being drowned, while I do not possess the gene, and stand on the bank and watch the child drown. If the child is your own child or your brother or sister, there is an even chance that the child will also have the gene, so five such genes will be saved in children for one lost in an adult. If you save a grandchild or nephew the advantage is only two and a half to one. If you only save a first cousin, the effect is very slight. If you try to save your first cousin once removed the population is more likely to lose this valuable gene than to gain it.   (Haldane, 1955, p. 44)

He went on, however, to suggest that this idea was probably more applicable to insects than to humans:

But on the two occasions when I have pulled possibly drowning people out of the water (at an infinitesimal risk to myself) I had no time to make such calculations. Palaeolithic men did not make them. It is clear that genes making for conduct of this kind would only have a chance of spreading in rather small populations where most of the children were fairly near relatives of the man who risked his life. It is not easy to see how, except in small populations, such genes could have been established. Of course the conditions are even better in a community such as a beehive or an ants' nest, whose members are all literally brothers and sisters.
(Haldane, 1955, p. 44)

Although Haldane never captured these thoughts in a mathematical model, we can see in this verbal description the subtlety of his thinking. He saw a gene for altruism might spread if the benefits fell differentially on other bearers of the gene, but he also realized that a mechanism that relied on individual organisms consciously calculating degrees of kinship was implausible. His proposed solution was 'small populations': if a population is so small that everyone is a close relative of everyone else, the benefits of altruism will tend to fall on genetically similar individuals without the need for any conscious calculation.

The Orange Tree was demolished in the spring of 1963. In the aftermath of the demolition, the Beatles arrived for a photoshoot, and a shot of them leaping above the rubble of Haldane's old haunt would be used as the cover for their 1963 EP, *Twist and Shout*.[3] Elsewhere in London,

---

[3] The photoshoot is documented by Schreuders et al. (2008, pp. 55–7). To my knowledge, no one has previously noted the Haldane connection. The site directly adjoins Tolmers Square, where, in the 1970s, a battle raged between developers and squatters over the fate of the old Victorian tenements (Wates, 1976). One of the squatters was George Price (of the 'Price equation'), who lived there in the months prior to his death in 1975 (Harman, 2010).

probably on a bus or in a railway station, a graduate student called Bill Hamilton was making leaps of a different kind.[4] He was busily preparing a manuscript for submission to the *Journal of Theoretical Biology*, entitled 'The Genetical Evolution of Social Behaviour', which he intended to complement a short note (entitled 'The Evolution of Altruistic Behavior') that had just been accepted by *The American Naturalist*.

Hamilton had independently arrived at a more general form of Haldane's insight, and he had formalized it in a rigorous and detailed mathematical framework. Crucially, he showed that the general sort of process Haldane had described did not require 'rare genes' or 'rather small populations'. Whenever organisms interact differentially with relatives—whether this is due to active kin recognition, or simply due to ecological mechanisms that keep organisms fairly close to their birth site—the conditions are potentially apt for the evolution of altruism. Hamilton also realized that the same framework could extend beyond altruism to explain other kinds of social behaviour: behaviour that was selfish, spiteful, or mutually beneficial. That 1964 paper became one of the most influential in the history of evolutionary theory. The ideas it contained—ideas now known as Hamilton's rule, kin selection and inclusive fitness—changed the way we think about the evolution of social behaviour.

Maynard Smith, by this time a lecturer at UCL, played a pivotal role in getting Hamilton's 1964 paper accepted, and in bringing Hamilton's ideas to a wider audience (Maynard Smith, 1964), but he infuriated Hamilton by attributing the basic idea of kin selection to Haldane (Segerstrale, 2013, Ch. 12). The 1955 article makes it clear that Haldane did conceive of a form of kin selection in an informal and imprecise way, but perhaps not with the sort of quantitative precision he displayed in the alleged pub quip. In any case, there is no doubt that Hamilton deserves the credit—and probably more credit than Maynard Smith gave him—for developing a formal theory of social evolution with that simple idea at its centre.

---

[4] Hamilton's institutional affiliation at this time was somewhat ambiguous. His graduate work was funded through a Leverhulme scholarship in the Department of Sociology at the LSE, and his 1963 paper carries that address. But he was also part-registered with the Galton Laboratory at UCL, and he gave this as the address for his 1964 paper. He appears to have preferred to work in his rented bedsit in 14 Hadley Gardens, Chiswick, on the top of buses, and in Waterloo station (Segerstrale, 2013).

Hamilton's pioneering work kickstarted a research program now known as social evolution theory—a program in which the concepts of relatedness, kin selection and inclusive fitness continue to play a central role (Frank, 1998; Wenseleers et al., 2010; Bourke, 2011; Marshall, 2015). This is a book about the conceptual foundations and future prospects of that program. I aim to defend the value of Hamilton's basic insights in the face of recent criticism, to clarify a number of thorny issues concerning the structure of social evolution theory as it is today, and to argue that the theory, when suitably extended, has the resources to explain phenomena at first glance far removed from the beehive and the ants' nest, including cooperation in microbes, cooperation among the cells of a multicellular organism, and culturally evolved cooperation among the 'Palaeolithic men' (and women) who evidently occupied Haldane's thoughts.

0.1 Proximate and Ultimate

On 1 February 1961, while Hamilton was struggling with his early models, Ernst Mayr, a professor of Zoology at Harvard, gave a lecture at MIT called 'Cause and Effect in Biology', his contribution to a longer series of lectures on the theme of 'cause and effect' (Mayr, 1961; Lerner, 1965). In that lecture, Mayr drew what would become a highly influential distinction between two types of biological cause.

Underlying Mayr's distinction was the idea that animal behaviour is controlled by a genetic program. This concept of a genetic program leads naturally to a distinction between those causes, such as natural selection, that are responsible for the gradual shaping of genetic programs over evolutionary time; and those causes, such as developmental, physiological, and cognitive mechanisms, that are responsible for decoding and executing the genetic program during the life cycle of a particular organism.[5] Mayr referred to the former as *ultimate causes* and the latter as *proximate causes*. He regarded the former as the proper subject matter of evolutionary biology.

---

[5] See Mayr (1993) for a particularly clear statement of how Mayr understood the proximate-ultimate distinction. The close connection of this distinction to the concept of a genetic program—already very clear in Mayr (1961)—is set out even more transparently here.

Social evolution theory is concerned with ultimate causes, and so is this book. However, my conception of 'ultimate causes' is somewhat more liberal than Mayr's. Recently, Kevin Laland and colleagues (2011, 2013) have questioned whether the proximate-ultimate distinction is useful at all. They cite processes such as niche construction (Odling-Smee et al., 2003), developmental plasticity (West-Eberhard, 2003), and social learning (Heyes and Galef, 1996; Avital and Jablonka, 2000; Richerson and Boyd, 2005): processes that clearly matter to both evolution and development, but that seem to involve neither the writing nor the execution of a genetic program. I agree with Laland et al. about the importance of these processes, and about the misleading nature of the 'genetic program' concept—and hence of the proximate-ultimate distinction as Mayr conceived it—when these processes are at work. But I see this as a reason to frame the proximate-ultimate distinction in a different way—a way more accommodating of the sorts of processes Laland et al. highlight—rather than a reason to abandon it altogether.

The key, I suggest, is to drop any reference to genetic programs. All we really need, in order to draw a useful proximate-ultimate distinction, is the idea that a behavioural phenotype has an associated *transmissible basis*—a basis which may be partially or even wholly non-genetic—that explains its recurrence across the generations. We can then say that the ultimate causes of a behavioural phenotype are those which explain the origin and maintenance, over evolutionary time, of its transmissible basis in a population of organisms; whereas the proximate causes of a behavioural phenotype are those which explain, in the context of the life cycle of a particular organism, the relationship between the phenotype's transmissible basis and its manifest form.

So, although genes are a very important form of transmissible basis, I think we should allow that in at least some cases—and perhaps especially in the case of humans—non-genetic processes of inheritance, such as cultural and ecological inheritance, also matter, and that the domain of proximate-causal explanation includes questions about how the manifest form of a phenotype relates to these non-genetic transmissible bases. Similarly, although natural selection is a particularly interesting and important cause of the origin and maintenance of the transmissible basis of phenotypes, we should allow that many other processes, including forms of cultural evolution and niche construction, can also be genuine ultimate causes.[6,7]

This pluralistic view about ultimate causes rarely surfaces in Part I of this book, Foundations, which focusses almost exclusively on one particular, much-studied type of ultimate cause: natural selection acting on parentally inherited genetic variation in a constant environment. I focus on this type of cause because it is the focus of Hamilton's work, and the overarching aim of Part I is to clarify the conceptual structure of the theory of social evolution we owe to Hamilton.

In Part II, however, I branch out in various directions, exploring the impact of 'horizontal' (i.e. nonparental) transmission on the genetic (Chapter 6) and cultural (Chapter 8) evolution of cooperation, as well as considering the feedback effects of group size on the evolution of social complexity (Chapter 7). A recurring theme of Part II is the ability of organisms to alter their social neighbourhoods (e.g. through gene mobility, through teaching others, or through promoting the growth of the group) in ways that feed back into the response to selection, an idea Powers et al. (2011) have termed 'social niche construction'. The overall argument of Part II is that Hamilton's ideas are even more powerful, and can explain even more about the natural world, when we relax some of the assumptions about inheritance that characterized his original models.

0.2 Foundations and Extensions

Here is a brief preview of what is to come. In Part I, Foundations, I aim to construct a coherent picture of the conceptual structure of social evolution theory, a picture that distinguishes the different explanatory

---

[6] My view here has affinities with the 'extended replicator' view of Sterelny et al. (1996), which also aims to make room for the fact that phenotypic traits can have non-genetic transmissible bases. However, I do not think the transmissible basis of phenotypic traits must take the form of replicators. For example, cultural transmission need not involve replicators (see Chapter 8). For further discussion of non-genetic inheritance, see Mameli (2004); Jablonka and Lamb (2005); Helanterä and Uller (2010).

[7] For further recent discussion of the proximate-ultimate distinction, see e.g. Calcott (2013); Dickins and Barton (2013); Gardner (2013); Haig (2013); Sterelny (2013a); Watt (2013); Otsuka (2015). The debate initiated by Laland et al. (2011) has brought to the surface a remarkable variety of ways in which philosophers and biologists have come to understand Mayr's distinction. I do not intend my own proposal to supplant all others; it is simply how I will construe the distinction for the purposes of this book.

roles of three distinct Hamiltonian innovations that are often conflated: Hamilton's rule, kin selection, and inclusive fitness. I assemble the picture gradually, focussing in each chapter on a separate key question:

- What are the main categories of social behaviour in the natural world, and how should they be defined? (Chapter 1)
- What is the role of the principle known as 'Hamilton's rule' in explaining social behaviour, and can the rule be defended in the face of recent criticism? (Chapters 2 and 3)
- What is the best way to think about the relationship between kin selection and group (or multi-level) selection? (Chapter 4)
- How should we conceptualize an organism's fitness in the context of social evolution? (Chapter 5)

I argue for a set of interlinked answers to these questions. In Chapter 1, I argue that we should re-interpret Hamilton's famous four-part classification of types of social behaviour as a classification based on recent selection history rather than current fitness effects. This is, in effect, to classify behaviours by their function, if one also endorses a recent history account of function. In Chapter 2, I argue that we should think of Hamilton's rule as an *organizing framework* for social evolution research: a framework that helps us compare and interpret the causal explanations of change provided by more detailed models. In Chapter 3, I argue that recent criticisms of the rule, although they do undermine other conceptions of its explanatory role, do not diminish its value as an organizing framework, and I argue that it still compares favourably to other possible organizing frameworks.

In Chapter 4, I turn to the relationship between kin and group selection, arguing for a proposal—inspired by Hamilton's own brief comments—on which these processes are conceived as varieties of selection on indirect fitness differences, distinguished by their commitments regarding population structure. In Chapter 5, I contrast Hamilton's two alternative conceptions of individual fitness—'neighbour-modulated fitness' and 'inclusive fitness'—and argue that inclusive fitness has distinctive advantages, in so far as it provides a stable criterion for improvement and a standard for optimality in a process of cumulative adaptation.

The overarching message of Part I is that Hamilton's conceptual innovations still provide us with a compelling and explanatorily powerful way of organizing our thinking about the ultimate causes of social behaviour. I hope that, by bringing a degree of clarity to areas in which rival camps of theorists have often talked past each other, this part of the book will help defuse some of the controversies Hamilton's work has provoked in recent years, while at the same time identifying areas in which further productive debate is possible.

As the field of social evolution research has progressed, its explanatory scope has steadily increased, pushing well beyond behavioural ecology's traditional heartland of insects, birds, and mammals to incorporate a hugely disparate range of biological phenomena under the umbrella of the 'social'. As Andrew Bourke (2011, p. 7) notes, the field 'has grown outwards from the study of the beehive and the baboon troop to embrace the entire sweep of biological organization. It claims as its subject matter not just the evolution of social systems narrowly defined, but the evolution of all forms of stable biological grouping, from genomes and eukaryotic unicells to multicellular organisms, animal societies, and interspecific mutualisms'. In the second part of the book, Extensions, I turn to the ways in which recent expansions in the explanatory domain of social evolution theory have generated new conceptual challenges. I ask:

- What are the consequences of horizontal gene transfer for the evolution of cooperation, and for the very concept of relatedness, in the microbial world? (Chapter 6)
- Can social evolution theory shed light on the origins of complex multicellular life forms, such as plants, animals, and fungi? (Chapter 7)
- Can a concept of cultural relatedness help illuminate the origin and stability of cooperation in humans? (Chapter 8)

In Chapter 6, I argue that horizontal transmission, and the opportunities it creates for altruism-promoting genes to help their potential future bearers, should lead us to revise our concept of relatedness so that it tracks genetic similarity across time, rather than at a single time. In Chapter 7, I defend the idea that we can usefully think of the multicellular organism as a social phenomenon, especially when thinking about the transition from unicellular to multicellular life. I suggest that thinking about this transition in terms of 'the economy of the cell state' can yield distinctive insights into the feedback effects that promote and limit the division of labour among cells. In Chapter 8, I turn to the cultural evolution of human cooperation. I develop a concept of cultural relatedness, and I argue that a cultural version of Hamilton's rule can provide an organizing framework for the study of early human social evolution. I propose (and tentatively defend) a speculative 'cultural relatedness hypothesis' regarding the evolution of cooperation in Palaeolithic human populations.

While these 'extensions' may initially seem unrelated, there are important connections. As noted above, the ability of organisms to influence the selection pressures they face is one theme. The concept of relatedness is another. Microbial evolution pushes us to change the way we think about genetic relatedness, while regarding the multicellular organism as a social phenomenon pushes us to take seriously the genetic relatedness that exists within, as well as between, organisms. Human evolution, meanwhile, pushes us to recognize a fundamentally different kind of relatedness made possible by the evolutionarily novel mode of inheritance—culture—our Palaeolithic ancestors mastered. Yet the basic role of relatedness in stabilizing altruism remains essentially the same in all three cases.

The overall message of Part II is optimistic: I argue that the Hamiltonian organizing framework set out in Part I, if suitably revised and expanded, can help us understand far more about the natural world than one might initially suppose. We can make real progress in understanding microbial evolution, evolutionary transitions, and cultural change by viewing them through the lens of social evolution theory, provided the theory is properly understood and adapted where necessary.

This book is a work of philosophy of science.[8] In both parts, the focus is on central theoretical concepts, such as relatedness and inclusive fitness, and on abstract theoretical principles, such as Hamilton's rule and the Price equation. The questions I explore concern how these ideas relate to each other, how they can be used to explain social evolution, and how they can be extended to novel cases. Experimental research is not the main focus of the book. Yet in working on microbial evolution, evolutionary transitions, and cultural evolution, I have found that issues which initially seem to be of purely theoretical or philosophical interest turn out to bring

---

[8] To be more precise, the book belongs to a tradition in philosophy of science that engages closely with the theoretical foundations of a scientific discipline and addresses questions specific to that discipline (as opposed to addressing very general questions about, say, the scientific method or the nature of causation). Landmarks in this tradition, from which I have learned a great deal, include Sober (1984); Lloyd (1988); Brandon (1990); Okasha (2006), and Godfrey-Smith (2009b).

novel, testable hypotheses into view. In Extensions, I put forward several speculative hypotheses I see as interesting and promising. This is not a work of experimental biology, and I have not attempted to verify these hypotheses empirically. But I aim to show that reflecting on the conceptual structure of social evolution theory, by giving us a better understanding of the theory, can also open up new directions for experimental work.

I hope the book can serve as an entry point, for philosophers and biologists, to a range of debates about the conceptual foundations of social evolution theory—some of which have been running for decades, others of which have barely begun. With this in mind, I have assumed no prior knowledge of social evolution theory and tried to avoid inessential mathematical detail. There are a few, fairly self-contained sections containing mathematical arguments (Sections 2.1, 5.2, 6.3, and 8.4): readers are encouraged to work through them, but are also welcome to skip to the key results, which I have tried to indicate clearly.

That said, the book is not a textbook or an introduction. For readers seeking an introduction to the mathematical methods employed in modelling social evolution, or a survey of the empirical literature, there are better books out there.[9] This book is intended as 'one long argument' for the cogency and explanatory power of Hamilton's ideas, not just as a way of understanding natural selection acting on parentally inherited genetic variation in a constant environment, but also as a way of organizing our thinking about the ultimate causes of cooperation among microbes, among the cells of our bodies, and among enculturated human beings.

---

[9] See e.g. Marshall (2015) or McElreath and Boyd (2007) for an introduction to mathematical methods, and Bourke (2011) for a synthesis of the empirical literature.

PART I

Foundations

1

Conceptualizing Social Behaviour

1.1 Some Examples

When we talk about social behaviour in the natural world, what are we talking about? What distinguishes a social trait from a non-social trait, and what distinguishes biological altruism from biological selfishness? I will set out and defend a way of thinking about these questions that puts a trait's recent evolutionary history at the centre of the picture. First, however, a few examples will help set the scene.

1.1.1 Empire of the leafcutters

The eusocial Hymenoptera provide some of the most celebrated instances of cooperation in nature, and perhaps the most remarkable of all are the leafcutter ants of the genera *Atta* and *Acromyrmex* (Hölldobler and Wilson, 2009, 2011). As their common name suggests, the leafcutters specialize in cutting and retrieving fragments of leaves—a task they undertake with great efficiency and precision (Figure 1.1)—but this is only part of the story. The leaves are not food for the leafcutters, nor are they building material. Instead, the ants use the leaves to cultivate subterranean fungus gardens, stocked with a special fungal cultivar passed from one generation to the next. Farming the fungus is a joint endeavour on a colossal scale: the ants plant the fungus in purpose-built chambers, spray it with growth hormones, protect it against parasites and other fungal strains, and supply it with appropriate food. Without the coordinated contributions of vast numbers of workers (leafcutter colonies often number in the millions; see Hölldobler and Wilson, 2009), the fungus could never be cultivated in sufficient volumes to feed the queen's larvae. The relationship is one of nature's great mutualisms: the ants rely on thriving

Figure 1.1 Workers of the leafcutter ant species *Atta colombica* (photograph by bandwagonman at English Wikipedia, cropped and reproduced under Creative Commons licence CC BY-SA 3.0).

fungus gardens to provide the queen's larvae with food, while the fungus relies on the steady stream of leaf matter brought by the ants from the world outside. It is also a remarkable example of biological altruism, in which workers forego reproduction to raise their sisters.

1.1.2 Microbial towers

Cooperative phenomena are extremely widespread in the microbial world, and the feats of cooperation performed by microbes are no less spectacular than those undertaken by larger and more familiar creatures (Crespi, 2001; West et al., 2007a). One useful model organism for the growing field of 'sociomicrobiology' is the social amoeba, or slime mould, *Dictyostelium discoideum* (Bonner, 1959; Strassmann et al., 2000; Strassmann and Queller, 2011). For much of their life cycle, these amoebae conform to our usual expectations of amoebae: they live in the soil, they engulf bacteria, they divide mitotically. When food gets scarce, however, things get interesting: if the amoebae are present in sufficient density, the starving amoebae aggregate to form a mobile 'slug'. The slug moves as one—and moves further and faster than any individual amoeba could—in the direction of heat and light. On reaching a favourable location, the slug stops and begins to transform into a fruiting body (Figure 1.2). Around a fifth of the amoebae sacrifice their lives in this process, forming a hardy, cellulose stalk of dead cells. The remaining four-fifths cluster at the tip of the stalk, where they generate and release spores. The spores are dispersed

Figure 1.2 Fruiting bodies of the social amoeba *Dictyostelium discoideum* (photograph by Scott Solomon, reprinted with permission).

through the environment, reducing the probability that the amoebae they ultimately produce will encounter the same harsh conditions their parents endured. The generation of fruiting bodies through the aggregation of previously separate cells is by no means unique to *D. discoideum*, nor is it unique to amoebae: similar behaviour is also found in the social bacterium *Myxococcus xanthus* (Velicer and Vos, 2009).[1]

1.1.3 Pack hunters

By working together in structured and organized ways, groups of predators are able to tackle bigger prey or to predate more efficiently than they ever could alone. Examples include bands of humans (*Homo sapiens*), troops of chimpanzees (*Pan troglodytes*), prides of lions (*Panthera leo*), and packs of wolves (*Canis lupus*) (Anderson and Franks, 2001). A particularly spectacular example is provided by pods of humpback whales (*Megaptera novaeangliae*), some of which employ a tactic known as 'bubble-net feeding'. A shoal of herring is located and driven upwards

---

[1] Microbial cooperation will be the subject of Chapter 6.

Figure 1.3 Bubble-net feeding by the humpback whale *Megaptera novaeangliae* (public domain photograph by Evadb at English Wikipedia).

from the sea floor by a group of whales; then a separate whale swims around the fleeing shoal, encircling it with a curtain of bubbles. The herring will not swim through the curtain of air; instead, they continue to swim upwards towards the surface, where they are trapped and devoured by the chasing group (Figure 1.3; Sharpe and Dill, 1997; Anderson and Franks, 2001).

Pack hunting is by no means the sole preserve of vertebrates, however, and it may not even be the sole preserve of multicellular organisms. Recent work on *M. xanthus* has revealed a mysterious behaviour in which the bacteria move collectively in a 'ripple' formation, like waves on the sea (Berleman and Kirby, 2009). There is good evidence that rippling is a predatory behaviour, triggered by the proximity of food; but the question remains open as to what predatory advantage, if any, it provides for the bacteria. One hypothesis is that the formation is a kind of battle tactic: by rippling underneath a prey colony, the *M. xanthus* swarm is able to disrupt and dislodge its prey more effectively, enabling its rapid consumption.

1.1.4 Sperm cells swim together

Some of the most striking examples of apparently cooperative phenomena occur not between organisms, but within them: almost everywhere we look, we find cells interacting in ways which make the language of cooperation difficult to resist (see Chapter 7 and Queller, 1997; Queller and Strassmann, 2009; Strassmann and Queller, 2010, 2011; Bourke, 2011). Sperm cells provide some memorable examples. We tend to imagine sperm as solitary swimmers, competing with one another to fertilize an egg. In the case of human sperm, this is more or less correct, but the picture changes when we consider species in which females mate with multiple males in quick succession. In these cases, the closely related sperm of a particular male stand a greater chance of winning the race against the unrelated sperm of rival males if they work together; as a result, we often find that selection has favoured cooperation within groups of sperm. For example, in the American opossum, *Monodelphis domesticus*, sperm swim together in pairs, touching at the head: an arrangement which enables faster and straighter swimming (Moore and Moore, 2002; Moore and Taggart, 1995; Pizzari and Foster, 2008). In rodents such as the Norway rat (*Rattus norvegicus*) and the wood mouse (*Apodemus sylvaticus*), we see even more dramatic feats of sperm organization: the sperm use tiny hooks on their heads to latch together into balls, and propel themselves forward with aligned and synchronized beating of their tails (Moore et al., 2002; Immler et al., 2007; Pizzari and Foster, 2008).

1.2 Hamilton's Four-Part Schema

Social evolution theorists aim to model the evolutionary processes that can, over extended periods of evolutionary time, lead to extraordinary natural phenomena such as these. For this purpose, from Hamilton (1964) onwards, they have tended to work with a more abstract characterization of social behaviour—a characterization that abstracts away from the rich detail of the actual examples we find in the natural world in order to capture the core evolutionary features they have in common, and that a good model of the evolution of social behaviour needs to incorporate.

We can turn to West et al. (2007c) for a typical definition. They write that, 'from an evolutionary point of view, a behaviour is social if it has fitness consequences for both the individual that performs the behaviour (the actor) and another individual (the recipient)' (West et al., 2007c, p. 418). The basic picture here, which we owe to Hamilton (1964), is of social behaviour as an interaction between two organisms, an actor and

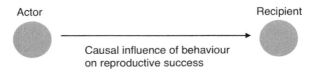

Figure 1.4 Social behaviour as a fitness-affecting interaction.

a recipient, in which the behaviour of the former causally influences the reproductive success of the latter (Figure 1.4).[2]

The picture in Figure 1.4 involves one obvious simplifying assumption: it depicts an interaction involving a single actor and a single recipient. In fact, this simplifying assumption is shared by many formal models of the evolution of social behaviour. But it should be recognized for what it is: an assumption that is rarely true of interesting examples of sociality in nature, which often involve multiple actors working in concert and/or multiple recipients being affected by their actions. Our examples from the preceding section are all feats of multi-actor *collaboration*, in which focussing on any single pair of individuals in isolation from the surrounding collaborative context would fail to do justice to the complexity of the phenomenon. I will set aside this complication for now, and revisit it at the end of the chapter (see Section 1.6).

Viewing social behaviour as fitness-affecting interaction leads naturally to the thought that we can classify different types of social behaviour by the sign of their effects on the reproductive success of actor and recipient. The result is a four-part schema, first introduced by Hamilton (1964), that categorizes social behaviours as mutually beneficial, selfish, altruistic, or spiteful (Table 1.1). These categories are most intuitive when individuals interact in pairs; but they can, in principle, apply to more complex interactions (see Section 1.6).

The effects that are relevant for Hamilton's schema are effects on the lifetime, absolute reproductive output of an individual organism. The focus on lifetime output means that so-called 'reciprocal altruism'—in which an actor cooperates at a short-term cost to itself but reaps long-term benefits as a consequence—does not qualify as 'altruism' on this conception (West et al., 2007c; Bowles and Gintis, 2011;

---

[2] I largely avoid the term 'fitness' in this chapter, so as not to pre-judge the issue of how fitness should be defined in the context of social evolution. This is the topic of Chapter 5.

Table 1.1 Hamilton's (1964) classification of the types of social behaviour: Row labels refer to the sign of the effect of the behaviour on the reproductive success of the actor; column labels refer to the sign of the effect of the behaviour on the reproductive success of the recipient.

	+	−
+	MUTUAL BENEFIT	SELFISHNESS
−	ALTRUISM	SPITE

Ramsey and Brandon, 2011). The focus on absolute output means that one's relative output in comparison to other organisms is not directly relevant. D. S. Wilson (1977, 1980, 1990) takes a different approach, distinguishing 'weak' and 'strong' altruism such that the latter requires an absolute cost to the actor, whereas the former requires only a relative cost to the actor in relation to the rest of its social group. The altruism category in Table 1.1 corresponds only to Wilson's strong altruism: his weak altruism would be categorized as a form of mutual benefit.

There are examples of all four of Hamilton's categories of social behaviour in nature. We have already encountered two examples credibly regarded as cases of altruism (leafcutter workers raising their sisters, and social amoebae giving their lives to form the stalk in a fruiting body) and two examples credibly regarded as a case of interaction for mutual benefit (bubble-net feeding, and the opossum sperm swimming together). Credible examples of biological selfishness are commonplace in nature: consider sharks fighting over food, or stags fighting over a mate.

The rarest category of social behaviour in nature is almost certainly spite. One might initially assume that spite cannot be reconciled with Darwinian logic, since it involves diminished reproduction for both actor and recipient. In fact, for reasons that will become clearer in Chapter 2, spite can evolve by natural selection when the relatedness between actors and recipients is negative (Hamilton, 1970). This is not a mere theoretical possibility. Andy Gardner and Stuart A. West (2006) describe several credible examples in bacteria, ants, and wasps: for example, bacteria of numerous species will sometimes 'explode in a shower of antibacterial toxins (bacteriocins) in order to kill their competitors' (Gardner and

West, 2006, p. R663). As Gardner and West point out, such behaviour can sometimes be conceptualized as a form of indirect altruism, in which an actor harms unrelated (or distantly related) social partners in order to benefit more closely related organisms. In principle, though, spite can evolve even if no individual gains an absolute benefit (see Chapter 2).

1.3 The Importance of Recent Selection History

Hamilton's four-part schema classifies social behaviours as selfish, spiteful, altruistic, or mutually beneficial according to their effects on reproduction. But where does cooperation fit into this picture? Traditionally, cooperation is defined as any social behaviour that confers a positive fitness benefit on a recipient, regardless of the sign of its fitness effects on the actor (Hamilton, 1964; Trivers, 1985; Bourke and Franks, 1995). In the four-part schema, this corresponds to any social behaviour that falls within the altruism or mutual benefit boxes.

More recently, West et al. (2007c) have departed from this tradition by proposing a somewhat more restrictive definition. Their motivation is the need to rule out behaviour that merely confers a fortuitous benefit on another organism. Suppose, for instance, that an elephant confers a fortuitous benefit on a nearby dung beetle by producing dung in its vicinity. We would not intuitively describe the elephant as cooperating with the dung beetle: we would sooner say that the dung beetle is merely exploiting a by-product of the elephant's digestive system (West et al., 2007c, p. 419). More importantly, it seems unreasonable to expect a theory of social evolution by natural selection to explain this kind of behaviour, because there is no reason to think the egestive behaviour of the elephant has been shaped by selection for its effects on the dung beetle.

To rule out such cases, West et al. suggest that a behaviour should not be classified as cooperative unless it is currently selected for in virtue of the benefit it confers. Accordingly, they define cooperation as 'A behaviour which provides a benefit to another individual (recipient), and which is selected for because of its beneficial effect on the recipient' (West et al., 2007c, p. 419). The 'selected for' criterion, they argue, gives us a principled basis on which to exclude cases of fortuitous benefit from the explanatory domain of social evolution theory.[3] As West et al. note, there is a parallel

---

[3] On the notion of 'selection for', see Sober (1984). The idea is that the behaviour is not simply positively selected, but positively selected *because of its causal effects on fitness*

here with Maynard Smith and Harper's (2003) distinction between signals and cues, and with historical definitions of 'adaptation' (Rose and Lauder, 1996); there is also an echo of Williams's (1966) distinction between group adaptation and fortuitous group benefit.

I agree with West et al. that we need some criterion to distinguish cooperation from fortuitous benefit, and I think they are on the right lines in appealing to natural selection to make sense of this. However, I disagree with their decision to focus on the selection pressures *currently* operating on a trait. We need to make room for cooperative traits that are not currently under selection because they do not currently vary, or because their link to fitness has been severed by recent ecological change. Human cooperation arguably falls into this latter category. The dispositions underlying human cooperation are widely thought to fall within the scope of social evolution theory (see Chapter 8). Yet we might doubt whether this behaviour is *currently* subject to selection, at least when selection is defined in genetic terms, because we live in a social world in which our actions are largely decoupled from reproductive consequences. We also need to make room for cooperative traits that were once selected for in virtue of their effects on the recipient, but which are now under selection only in virtue of their effects on the actor. Once a cooperative trait that is costly for the actor has gone to fixation, selection may subsequently favour variants that reduce the cost of performing the behaviour, leaving the beneficial effect on the recipient unaltered. Yet it would be strange to claim that trait has ceased to be cooperative simply because selection is currently targeting only its actor-directed effects.

A natural move here is to appeal to selection history. For example, we could spell out the 'selected for' condition as the condition that the trait has, at some point in its evolutionary history, been selected for in virtue of its beneficial effect on the recipient. This would adequately handle the dung beetle case, and it would also make room for cooperative traits that are not currently under selection by virtue of their effects on the recipient. West et al. resist this move, however, citing the need to distinguish between the reasons for a trait's current maintenance and the reasons for its origin. What makes a trait cooperative, they argue, is that it is

(and not, for example, because it is linked to another trait that causally promotes fitness). In the context of social behaviour, we need to allow that the 'effects on fitness' may be effects on the fitness of another organism.

maintained by virtue of its beneficial effects on other organisms, not that it originated for that reason.

At this point, it helps to borrow a move from the literature on 'etiological' (i.e. causal-historical) theories of function (Allen et al., 1998; Buller, 1999). One influential position in the functions debate is that biological function is a matter of 'modern' or 'recent' selection history: a trait's function is, roughly speaking, the effect in virtue of which it has been maintained by natural selection in its recent evolutionary past (Godfrey-Smith, 1994). This allows for cases in which a trait is not currently subject to selection for that effect, but it also respects the distinction between a trait's maintenance and its origin, since a trait's recent selection history explains its maintenance but not necessarily its origin.

I suggest that we define cooperation in similar terms: a cooperative behaviour is one which, in its recent selection history, has been maintained in the population by natural selection in virtue of its positive effect on the reproductive success of other organisms. As well as respecting both the distinction between cooperation and fortuitous benefit and the distinction between maintenance and origin, this proposal has a further advantage: it shows why it is explanatory to successfully classify a social behaviour. For an accurate classification, like an accurate attribution of a function, provides a reason why a trait has recently been maintained, and thereby provides a causal explanation (admittedly, a minimal one, but an explanation nonetheless) for its current presence in a population.

How recent is 'recent'? Godfrey-Smith (1994, pp. 356–7) takes a pragmatic line on this:

Some might wonder how recent the selective episodes relevant to functional status have to be. The answer is not in terms of a fixed time—a week, or a thousand years. Relevance fades. Episodes of selection become increasingly irrelevant to an assignment of functions at some time, the further away we get.

I am inclined to take the same line in the case of cooperation. The selection history that matters is the selection history relevant to explaining the recent maintenance of the trait. To the extent that this is sensitive to our explanatory interests, so is the classification of social behaviour.[4]

---

[4] Griffiths (1993, p. 417) suggests a more principled way of delimiting a trait's recent selection history (in his terminology, an 'evolutionarily significant period'), whereby this encompasses a length of time such that we would expect the trait to be eroded by the accumulation of mutations in the absence of any selection in its favour during that

I further suggest that this 'recent history' version of the 'selected for' criterion removes the need for the first part of the West et al. definition: we should describe *any* trait that has been maintained in recent history by natural selection in virtue of its beneficial effects on a recipient as cooperative, regardless of its current effects. This makes room for cooperative traits that currently fail to have any beneficial fitness effects because they are currently being expressed outside the ecological environment in which they evolved. West et al. do not comment on whether their 'selected for' criterion should apply to the four categories of social behaviour represented in Table 1.1, or just to cooperation. I propose that the 'recent history' version of the criterion should indeed apply to these four categories. In other words, I propose that we think of mutual benefit, altruism, selfishness, and spite as defined not in terms of their current effects but rather in terms of their recent selection history. For example, we might say (subject to the refinements in the next two sections) that a behaviour is altruistic if and only if it has, in recent history, been maintained by selection because of its positive effect on the reproductive success of other organisms, and despite its negative effect on the reproductive success of the actor.

1.4 Objections to Historical Definitions

There are various possible objections to the idea that we should classify social behaviours by their recent selection history. However, since these objections mirror well-known and timeworn objections to etiological theories of function and adaptation, they can be resisted in much the same way. Before I introduce any further refinements to my approach, I will briefly consider three of these objections.

One is that, in bringing natural selection into the definition of cooperation, we make it true by definition that any behaviour that is cooperative has been maintained in recent history by natural selection, when this should be a substantive explanatory hypothesis (see Wilson 2002 for a version of this objection). Daniel C. Fisher (1985) made a similar point with reference to the concept of adaptation. He observed that, if we define an adaptation in historical terms, as a trait that was shaped by natural

time. Readers unpersuaded by Godfrey-Smith's pragmatic answer may find this one more satisfactory.

selection for its current function, then the claim that natural selection explains the origin of adaptations becomes trivially true. Yet it was surely a non-trivial breakthrough, on Darwin's part, to discover that natural selection can explain the origin of adaptations.

However, as Tim Lewens (2007a) notes, it is helpful in this context to distinguish the theoretical notion of adaptation from a more intuitive notion—call it 'adaptedness'—that denotes the apparent 'good fit' between an organism's phenotypic traits and its environment. It was certainly no trivial discovery that natural selection explains adaptedness. But this discovery, once made, provided a rationale for introducing a theoretical notion of adaptation in which the role of natural selection in generating such traits was made explicit. Adaptation thus became an explanatory category in its own right—one that carries implications about the origins of a trait—and not simply an intuitive description of a phenomenon.

Similar considerations apply in the case of cooperation. We should take care to distinguish the theoretical notion of cooperation, which I define in terms of recent selection history, from the more intuitive idea of an action that benefits other organisms. Obviously, the discovery that natural selection can explain the maintenance of actions that benefit other organisms, even at a cost to the actor, was a non-trivial breakthrough, in this case one properly credited to Hamilton (1964). But, as with adaptation, this discovery now provides us with a rationale for introducing a theoretical notion of cooperation in which the role of selection is made explicit. This theoretical notion is an explanatory category: to classify a behaviour as cooperative is to assign it to a class of behaviours whose maintenance under selection is explained by their positive effect on the reproduction of other organisms.

It is also helpful to stress again here the distinction between a trait's origin and its recent maintenance. It may be a definitional truth that a behaviour that is cooperative has been maintained by selection in recent history, but it remains, for any particular cooperative behaviour, a substantive explanatory hypothesis that selection explains the origin of that behaviour. It therefore remains a substantive explanatory hypothesis that the behaviour is an adaptation (rather than, say, an 'exaptation' in the sense of Gould and Vrba, 1982).

A second concern is that a historical definition of cooperation faces a version of the infamous 'swampman' objection to etiological theories of function and mental content (Braddon-Mitchell and Jackson, 2007). Suppose an object physically indistinguishable from a living human being comes together through chance quantum fluctuations in a swamp. Being a product of chance, this creature has no selection history. Nevertheless, can we not legitimately attribute functions to its parts? And, relevantly for our purposes, can we not legitimately describe its actions as being cooperative, altruistic, selfish, and so on? The standard, and to my mind effective, reply is that this objection places excessive weight on armchair intuitions regarding merely possible cases (Neander, 1996; Papineau, 2001).

A third concern, in my view more serious than the others, is that a historical definition of cooperation sets a high evidential bar for knowing whether or not an action is cooperative: if we are ignorant of its recent selection history, then we are not in a position to know whether or not it is an instance of biological cooperation (again, see Wilson 2002 for a version of this objection). A similar worry is sometimes raised for etiological accounts of function, which set a high evidential bar for the attribution of functions (Lewens, 2007b). Defenders of such accounts reply that, given the importance attached to function attributions, and given the explanatory role they serve in explaining the maintenance of traits, the concept should be seen as an onerous one, and we should not invoke it before we understand the selection pressures that have operated on the trait of interest (cf. Williams, 1966 on adaptation).

I suggest that same should apply to cooperation. This too is an onerous concept: one that carries implication about how a trait functions in the social lives of its bearers, and about why it has been maintained by natural selection. We should not describe a trait as cooperative (or altruistic, selfish, etc.) before we understand the selection pressures responsible for its recent maintenance. We should therefore not underestimate the amount of empirical work required to determine conclusively that an action is cooperative. Like 'function' and 'adaptation', 'cooperation' and related notions are onerous concepts that should be treated with caution in the absence of knowledge of selection history.

To summarize the argument so far: West and colleagues' 'selected for' criterion is well motivated, but it does not go far enough. For the purposes of social evolution theory, we should characterize biological cooperation, and all other categories of social behaviour, in terms of their recent selection history. This is, in effect, to characterize them by their function, if we also endorse a recent-history theory of function (along the lines of Godfrey-Smith, 1994). My proposal consequently inherits all the drawbacks of that theory, but these drawbacks are outweighed by the advantages.

1.5 Actions and Strategies

There are, however, two important complications that still need to be addressed. Here is one. Throughout this chapter we have been concerned with categorizing types of social behaviour, but the examples of 'behaviour' we have been considering are examples of individual social actions. Yet particular actions are rarely the immediate target of evolutionary explanations. More often than not, the explanatory target is a *strategy* that involves a variety of actions across a range of environmental conditions. But what exactly is a strategy? And should strategies or actions be the main targets of classification?

Talk of strategies, though extremely widespread, has sometimes been regarded as controversial. For example, Kramer (1984) complained that such talk imputes to insects, bacteria, and other social organisms a dubious capacity for planning and foresight. Social evolution theorists have typically sought to evade such concerns by characterizing the notion of a strategy in terms that imply no commitment to foresight on the part of social actors. For example, Maynard Smith (1982, p. 10) defines a strategy as 'a behavioural phenotype; i.e., it is a specification of what an individual will do in any situation in which it may find itself.' The idea here is that we think of a strategy as a *pattern* of behaviour, a pattern that can be captured by a function mapping the 'situation' an organism is in to the action it performs (on the reality of patterns, see Dennett, 1991, 1995). If strategies are simply patterns of behaviour, then no capacity for foresight is required in order to possess one, and Kramer's worry is defused.

However, there may be a lingering concern that talk of 'strategies' still involves a controversial commitment, namely a commitment to the idea that an organism's behaviour is in some sense 'programmed' by its genome. As we saw in the book's introduction, this idea, famously advocated by Mayr (1964, 1974), has come in for severe criticism in recent philosophy of biology. There is now a widespread view that, although it is reasonable to suggest that the genome 'codes for' specific RNA molecules and polypeptides, talking of whole-organism behaviours as 'programmed' stretches a seductive metaphor to breaking point, given the substantial influence of environmental and epigenetic processes on realized phenotypes (Godfrey-Smith, 2000, 2007b; Griffiths, 2001).

I suggest, however, that this worry is misplaced, not because the criticisms of the 'genetic program' metaphor are unsound, but simply because talk of 'strategies' does not imply a commitment to the validity of this metaphor. True, it is tempting to envision a strategy as a program that 'tells the organism what to do' in the various environmental scenarios it may encounter over its lifetime. This informal talk is particularly appealing in the context of computer models of social evolution, since in such models strategies are literally programmed. But all of this informal 'program' talk is dispensable. In taking strategies as our primary explanatory targets, all we are really presupposing is that (i) organisms objectively manifest patterns of behaviour and that (ii) these patterns of behaviour are transmitted across generations in a way that makes them appropriate targets for natural selection and evolutionary explanation. The concept of a strategy, construed in this minimal way, is compatible with explanations of the transmission of patterns of behaviour that eschew concepts of programming or coding.

The concept of a strategy is invaluable in social evolution research, because it is often the case that we can only understand the ultimate explanation for an action by considering the wider strategy of which it is a part. 'Axelrod's tournaments' provide a famous example of this. In the 1980s Robert Axelrod ran computer simulations to establish which strategies were more successful than others in a game called the repeated (or iterated) prisoner's dilemma (Axelrod and Hamilton, 1981; Axelrod, 1984). As in a one-shot prisoner's dilemma, players choose whether to cooperate or defect, but in the repeated version they play the game repeatedly, not just once. The headline result was that a strategy called 'Tit-for-Tat', which involved reciprocal cooperation with players who have cooperated in the past, along with reciprocal defection on players who have defected in the past, won both tournaments (though see Nowak and Sigmund, 1993; Imhof et al., 2007 for a strategy that does even better under certain conditions). Crucially, 'Tit-for-Tat' outperformed 'Always Cooperate', a strategy of unconditional cooperation. This is a case in which cooperating as a part of a strategy of unconditional cooperation is selected against, but cooperating conditionally as part of a strategy of reciprocity is selected for. The action of cooperating itself is neither selected for nor selected against: selection favours one strategy involving cooperative actions while disfavouring another.

This observation allows a further refining of our definition of cooperation and related phenomena: if actions are maintained by selection only as parts of strategies, and if they are to be classified by their recent selection history, then the cooperative (or altruistic, spiteful, etc.) character of an action depends on the explanation for why the strategy of which it is a part has been maintained. For example, we might say that a type of action A is cooperative if and only if the strategy of which A is a part was, in recent history, maintained in the population by natural selection at least in part because of the fitness benefits conferred by A on other organisms, when A was performed as part of that strategy. This is close, I think, to a satisfactory definition, subject to one further refinement (see the next section).

Note that, on this proposal, it is still actions, not strategies, that are classified as cooperative, altruistic, and so on; it is simply that the character of the action depends on the strategy of which it is a part. Why not entirely switch the focus to strategies, and talk of 'altruistic strategies', 'selfish strategies', and so on? Biologists, notably in the context of evolutionary game theory, often talk in these terms. Sometimes they are labels introduced stipulatively to name particular strategies in an evolutionary game, but sometimes they are used in a looser sense, with the aim of describing the overall character of a strategy. I do not seriously object to such talk (indeed, I will often use it myself in this book); however, we should recognize that it is potentially misleading. A strategy can encompass a wide variety of actions under a wide variety of conditions, and the same strategy may lead to altruistic actions in some contexts and selfish actions in others. If a strategy is unconditionally altruistic, that is, involves performing altruistic behaviours in all circumstances, then we could reasonably gloss it as an 'altruistic strategy'; but altruism in the real world rarely, if ever, works like this. Most of the strategies that we informally describe as 'altruistic' are in fact only conditionally altruistic: they dispose an organism to act altruistically in some—but not all—social and environmental circumstances.

1.6 The Collaborative Context

Here is the second complication, which we noted and set aside earlier. So far, we have been assuming that it makes sense to talk of 'the effects of a type of action on reproductive success' without reference to the actions of others. However, reflecting on real-world examples, such as bubble-net feeding, makes it immediately apparent that the fitness consequences of a type of action can be highly sensitive to the actions of others.

Patrick Forber and Rory Smead (2015) have recently argued that this problem seriously undermines Hamilton's four-part schema. They focus on a simple model of collaboration known as the 'stag hunt', a two-player game in which each player must choose whether to hunt a stag or whether to hunt a hare (Skyrms, 2004). The payoff structure rewards coordination: both must hunt the stag together in order to receive the maximum payoff. In such a game, the fitness effects of one player's action clearly depend on how the other player behaves, in a way that seems as though it should make a difference to the classification of that action. A good classification scheme, it seems, should allow us to say that hunting the stag in collaboration with the other player is a case of mutually beneficial cooperation, whereas hunting the stag when the other player is hunting the hare is not.[5]

It can hardly be denied that, in cases where two or more social actors collaborate to generate a benefit in an interaction with the structure of a stag hunt (or a pure coordination game), the fitness effects of an action depend on the actions of others. However, I question the moral Forber and Smead draw from this. The moral they draw is that we should stop classifying particular social actions and instead classify whole payoff matrices. For example, the stag hunt game can be characterized as a special case of a more general type of game, namely a coordination game. It is more illuminating, Forber and Smead suggest, to classify a certain type of interaction as a coordination game than to classify a specific action within that game as mutually beneficial cooperation.

I take the view that both approaches to classifying social behaviour have their uses and their limitations. The drawback to classifying whole payoff matrices rather than individual actions is the proliferation of categories once we move beyond symmetric two-player games to consider more complex payoff structures and larger numbers of actors and recipients. As Forber and Smead note, classifying games in which players have three strategic options (rather than two, as in the stag hunt) by their overall payoff structure leads to a scheme with forty-seven categories, leading them to concede that 'as interactions become more complicated, classification will become significantly more difficult and, most likely,

---

[5] A similar point can be made using a pure coordination game. In such a game, no player receives any payoff unless both choose the same strategy. The need for context-sensitive classification is arguably even more striking here: it seems appropriate to say that in a pure coordination game an action is cooperative if and only if both players perform it.

less helpful for drawing conclusions of evolutionary significance' (Forber and Smead, 2015, p. 413).

By contrast, classifying actions, although less informative about payoff structures, gives us a set of categories that apply across a wide range of different structures, helping to bring out the underlying functional similarities between actions that initially seem very different. We should, however, concede the point that, because the fitness consequences of an action often depend on its coordination (or lack of coordination) with the actions of others, the classification of an action should be relativized to a *collaborative context*. This allows for the possibility that the same type of action, such as pursuing a stag, might be cooperative when performed in one collaborative context and non-cooperative when performed in another.

However, we cannot simply leave things there. The notion of 'the collaborative context' needs further elaboration. In two-player coordination games, this idea has an obvious meaning: it is simply the strategy of the other player. However, many real-world collaborative phenomena are not well modelled as two-player coordination games: they involve many actors and/or many recipients. We encountered three striking examples at the beginning of the chapter: fruiting-body formation in *D. discoideum*, social foraging and fungal cultivation in the leafcutter ants, and bubble-net feeding in humpback whales (Section 1.1).

What does relativizing our classifications to a collaborative context mean in such cases? If what is needed is a complete specification of what every other actor or recipient is doing, collaborative contexts will be very fine-grained, and the worry arises that a particular collaborative context will not recur often enough for it to make sense to regard the expression of a behaviour in that context as having a selection history. Collaborative contexts need to be specified in such a way as to be coarse-grained enough to recur regularly in the life history of an organism, but fine-grained enough to facilitate biologically meaningful classifications of social behaviour.

The crucial concept here, I suggest, is that of a *task*. Think of hunting a stag: this is a task that requires contributions from two more actors for its completion. In the context of that task, certain actions, performed in a specific way at a specific time (e.g. throwing a spear at a crucial moment) lead causally to positive fitness consequences. Performed outside the context of that task, those same actions may be ineffectual or even harmful. Bubble-net feeding has a similar structure: a number of organisms undertake a task, and in the context of that task certain actions, performed in a specific way at a specific time (e.g. producing a curtain of bubbles around the target shoal), lead causally to successful feeding.

In a seminal series of papers, Carl Anderson, Nigel Franks, and Daniel McShea argue for the importance of the concept of a task in social evolution research in general, and especially in the social insects (Anderson and McShea, 2001; Anderson and Franks, 2001; Anderson et al., 2001). Consider, for example, the collaboration between members of the major (large) and minor (small) castes in the dimorphic ant *Pheidole pallidula*: when the colony is threatened by an intruder, the ants form teams comprising one major ant and many minor ants; the minors then pin down the intruder so that the major can deploy its strong jaws to decapitate it (Detrain and Pasteels, 1992; Anderson and Franks, 2001). Or consider the army ants *Eciton burchelli* and *Dorlyus wilverthi*, which form teams of two or more individuals (one at the front, the rest at the back) to retrieve prey items that are too heavy for any single ant to carry alone (Franks, 1986, 1987; Anderson and Franks, 2001). These teams are 'superefficient', in the sense that they are able to carry items heavier even than the sum of the weights each team member could carry by itself (Franks, 1986; Anderson and Franks, 2001). In all these cases, the actions performed as parts of these tasks seem clearly cooperative, but they yield positive fitness consequences only in conjunction with the actions of others.

What can be said in general about the nature of tasks? Anderson and Franks propose that 'a task is an item of work that potentially makes a positive contribution, however small, to inclusive fitness' (Anderson and Franks, 2001, p. 534). This characterization, although a reasonable first pass, has two main drawbacks. The first is that, for reasons I will discuss in Chapter 5, defining the notion 'inclusive fitness' in the context of task-structured cooperation raises some difficulties that, for now at least, we should set aside. So I suggest that, for the purposes of defining task-structured cooperation, we instead take the effect on the reproductive success of recipients as the relevant effect. I also want to allow that the effects of tasks on reproductive success can be negative as well as positive (consider, for example, warfare in humans).

The second drawback is that the notion of an 'item of work' seems too imprecise. In particular, it draws no distinction between a whole task and its component steps. For example, suppose a humpback whale produces a ring of bubbles around a shoal of fish. This is an item of work, and there is a sense in which it *potentially* contributes to reproductive success, in so far as it enables the humpback and its neighbours to feed when performed as part of the bubble-net feeding procedure. Is it therefore a whole task in its own right? Or is it, as intuition would suggest, a mere component of a larger task? The Anderson et al. definition does not help us settle such questions.

We can remedy this second problem by drawing on an idea from Calcott (2006): tasks are *mechanisms* for the generation of benefit or harm. Machamer et al. (2000, p. 3) characterize mechanisms in biology as composed of 'entities and activities, organized such that they are productive of regular changes from start or set-up to finish or termination conditions'. Calcott suggests that collaborative tasks fit this description: they are mechanisms composed of entities and activities organized such that they are productive of regular benefits or harms, typically in the form of resources (e.g. food resources) that promote reproductive success.[6]

If we think of tasks as benefit-generating (or harm-generating) mechanisms, then identifying distinct tasks is a matter of identifying mechanisms. While this is not always easy, it is a feat biologists accomplish in many different areas of biology. In the case of the humpback whales, we can see that, while bubble-net feeding qualifies as a mechanism that produces regular benefits in the form of food resources, its component steps do not qualify as tasks in their own right, since they lead to regular benefits only if the other component steps are also completed in the correct order.

This conception of a task may give the impression that some social behaviour is task-structured and some is not. I think it would be more accurate, however, to say that *all* social behaviour takes the form of tasks—that is, all social behaviour consists in the implementation of mechanisms that generate benefit or harm—but some tasks are simple enough to require only one action from one organism for their implementation (Anderson and McShea call such tasks 'individual tasks'). Many, however, including the examples introduced earlier, require multiple contributions in order

---

[6] I want to allow that selfish or spiteful behaviour can take the form of tasks that are productive of regular harms to other organisms, so I allow that tasks may be productive of regular harms. However, the examples of tasks I discuss here all involve the generation of benefit.

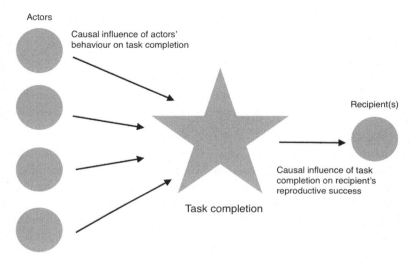

Figure 1.5 The generation of benefit in a collaborative task.

to generate benefit. In such cases, the causal structure of the task does not match the simple picture of a single actor conferring a benefit on a recipient (Figure 1.4): rather, it is one of many actors collaborating to confer a benefit through task completion (Figure 1.5). The recipients may be the same individuals as the actors (as in the case of a task performed by a number of individuals for their mutual benefit) but they need not be; indeed, in eusocial insect societies the recipients (queens) rarely participate in any collaborative tasks, and the actors (workers) rarely gain any benefit from their efforts.

With this in mind, let us return to the problem of specifying the 'collaborative context' in which a social action is expressed. I suggest that, for the purpose of classifying social behaviour, the context that matters is the task within which the action is performed. We should therefore classify not actions *simpliciter*, but *actions-in-tasks*. A task-relative classification of behaviour gets the grain of analysis right: tasks supervene on distributions of individual behavioural phenotypes without completely determining them, allowing for the same task to recur many times in slightly different ways, but they are fine-grained enough to capture the elements of the wider context that make a difference to the fitness consequences of an action.

With all the necessary refinements now in place, here (at last) is my favoured conception of biological cooperation:

Biological cooperation: An action A, performed as part of a strategy S in a task T, is *cooperative* if and only if S has, in recent history, been maintained by selection at least in part because of the positive effect of performing A in T on the reproductive success of other organisms.

While, all else being equal, a simpler definition might be preferable, I maintain that the relative intricacy of this definition is well motivated. The underlying rationale is that an individual cooperative action is neither the primary target of selection nor a complete mechanism for the generation of benefit or harm. Rather, strategies are selected for, tasks generate benefit or harm, and cooperative actions are performed as parts of both strategies and tasks.

In special cases, it may be that $A = T$, because the action generates benefit by itself; it may also be that $A = S$, because the organism's strategy is simple and unconditional. There may even be cases in which $A = T = S$. But I contend that such cases are the exception rather than the rule. In general, it is important to distinguish actions from strategies and tasks, and to relativize the cooperative or non-cooperative character of an action to the strategy and task within which it is expressed. It is straightforward to construct corresponding definitions for related categories of social behaviour (Box 1.1).

Box 1.1 Classifying actions by task, strategy, and recent selection history

An action A, performed as part of a task T and a strategy S, is:

cooperative if and only if S has, in recent history, been maintained by selection at least in part because of the positive effect of performing A in T on the reproductive success of other organisms.

altruistic if and only if S has, in recent history, been maintained by selection at least in part because of the positive effect of performing A in T on the reproductive success of other organisms, and despite the negative effect of performing A in T on the reproductive success of the actor.

mutually beneficial if and only if *S* has, in recent history, been maintained by selection at least in part because of the positive effect of performing *A* in *T* on the reproductive success of other organisms, and also at least in part because of the positive effects of performing *A* in *T* on the reproductive success of the actor.

selfish if and only if *S* has, in recent history, been maintained by selection at least in part because of the positive effect of performing *A* in *T* on the reproductive success of the actor, and despite or also in part because of the negative effects of performing *A* in *T* on the reproductive success of other organisms.

spiteful if and only if *S* has, in recent history, been maintained by selection at least in part because of the negative effect of performing *A* in *T* on the reproductive success of other organisms, and despite the negative effects of performing *A* in *T* on the reproductive success of the actor.

1.7 Summary of Chapter 1

Hamilton (1964) proposed classifying social behaviours by the sign of their effects on the reproductive success of the actor and the recipient, leading to a four-part schema that categorizes behaviour as altruistic, selfish, mutually beneficial, or spiteful. West et al. (2007c), while broadly endorsing Hamilton's approach, suggested that, in order to distinguish cooperation from the fortuitous conferral of benefit, we should define cooperation in terms of the selection pressures currently acting on a behaviour.

I have argued that we should characterize cooperation, and all other categories of social behaviour, in terms of the selection processes that have maintained the behaviour in recent history. If one also endorses a recent history account of function, this is simply to characterize them by their function. This preserves a difference between cooperation and fortuitous benefit, and it shows why it is explanatory to identify some phenomenon as an instance of cooperation.

Given its close affinity with a recent history theory of function, a recent history classification of social behaviour faces objections that parallel the well-known objections to the former theory—but parallel responses are also available. The objection that the account turns an explanatory connection into a definitional truth can be rejected, as can a version of the infamous 'swampman' objection.

In response to the objection that the account sets a high evidential bar for attributions of cooperation (or altruism, etc.), we can only say that it does indeed, but that this is something we should accept. The recent history account makes the concept of cooperation (like function and adaptation) explanatory but empirically onerous. We cannot conclude that a behaviour is cooperative (or altruistic, etc.) in the absence of knowledge regarding the selection processes that have maintained it in recent history.

In the last two sections, I further argued that the classification of an action should be (i) strategy-relative and (ii) task-relative. Since it is strategies that are selected for, rather than specific social actions, we should classify actions by the selection history of the wider strategy to which they belong. Since actions often contribute to the generation of harm or benefit as part of collaborative tasks, and not in isolation, we should consider the past fitness effects of actions-in-tasks, recognizing that the same action may have very different fitness effects when performed in different collaborative contexts.

2

Hamilton's Rule as an Organizing Framework

Hamilton's rule, on the face of it, is a very simple statement of the conditions under which natural selection will favour the genes underlying a behavioural strategy. What the rule says, in a nutshell, is that selection favours the genes for a particular strategy when $rb > c$, where c is the fitness cost imposed on the actor, b is the fitness benefit conferred on a recipient, and r is the coefficient of relatedness between actors and recipients (Hamilton, 1963, 1964). In plain terms, the rule tells us that the genes for a strategy are favoured when the cost to the actor is offset by a sufficient benefit to sufficiently related recipients. Figure 2.1 provides a visualization of what the rule says, although (as we will soon see) it is in some ways a misleading visualization.

This principle is one of the most important ideas in social evolution theory. It is also, for all its apparent simplicity, one of the most controversial. In a strongly worded (2010) *Nature* article, Martin A. Nowak, Corina E. Tarnita, and Edward O. Wilson claimed that 'Hamilton's rule almost never holds', in the sense that it almost never provides a correct statement of the conditions for the evolution by natural selection of a social behaviour (Nowak et al., 2010, p. 1059). In 2011, *Nature* published five rebuttals, one of which asserted in no uncertain terms that Nowak and colleagues' arguments 'are based on a misunderstanding of evolutionary theory' (Abbot and 136 others, 2011, p. E1). The letter was signed by 137 social evolution researchers. Later that year, in a detailed defence of the rule, Andy Gardner, Stuart West, and Geoff Wild (2011, p. 1038) wrote that 'it is simply incorrect to claim that Hamilton's rule requires restrictive assumptions or that it almost never holds'. Nowak, Wilson, and colleagues were not persuaded (Nowak et al., 2011), and an article by Ben Allen, Nowak, and Wilson (2013) provided a second barrage of criticism of Hamilton's rule, partly in response to Gardner et al. (2011).

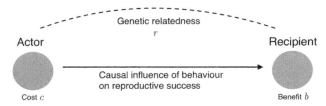

Figure 2.1 Hamilton's rule, informally. Roughly speaking, the genes for a social behaviour are favoured by natural selection if and only if $rb > c$, where b is the benefit the behaviour confers on a recipient, c is the cost its expression imposes on the actor, and r is the coefficient of relatedness between actor and recipient.

I have weighed into this on-going debate before, seeking to bring out its connections to philosophical debates about causality and explanation (Birch, 2014b; Birch and Okasha, 2015). Here I provide an updated assessment of the status of Hamilton's rule, again stressing the philosophical dimensions of the debate.[1] My aim is to defend the use of a particular version of Hamilton's rule (David Queller's 1992a 'general model', which I call 'HRG') for a particular explanatory purpose: that of an *organizing framework* for social evolution research. Queller (1992a) found a way of deriving Hamilton's rule that was more general than Hamilton's own derivations, and this version of the rule has since become a standard version in the theoretical literature (Gardner et al., 2011). This chapter sets out the mathematical basis of Queller's general model, and explains why it is apt to serve as an organizing framework. The next chapter defends it from criticism and compares it with alternative frameworks.

2.1 Queller's 'General Model' (HRG)

First, I will set out the key details of Queller's (1992a) general model. I will go somewhat more slowly than Queller's original paper, in the hope that readers with no familiarity with this sort of argument can follow it. However, readers who wish to avoid mathematical details altogether may

---

[1] This chapter differs substantively and not just presentationally from my (2014b) article. Perhaps most significantly, I no longer think the value of Hamilton's rule as an organizing framework relies on the cost and benefit coefficients being interpretable as quantitative measures of direct causal influence (see Section 2.3).

safely skip most of this section (but please note the key result at the end, labelled 'HRG').

Queller's (1992a) argument begins with the Price equation (Price, 1970, 1972a), an abstract mathematical description of the evolutionary change in the frequency of a gene between earlier ('ancestral') and later ('descendant') populations (e.g. consecutive generations in a discrete generations model, or earlier and later census points in an overlapping generations model):

$$\Delta \bar{p} = \frac{1}{\bar{w}} \left[\mathrm{Cov}(w_i, p_i) + \mathrm{E}(w_i \Delta p_i) \right] \qquad (2.1)$$

The derivation of the Price equation is discussed in the book's appendix (see also Price, 1970, 1972a; Frank, 1995, 1998, 2012; Rice, 2004; Okasha, 2006; Gardner, 2008). Here I will simply explain what the equation means. The variable p_i represents the individual gene frequency (or, for short, genic value) of the ith individual in the population with respect to the allele of interest.[2] The mean value of p_i over all individuals, $\bar{p}$, is simply the population frequency of the gene. The variable w_i is the number of descendants contributed to the descendant population by the ith member of the ancestral population. This can be glossed for now as a measure of 'individual fitness', although the subject of fitness, and the different ways in which it may be conceptualized in the context of social evolution, will be considered in detail in Chapter 5. The mean value of w_i over all individuals, $\bar{w}$, is thus the mean individual fitness in the population.

The Price equation states that the overall change in population frequency of the gene between the ancestral and descendant populations ($\Delta \bar{p}$) is equal to the sum of two population statistics (both divided by the mean fitness, $\bar{w}$): $\mathrm{Cov}(w_i, p_i)$, the covariance in the ancestral population between individual gene frequency and individual fitness; and $\mathrm{E}(w_i \Delta p_i)$, the expectation, across all ancestor-descendant pairs, of the change in p_i between an ancestor and one of its descendants.

The derivation of the equation requires few assumptions about the evolving population it describes. Inward migration is assumed absent, since all members of the descendant population must have ancestors in

---

[2] An individual's 'individual gene frequency' for some allele is the number of copies of the allele it possesses at the relevant locus, divided by its ploidy. In other words, it is its number of copies expressed as a fraction of the maximum number of copies it could have at that locus.

the ancestral population. It must also be the case that all descendants have the same number of ancestors,[3] that every individual in the ancestral population has a well-defined value for individual fitness (w_i), and that every individual in both the ancestral and descendant populations has a well-defined value for individual gene frequency (p_i), but nothing else is assumed.

From this starting point, Queller makes (in the space of two sentences) three crucial moves. First, he notes that the Price equation is true not only when p_i is interpreted as an individual gene frequency, but also when p_i is interpreted as a linear combination of such frequencies over multiple alleles at multiple loci. One such linear combination is the 'breeding value' of quantitative genetics, which is essentially an individual's trait value for a specific phenotypic character as predicted by the sum of average effects (in the sense of Fisher, 1930, 1941) of all relevant alleles (Falconer and Mackay, 1996; Gardner et al., 2011).[4] When p_i is interpreted as the ith individual's breeding value for a phenotypic character, $\Delta\bar{p}$ is interpretable as the change in the population mean of the breeding value; and, given a further technical assumption I will not discuss here, $\Delta\bar{p}$ is equal to the change in the population mean of the phenotypic character itself (Frank, 1998, p. 17). Interpreting p_i as a breeding value is important if we want a version of Hamilton's rule that describes the evolutionary change in the population means of quantitative, polygenic traits, and not simply in the frequencies of individual genes.

Second, Queller assumes that $E(w_i\Delta p_i) = 0$, so that the expectation term of the Price equation disappears, leaving:

$$\Delta\bar{p} = \frac{1}{\bar{w}}\left[\text{Cov}(w_i, p_i)\right] \tag{2.2}$$

He takes this to follow from 'neglecting meiotic drive and genetic drift' (p. 376), but this is not quite correct. When we interpret p_i as a breeding value, the assumption that there is no systematic change in p_i across

---

[3] See Kerr and Godfrey-Smith (2009) for an extended version of the Price equation that relaxes this assumption, as well as the 'no inward migration' assumption.

[4] These formal arguments assume nothing about the nature of the phenotypic character of interest. It may be a qualitative, all-or-nothing character, such as the presence or absence of a particular strategy, in which case we assign organisms a phenotypic value of 1 if they have it and 0 is they do not. It may also be a quantitative, continuously varying character, such as the probability with which an organism adopts a particular strategy.

ancestor-descendant pairs requires not only that genes are transmitted without bias (hence no meiotic drive, no gametic selection, and no random bias due to drift or mutation) but also that the average effects of alleles on the phenotype of interest are constant (Frank, 1998). Since the average effects of alleles can change simply due to changes in the frequency of dominance and epistatic effects, as well as due to changes in the ecological environment, this is a substantial assumption. We might think of it as the assumption that the 'genic environment' is held fixed.[5]

There is a certain amount of interpretative leeway regarding the meaning of assuming that $E(w_i \Delta p_i) = 0$. If we regard ourselves to be representing biased transmission and changes in average effects as absent, then we are making *idealizations* (in the sense of Thomson-Jones, 2005), since we know these assumptions will often be false in real populations. However, we might also think of ourselves as simply choosing to focus on the part of the evolutionary change that is independent of transmission biases and changes in average effects, in order to isolate the effects directly attributable to natural selection acting in a constant genic environment, while making no commitments about the contribution made by other processes to the total change. This is the interpretation favoured by Steven A. Frank (1998) and Gardner et al. (2011), among others. On this interpretation, the neglect of $E(w_i \Delta p_i)$ is an exercise in *abstraction* (again, in the sense of Thomson-Jones, 2005): we are not representing certain causal factors as absent, but simply omitting them from our analysis in order to focus on the effects of causes we especially want to understand.[6]

Queller's third move is to interpret the term that remains, $Cov(w_i, p_i)$, as capturing the effects of natural selection on the evolution of the character of interest (it is, as he puts it, the 'selective change' in the character). We should qualify this: $Cov(w_i, p_i)$ captures the effects directly attributable to natural selection acting in a constant genic environment, but it does

---

[5] This issue is often discussed in the context of Fisher's (1930) 'fundamental theorem of natural selection', which similarly relies on 'holding fixed' the average effects of alleles, which can be interpreted as holding fixed the 'genic environment'. See Price (1972b); Edwards (1994); Frank (1997b); Okasha (2008); Ewens (2011); Birch (2016b) and references therein for further discussion. I also revisit this crucial notion of the 'genic environment' in the book's conclusion.

[6] See Thomson-Jones (2005) on the difference between idealization and abstraction, Godfrey-Smith (2009a) on the application of this distinction in evolutionary biology, and Potochnik (2009) for a related discussion in the context of optimality modelling.

not capture the ways in which selection may alter the genic environment. Moreover, in the presence of drift even this qualified interpretation would be questionable, since drift can give rise to random covariance between one's genes and one's number of descendants (see Okasha, 2006, Ch. 1), but on the assumption that drift is absent, it is reasonable.[7]

To get from equation (2.2) to a version of Hamilton's rule, we partition the covariance term into two components: one corresponding to rb, the other to $-c$. The first step is to write a linear regression model for the fitness of the ith individual. This expresses its fitness as a linear function of its own individual gene frequency (p_i) and the average individual gene frequency of its social partners $(\hat{p}_i)$, in which each quantity is weighted by a partial regression coefficient:[8]

$$w_i = \alpha + \beta_1 p_i + \beta_2 \hat{p}_i + \epsilon_{w_i} \tag{2.3}$$

Here, β_1 is the partial regression of one's fitness on one's own individual gene frequency, controlling for one's social partner's individual gene frequency; β_2 is the partial regression of one's fitness on one's social partner's individual gene frequency, controlling for one's own. α is a constant and is interpretable as the baseline 'non-social' component of fitness, assumed to be the same for every individual. The residual, ϵ_{w_i}, quantifies the extent to which the ith individual's fitness departs from the value predicted by the regression model.

This regression model can be visualized intuitively as the 'plane of best fit' through the population data when one plots w_i as a dependent variable against p_i and $\hat{p}_i$ for every individual in the population. It is important to see that, because the regression model includes a residual term, it is compatible in principle with *any* set of population data. Naturally, the regression model will fit some populations better than others (i.e. the residuals will be larger in some cases than others), but there can be no

---

[7] Grafen (2000) formulates a version of the Price equation that makes room for drift by looking at the expected values of $Cov(w_i, p_i)$ and $E(w_i \Delta p_i)$ across a measure space of possible outcomes, and Rice (2008) provides further developments of the Price equation to incorporate stochastic effects, but these formulations introduce complications I intend to leave aside here.

[8] The technique of decomposing the response to selection using a regression model of fitness was originally developed by Lande and Arnold (1983) and Arnold and Wade (1984a, b). Queller's innovation was to apply the technique to recover a version of Hamilton's rule.

individual in any population, real or modelled, of which the regression equation is false.[9]

I should also emphasize, foreshadowing the discussion of the next section, that the statistical associations captured in the regression coefficients, being population statistics and not sample statistics, are properties of populations that exist independently of whether there is anyone around to estimate them: although it is natural to *visualize* the regression model as a plane of best fit through a set of population data, the model is still true of populations for which we have no data.

We then substitute our regression model of fitness into the Price equation, obtaining the following partition:[10]

$$\overline{w}\Delta\overline{p} = \mathrm{Cov}(\alpha, p_i) + \beta_1\mathrm{Var}(p_i) + \beta_2\mathrm{Cov}(\hat{p}_i, p_i) + \mathrm{Cov}(\epsilon_{w_i}, p_i) \quad (2.4)$$

We can simplify this by noting firstly that p_i cannot co-vary with the constant α, and secondly that p_i, by virtue of being a predictor in the regression model, cannot co-vary with the residual ϵ_{w_i}. Eliminating these terms leaves us with a simplified partition:

$$\overline{w}\Delta\overline{p} = \beta_1\mathrm{Var}(p_i) + \beta_2\mathrm{Cov}(\hat{p}_i, p_i) \quad (2.5)$$

We rearrange this to yield:

$$\overline{w}\Delta\overline{p} = \left\{ \beta_1 + \beta_2 \frac{\mathrm{Cov}(\hat{p}_i, p_i)}{\mathrm{Var}(p_i)} \right\} \mathrm{Var}(p_i) \quad (2.6)$$

Finally, because neither $\overline{w}$ nor $\mathrm{Var}(p_i)$ can be negative, we can derive from this a condition for an increase in the population mean of the character:

$$\Delta\overline{p} > 0 \iff \frac{\mathrm{Cov}(\hat{p}_i, p_i)}{\mathrm{Var}(p_i)}\beta_2 > -\beta_1, \text{ provided } \mathrm{Var}(p_i) \neq 0 \quad (2.7)$$

---

[9] A caveat: the partial regression coefficients are defined only if (i) there is non-zero variance in both predictor variables and (ii) the two predictor variables are not perfectly collinear. These are fairly minimal conditions, and it is reasonable to assume that they will be met in a very wide range of cases.

[10] Note that the covariance between p_i and itself is simply the variance in p_i.

To obtain the rule in its familiar $rb > c$ form, we introduce the following notation:

$$r = \text{Cov}(\hat{p}_i, p_i)/\text{Var}(p_i)$$
$$b = \beta_2$$
$$c = -\beta_1$$

This simplified notation allows us to rewrite (2.7) as:

$$\Delta \bar{p} > 0 \iff rb > c, \text{ provided Var}(p_i) \neq 0 \qquad \text{(HRG)}$$

In my (2014b) article, I called this formulation of the rule 'HRG' ('G' for 'General', following Queller's description, although it could equally be for 'Genic'). The description of HRG as a 'general' result is in some ways misleading, to the extent that it downplays the assumption of $E(w_i \Delta p_i) = 0$ and the neglect of drift and migration. However, I will keep this label here. I called Queller's formulation HRG to contrast it with the plethora of alternative formulations of Hamilton's rule that require further assumptions: for example, an assumption of weak selection or assumptions regarding the payoff structure of social interaction. Some of these assumptions, and their relationship to the concept of inclusive fitness, will be discussed in Chapter 5. Here I simply want to note that, as Queller (1992a) emphasized, such assumptions are not required by HRG, which can be interpreted as a general mathematical truth about the action of natural selection in a constant genic environment.

2.2 Cost, Benefit, and Relatedness as Population Statistics

Let us consider more closely the meaning of r, b, and c, or, as they are commonly known, the coefficients of relatedness, benefit, and cost. Intuitively, one might take these coefficients to be referring to features of a specific social interaction on a particular occasion (what one might call, borrowing some philosophical jargon, a 'token' social interaction). One might assume that c and b denote the payoffs of that interaction for the actor and recipient, and that r denotes some measure of the degree of genetic relatedness between them, as suggested by Figure 2.1.

However, I noted from the outset that the figure was misleading, and it is time to explain why. While the above is often harmless as an informal gloss on what the coefficients in HRG mean, it is not how they are formally defined. Formally, they are not properties of token interactions at all, but population statistics—specifically, regression coefficients—computed by averaging over the whole population. In broad terms, r can be visualized as the 'line of best fit' through a set of population data plotting $\hat{p}_i$ against p_i for every individual in the population; while, as noted above earlier, c and b can be visualized as specifying the 'plane of best fit' through a set of population data plotting, for each individual in the population, w_i against p_i and $\hat{p}_i$.

The upshot is that the coefficients in HRG are properties of populations, not of individual organisms or token social interactions. Strictly speaking, it makes no sense to talk of the relatedness (in this sense) between one particular individual and its social partner in isolation, nor does it make sense to talk of the cost incurred or benefit received by a single individual on a particular occasion, assuming these terms are intended to have the meaning they have in HRG. Regression coefficients cannot be defined for a single data point. Of course, we can still talk of the payoff lost or gained by a particular organism on a particular occasion, or of the genealogical relationship between two organisms, but we should not equate these notions with the cost, benefit, and relatedness coefficients in HRG. Cost and benefit are not payoffs; relatedness is not genealogy (Grafen, 1985).

Thinking of cost, benefit, and relatedness as population statistics has some important and potentially counterintuitive consequences. One is that these quantities are all about differences: c and b quantify the *differential* fitness effects of having a higher than average value (in oneself or one's social partners) for the character of interest, and r quantifies the *differential* genetic similarity (at loci relevant to a social character of interest) between pairs of organisms that interact socially, relative to the average genetic similarity (at the relevant loci) of a randomly selected pair of individuals from the population (Grafen, 1985). If there is no variation at the relevant loci, r, b, and c are not even well-defined.[11]

---

[11] There is a popular misconception that relatedness is simply a matter of absolute numbers of shared genes, leading (for example) to the idea that, if humans share approximately 99% of our genes with chimpanzees, then $r \approx 0.99$, suggesting an extremely strong incentive to cooperate. As should now be clear, this rests on a misunderstanding of the meaning of r, which measures differential similarity at loci where there is genetic variation (Dawkins, 1979; Grafen, 1982).

Another consequence is that, since regression lines can slope downwards as well as upwards, all three coefficients can be negative. Hence, although talk of costs and benefits intuitively connotes that costs will detract from an agent's fitness while benefits increase it, this need not be the case: b and c can be positive or negative, and HRG still holds regardless of their sign. So, although Hamilton's rule is most often associated with the evolution of prosocial behaviour (i.e. mutually beneficial cooperation or altruism), HRG describes the conditions for any social behaviour—including antisocial (i.e. selfish or spiteful) behaviour—to be subject to positive selection.

That relatedness too can be negative is harder to see. In what sort of biological scenario might a negative value of relatedness arise? It would be one in which social partners are *less* genetically similar at relevant loci, on average, than a pair of individuals drawn at random from the population (Grafen, 1985). Hamilton (1970) suggested that such a scenario would be conducive to the evolution of spite: by inflicting harm on their social partners, even at a cost to themselves, individuals with the genes for spite could increase the relative representation of these genes in the next generation. HRG underwrites this prediction, since it implies that, when r is negative, a social behaviour can be favoured by selection even if its fitness effects on both actor and recipient are also negative (Gardner and West, 2004a, b, 2006; West and Gardner, 2010; Smead and Forber, 2013).

2.3 The Organizing Role of HRG

What is the explanatory role of HRG in social evolution research? As I noted from the outset, this is a contested issue, and the central issue of this chapter and the next. In the rest of this chapter, I will set out my favoured answer. In the next chapter, I will argue that recent criticisms of HRG, although they may undermine other ideas one might have about its explanatory role, do not undermine the picture I favour.

I have in the past argued that HRG serves as a 'unifying principle' for social evolution theory (Birch, 2014b). The suggestion here was that, in identifying a condition that is satisfied by all processes of social evolution by natural selection, HRG latches on to an important feature that these processes have in common. I should be clear, however, about the sort of 'unification' HRG achieves. The sort of 'unification' I have in mind is not 'unification' in Philip Kitcher's (1981; 1989) sense. Kitcher's notion of unification involves identifying 'argument patterns' that can be used over and over again to derive truths about various phenomena of interest. HRG, however, does not unify in this way. The relation between HRG and the models of particular ecological scenarios it unifies is not one of derivation: social evolution theorists do not use HRG to *derive* more detailed evolutionary models.[12]

Yet there is still an important sense in which HRG is 'unifying'. For HRG provides an *organizing framework* within which the results of more detailed models of particular evolutionary scenarios can be interpreted, compared, contrasted, and classified.[13] Social evolution theory is a broad church, encompassing a plethora of models that vary a great deal in both the formal methods they employ and the dynamical details of the evolutionary processes they aim to represent. On the face of it, for example, computer simulations of 'Tit-for-Tat' reciprocity (e.g. Axelrod and Hamilton, 1981) have little in common with analyses of kin selection based on solving partial differential equations (e.g. Taylor and Frank, 1996), and neither looks to have much in common with classical population-genetic models. But since we know that HRG is true of all these models, despite the variation in their mathematical details, we can interpret all of them as describing different ways in which the fundamental $rb > c$ condition

---

[12] Kitcher informally presents the unificationist view as the idea that understanding involves 'seeing connections, common patterns, in what initially appeared to be different situations' (Kitcher, 1989, p. 432). It seems to me that HRG fits this informal description better than it fits Kitcher's formal account.

[13] Morrison (2000) and Woodward (2014) have noted the plurality of forms of unification in the sciences. For example, Woodward (2014, Section 5.4) observes that

> unification, as it figures in science is a quite heterogeneous notion, covering many different sorts of achievements. Some kinds of unification consist in the creation of a common classificatory scheme or descriptive vocabulary where no satisfactory scheme previously existed, as when early investigators like Linnaeus constructed comprehensive and principled systems of biological classification. Another kind of unification involves the creation of a common mathematical framework or formalism which can be applied to many different sorts of phenomena, as when the systems of equations devised by Lagrange and [the physicist W. R.] Hamilton were first developed in connection with mechanics and then applied to domains like electromagnetism and thermodynamics.

The unification afforded by HRG contains elements of both of these kinds: it provides a classificatory scheme and a descriptive vocabulary that derive from the construction of a common mathematical framework (but see also Chapter 3, footnote 4).

can come to be satisfied. In other words, HRG shows how the results of many particular models, from diverse modelling traditions, can be seen as ways of satisfying a very general statistical condition for positive evolutionary change.

Because of this, HRG allows us to make useful comparisons between models: comparisons that highlight biologically significant similarities and differences in the processes they represent. For example, HRG allows us to see that mechanisms as diverse as kin discrimination, limited dispersal, recognition of phenotypic markers, shared habitat preference, and horizontal gene transfer can all play a similar role in promoting the evolution of social behaviour, since all of them can be viewed as sources of positive genetic assortment between social partners (see 'Indirect Fitness Explanations' later in the chapter). Similarly, it allows us to see that punishment, reward, reciprocity, pleiotropy, and linkage can play a relevantly similar role, because all can be viewed as ways of coupling the short-term costs of possessing the genes for a particular behaviour with longer-term direct fitness returns (see 'Direct Fitness Explanations' later in the chapter).

It will help here to be a little more precise about what I mean in calling HRG an 'organizing framework'. Suppose we have a set M comprising models of particular target systems (in this context, models of social evolution in particular ecological scenarios). The idea is that a model outside that set, Ω, is able to serve as an organizing framework for M if (i) Ω represents all the target systems represented by the members of M, but does so in less detail, (ii) Ω assumes nothing that is not assumed by all members of M, and (iii) there are relations between Ω and the members of M that enable us to classify the members of M in an illuminating way.

This three-part account allows us to see exactly why Queller's 'general model' is well-placed to serve as an organizing framework for a wide range of models of social evolution. First, because of the flexibility in the interpretation of p_i, HRG can be interpreted as a highly abstract representation of the evolutionary change between ancestral and descendant populations in any character that is genetically inherited from parents to offspring, so it satisfies condition (i) (moreover, see Chapter 6 for an extension to horizontal transmission, and Chapter 8 for an extension to non-genetic inheritance). Second, although the derivation of HRG does make some important assumptions—no drift, and $E(w_i \Delta p_i) = 0$—these are assumptions it shares with a wide range of models that focus on representing the change due to natural selection acting in a constant genic environment rather than the change attributable to other causes, so it satisfies condition (ii). Third, the partition of the selective change achieved by HRG—that is, its partitioning into an 'rb' component and a '$-c$' component—enables a useful classification of models and modelling results, because it allows us to classify them by their commitments regarding the sign and relative magnitude of these components. So Queller's general model has all of the key features we require of an organizing framework.

I should say more, however, about the nature of the classification afforded by HRG, and why it is useful. One way to visualize the classification HRG affords is in terms of a 'space of explanations' defined by rb on the x-axis and c on the y-axis (Figure 2.2). All models of genetic social evolution aim to provide explanations of positive change in the frequency of a gene, or in the population mean of a polygenic character, and all such explanations fall somewhere within this space. I will switch here to talking about 'potential explanations' rather than models, since the same model might be used to construct various different potential explanations of evolutionary change (e.g. by exploring different sets of parameter values), each with different commitments regarding the values of rb and c. However, once we specify a set of parameter values and

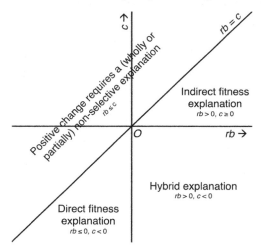

Figure 2.2 A space of explanations. Queller's general model allows us to distinguish four broad classes of explanation of positive evolutionary change in a social trait, defined by their commitments regarding the values of rb and c. All explanations of positive change lie somewhere in this space. The corresponding space for negative change is an inversion of this space (with O as the centre of inversion).

construct an adequately specified potential explanation, that explanation will be located somewhere in the space—in other words, it will have certain commitments regarding the sign and relative magnitudes of rb and c.[14] We can sort all such explanations into one of four categories on the basis of these commitments. The four categories are: indirect fitness explanations, direct fitness explanations, hybrid explanations, and non-selective explanations.[15]

Before illustrating these categories, I should note that I am not the first to emphasize this organizing role of HRG. I do not intend to present this view as radical or revisionary: rather, my aim is to articulate what I take to be the source of HRG's existing attraction in the eyes of its proponents (e.g. Gardner et al., 2007, 2011; West et al., 2007c; Marshall, 2015). For example, Gardner et al. (2007) write that:

The most powerful and simple approach to evolutionary problems is to start with a method such as population genetics, . . . game theory or direct-fitness maximiz-ation techniques. The results of these analyses can then be interpreted within the frameworks that Price's theorem and Hamilton's rule [HRG] provide. The correct use of these powerful theorems is to translate the results of such disparate analyses, conducted with a variety of methodologies and looking at very different problems, into the common language of social evolution theory.

(Gardner et al., 2007, p. 224)

This is another way of putting the point that HRG provides an organizing framework; I simply favour a different metaphor. In my terms, HRG organizes social evolution research by allowing us to locate specific mod-elling results in a space of explanations.

2.4 Indirect Fitness Explanations

To flesh out that metaphor, I will now briefly review the main sorts of models that provide explanations in each of the four categories. My aim is not to provide an exhaustive survey of the field. I simply aim to show

---

[14] These commitments are sometimes stated explicitly, but they are often left implicit in the model. For example, if a model contains no source of genetic assortment, it will be the case that $rb = 0$ in that model, but this may not be stated explicitly.

[15] Here I drop 'potential' and talk simply of 'explanations' rather than 'potential explan-ations', but I take it for granted that any potential explanation of a real-world case of evolu-tionary change requires empirical support before it can be regarded as a true explanation.

that there exists enough diversity among explanations of social evolution for an organizing framework to be desirable, and that HRG, by marking out a four-way distinction between indirect fitness explanations, direct fitness explanations, hybrid explanations, and non-selective explanations, provides such a framework. HRG is not the only such framework—I will discuss some of the alternatives in the next chapter—but, for reasons I will set out in due course, I take it to be a particularly useful one. The region of the space in which $rb > 0$, $c \geqslant 0$ and $rb > c$ contains indirect fitness explanations. What unites and distinguishes this class of explanations is a reliance on positive rb, either because both r and b are positive, as is needed for the evolution of altruism, or because both are negative, as is needed for the evolution of spite. I will focus in this subsection on indirect fitness explanations for the evolution of altruism. Such explanations rely on there being a mechanism that explains the systematic tendency for the benefits caused by the expression of genes for altruism to fall differentially on other bearers of those genes; in other words, they rely on positive genetic assortment at loci relevant to altruistic behaviour.

Among explanations for positive genetic assortment, we can usefully distinguish between those which rely on kinship—that is, shared genealogical ancestry—as a source of genetic similarity and those which do not. In the former category are *kin discrimination* and *limited dispersal*. Kin discrimination involves organisms detecting and preferentially interacting with kin. Note that this does not require any cognitive ability to recognize kin as kin, let alone a cognitive ability to estimate degrees of kinship. All that matters is that, for one reason or another, actors behave in a way that is sensitive to whether or not the recipient is a close genealogical relative. For example, long-tailed tits (*Aegithalos caudatus*), if they do not breed themselves, assist in raising the offspring of others. Using learned vocal cues, they are able to discriminate between relatives and non-relatives, and they preferentially help the former (Russell and Hatchwell, 2001; West et al., 2007b).[16]

By contrast, when relatedness arises through limited dispersal, the behaviour of social actors need not be sensitive to any properties of the recipient. The idea is simply that, for various ecological reasons, leaving one's birth site is sometimes hard, with the upshot that social partners

---

[16] I am indebted in this chapter to West et al. (2007b): several of the examples are drawn from their wide-ranging survey.

are differentially likely to have shared a birth site. This means they are differentially likely to have shared ancestry, resulting in genetic correlations. For example, meerkats (*Suricata suricatta*) appear not to discriminate actively between kin and non-kin. In the wild, however, limited dispersal ensures that groups are formed of close relatives (Clutton-Brock et al., 2000; West et al., 2007b). The drawback to limited dispersal as a source of relatedness, as regards the evolution of altruism, is that it can increase the strength of competition among relatives (Hamilton, 1971). In some cases, the increase in local competition may cancel out or even outweigh the selection for helping relatives (Wilson et al., 1992; Taylor, 1992; Queller, 1994). This competition effect can be conceptualized within HRG as a factor that erodes b, since the benefit conferred by the helping behaviour indirectly harms the competitors of the beneficiary, and these competitors are also relatives of the actor (Frank, 1985; West et al., 2002; Marshall, 2015).[17]

What about kinship-independent mechanisms? One might wonder how there could be positive r without kinship. Don't they mean the same thing? But they do not. We have already seen that, in social evolution theory, relatedness is defined as a regression coefficient that measures the genetic similarity between actors and recipients at the genomic loci relevant to the character of interest. Hence, if there are mechanisms that generate genetic similarity at relevant loci without relying on genealogical kinship, then these too will contribute to the value of r.

Richard Dawkins's (1976) 'greenbeard' thought experiment (based on a remark in Hamilton, 1964) provides one example. Dawkins asks us to consider a gene or gene-complex that causes its bearers to (a) grow a green beard, (b) recognize other bearers on the basis of their green beards, and (c) differentially help these individuals at a cost to themselves. Could such a trait ever be favoured by natural selection? Dawkins argues that it could. The key consideration is that, by causing its bearers to help other bearers of the same allele, the greenbeard gene may indirectly increase its genetic representation in the next generation, in spite of the cost it

---

[17] It can also, perhaps less intuitively, be conceptualized as a factor that erodes r, if we define r with reference to the subpopulation consisting of the recipient's competitors, not the global population (Queller, 1994). As competition becomes more local, the reference population of competitors becomes increasingly dominated by the focal individual's relatives, so the focal individual's *differential* relatedness to its social partners is eroded.

imposes on its bearer. This argument relies on the idea that there is positive relatedness—in the regression sense—between social partners with respect to the greenbeard locus. Note, however, that the mechanism does not require any genealogical kinship between bearers of the greenbeard gene. We can suppose, if we want to, that the initial bearers of the trait are genealogically unrelated, and that the greenbeard mutant appears independently in each of them.

The example is hypothetical, but strikingly similar effects (mediated not by literal green beards, but by phenotypic markers playing a similar role) have since been discovered empirically (Gardner and West, 2010; West and Gardner, 2010). For example, Keller and Ross (1998) discovered an allele in the fire ant *Solenopsis invicta* that (a) causes queens with the allele to emit a characteristic odour, and (b) causes workers with the allele to spare these queens while decapitating others. The 'green beard' in this scenario is the odour: a phenotypic marker, produced by a certain allele, that attracts a differential benefit (i.e. the benefit of being spared decapitation) from other bearers of that allele.

The essence of a greenbeard effect is that a social trait is connected, for genetic reasons, with some mechanism for generating positive assortment between bearers of the trait. The connection may arise through pleiotropy (i.e. multiple phenotypic effects from a single gene, as in the fire ant example) or through linkage between different genes. In a 'classic' greenbeard scenario, the assortative mechanism relies on a phenotypic marker, such as an odour. But other assortative mechanisms exist. For example, as Hamilton (1975) pointed out, a social trait may be linked to a gene promoting a certain kind of habitat preference (as in Wilson and Hölldobler's 2005 model of the evolution of eusociality, criticized by Foster et al., 2006). A recent model by Powers et al. (2011) provides another example: they show how assortment can arise when a gene for a social trait is linked to another that encodes a preference for social group size.

In microbes, a different way of generating locus-specific genetic correlations is through horizontal gene transfer, the transfer of genetic material between individuals by means other than reproduction (Nogueira et al., 2009; Rankin et al., 2011b; Mc Ginty et al., 2013; West and Gardner, 2013; Birch, 2014a). In Chapter 6, I will argue that this should cause us to rethink the very concept of genetic relatedness, but I do not want to pre-empt that discussion here. For now, let us simply note that this mechanism can generate genetic resemblance between social partners in a way that does not rely on genealogical kinship. From a certain oblique angle, we could describe this as another variety of greenbeard mechanism, since it provides another way in which a social trait can come to be linked to an assortative mechanism. However, this mechanism differs in important ways from classic greenbeard phenomena (see Chapter 6).

How important are kinship-independent mechanisms? One important feature all such mechanisms share is that they produce genetic correlations at specific genomic loci only; they do not generate genetic correlation at every locus in the genome. To the best of our knowledge, the only sources of whole-genome relatedness in nature are kinship-dependent mechanisms. This leads naturally to the thought that greenbeard genes (of any variety) are 'intragenomic outlaws', in the sense that the rest of the genome stands to gain by suppressing their expression. This line of argument suggests that kinship-dependent mechanisms have a special role to play in the evolution of altruism, since only these mechanisms align the interests of the whole genome, and so only these mechanisms can give rise to stable altruistic phenotypes (Dawkins, 1976; Grafen, 1985; Okasha, 2002).

As Mark Ridley and Alan Grafen (1981) have argued, there is something apt about the phrase 'intragenomic outlaws', but also something that is potentially misleading (see also Gardner and West, 2010). In most greenbeard scenarios, the selection pressures operating at other genomic loci are no different from the pressures operating at the greenbeard locus itself. This is because (a) selection at any locus would favour a 'falsebeard' allele that selectively suppressed the altruistic behaviour while retaining the associated marker; while (b) selection at other loci would favour an allele that suppressed the whole phenotype (i.e. both the marker and the altruism) if and only if such an allele would also be favoured at the greenbeard locus. To see the logic behind (b), note that if bearers of the greenbeard gene are fitter on average than non-bearers, then the rest of the genome does not stand to gain by suppressing the whole greenbeard phenotype, since, on average, it attracts benefits that outweigh the associated costs. Meanwhile, if bearers are less fit on average than non-bearers, then an allele suppressing the whole phenotype would be favoured even if it were to arise at the greenbeard locus itself.

However, even if we avoid the term 'intragenomic outlaws', it is important to emphasize that a greenbeard mechanism is always vulnerable to subversion by an allele that selectively suppresses the altruistic behaviour while retaining the associated marker that attracts benefits from others. In other words, it always pays to be a 'falsebeard', a free rider who subverts the assortative mechanism (Gardner and West, 2010). This alone provides a reason to doubt the evolutionary stability, in the long term, of altruistic traits that rely on greenbeard mechanisms. They will be stable only if, for some reason, the altruism cannot be suppressed without also suppressing the marker.[18]

2.5 Direct Fitness Explanations

Direct fitness explanations are united by their reliance on negative c, and by the absence of any reliance on positive rb. For many behaviours, the source of negative c is no mystery, because the behaviour has a clear direct advantage. This is especially true of many behaviours that benefit the actor at the expense of others. If, for example, we see a social predator such as a wolf or a hyena stealing food from a fellow group member, we need not look beyond direct fitness effects to explain this behaviour, because there is a clear advantage to feeding rather than starving.

Social evolution theorists have tended to focus on constructing direct fitness explanations for behaviour that benefits others (i.e. 'prosocial' behaviour). There are many situations in which a prosocial behaviour pays off for the actor over the course of its lifetime, even if it seems costly at the time it is performed. Direct fitness explanations of this general sort are widely thought to be particularly important in explaining the origins of human cooperation, because genetic relatedness in early human populations is estimated to have been low.[19] Here I will consider three broad classes of ways in which a short-term costly trait can come to be associated with direct fitness returns over the longer term. These are (i) *direct returns from task completion*; (ii) *reciprocity, reward, and punishment*; and (iii) *pleiotropy and linkage*.

---

[18] I revisit this point in Chapter 4, Section 4.4.

[19] A study of contemporary hunter-gatherers by Hill et al. (2011) estimates that $r \approx 0.05$ in these societies. While this is not conclusive evidence of low relatedness in Palaeolithic societies, it does suggest we should be wary of assuming greater degrees of relatedness. I revisit this issue in Chapter 8.

Direct returns from task completion describes a situation in which an actor participates in a collaborative task, incurring a short-term cost of some kind (e.g. in the form of expended energy, risk of injury, or simply an opportunity cost), but gains in the longer term provided the task is completed successfully. The $c < 0$ condition requires that the expected gain from participating exceeds the short-term cost, and this may sometimes be the case even in the absence of any positive genetic assortment between the participants. For example, in a stag hunt game, the strategy of hunting the stag can increase in frequency without positive assortment of any kind if the payoff for success is sufficiently large and the initial frequency of the strategy is sufficiently high. Such strategies can evolve more readily, however, when we introduce sources of phenotypic assortment, such as learning from neighbours or partner choice (i.e. cooperators choosing to interact with other known cooperators) (Skyrms, 2004). In the framework provided by HRG, these are all interpreted as ways of generating negative c, since, in the absence of genetic assortment, it remains the case that $rb = 0$.

This is arguably an underrated class of mechanisms for the evolution of cooperation. That said, it has received greater attention in recent years, especially in the context of human sociality (Skyrms, 2004; Tomasello et al., 2012; Tomasello, 2014; Forber and Smead, 2015; Sterelny, 2016). For example, Kim Sterelny (2016) argues that cooperation in early human populations initially evolved due to the immediate returns of social foraging. Participating in collaborative foraging tasks, he argues, was directly beneficial for participants, because it entailed immediate access to valuable food resources when they were acquired. He further contends that the 'free rider' problem in early human populations has been exaggerated: aspiring free riders would have lost out simply by virtue of being excluded from access to the immediate returns of successful cooperation.

Reciprocity, reward, and punishment provide less straightforward, more mediated ways in which the lifetime fitness cost of performing a social behaviour can be made negative, and they are widely thought to be especially important in humans. In a case of direct reciprocity, the beneficiary of a social behaviour returns the favour by conferring a reciprocal payoff on the actor, a phenomenon captured in formal modelling by the Tit-for-Tat strategy in the repeated prisoner's dilemma (Trivers, 1971; Axelrod and Hamilton, 1981). Outside human populations, examples of reciprocity are rare and contentious (Clutton-Brock, 2009; Melis and Semmann, 2010).

Vampire bats (*Desmodus rotundus*) provide a famous alleged example, whereby bats that have recently fed regurgitate blood and feed it to their hungry fellow group members (Wilkinson, 1984). The case remains controversial, however, since 'field studies do not provide unequivocal evidence that individuals are more likely to give blood to bats that previously have provided them with a meal' (Clutton-Brock, 2009, p. 54, although cf. Carter and Wilkinson, 2013).

In a case of indirect reciprocity, recipients do not directly reciprocate benefits, yet reputation ensures that 'what goes around comes around': actors with a reputation for cooperating will differentially receive the benefits of cooperation, whereas actors with a reputation for selfishness will be shunned (Nowak and Sigmund, 2005; Nowak, 2006). The cognitive demands of indirect reciprocity are comparatively high, since social actors must be able to assess the reputation of their fellow group members and update their assessments in light of observed (or reported) behaviour (Sigmund, 2012). Consequently, it is doubtful whether this mechanism ever operates outside humans (Melis and Semmann, 2010). Among humans, it may well have been one important driver of cooperation in Palaeolithic societies (Panchanathan and Boyd, 2004); indeed, according to some accounts, it lies at the heart of the evolution of morality (Alexander, 1987; Nowak and Sigmund, 2005; Joyce, 2006).

Both direct and indirect reciprocity may be regarded as ways of rewarding cooperators for their prosocial behaviour. But mechanisms of reward need not rely on reciprocity, if the latter is understood as requiring that recipients (or other group members) perform the same behaviour that the original actor performed. Rewards may also be distributed in other ways, for example by repaying a share of a public good to those who contributed to it (Sigmund et al., 2001; Hauert, 2010; Sasaki and Unemi, 2011).

The opposite of reward is *punishment*, the conditional imposition of direct fitness penalties on actors who behave in antisocial ways (or, in humans at least, on those who violate prevailing social norms). Since c quantifies differential cost, not absolute cost, this can lead to negative c for traits that adhere to the enforced patterns of behaviour. We find various examples of punishment in this minimal behavioural sense in animal societies, usually involving dominant individuals in a hierarchical social group punishing their subordinates (Clutton-Brock and Parker, 1995). For example, in primitively eusocial Polistes wasps, 'queens are regularly aggressive to inactive workers, chasing, biting, grappling or bumping them, and experimental removal or cooling of queens rapidly lowers the level of worker activity' (Clutton-Brock and Parker, 1995, p. 214).

In humans, of course, punishment tends to acquire explicitly moralistic overtones, and it is therefore unsurprising that this too (along with indirect reciprocity) features prominently in accounts of the evolution of morality (see Kitcher, 2011; Boehm, 2012, though cf. Sterelny, 2012b). Note, however, that punishment is itself a social behaviour, and it calls for explanation in its own right. If it is costly, as often seems to be the case in humans, the ultimate explanation of punishment practices may require some appeal to indirect fitness effects (Boyd et al., 2003; Bowles and Gintis, 2011).

Finally, *pleiotropy and linkage* can lead to negative *c*, if they lead to a situation in which a gene or gene-complex that promotes a costly social behaviour is associated with a different behaviour that causes a direct fitness advantage. For example, recall the fruiting bodies of the social amoeba *D. discoideum*, in which the cells included in the stalk sacrifice their lives so that those in the fruiting body above can sporulate (Chapter 1, Section 1.1). In a groundbreaking experimental study, Foster et al. (2004) identified a gene in this amoeba with two associated phenotypes. First, its bearers tend to opt out of prestalk formation, increasing their chances of entering the fruiting body. But then, later in the life cycle, its bearers tend to be competitively excluded from the spores by nonbearers. The second effect cancels out the individual advantage the first would otherwise have conferred. As Foster et al. suggest, this may help 'to limit cheating and ensure fair contribution to the stalk' (2004, p. 694). Effects of this sort, which have also been found in *Vibrio fischeri* and *Escherichia coli* bacteria (Foster et al., 2004), can more than cancel out the individual advantage defectors reap, thereby promoting the evolution of cooperation.

2.6 Hybrid and Partially Non-Selective Explanations

2.6.1 Hybrid explanations

The third category—hybrid explanations—combines the previous two, citing fitness effects on genetically related recipients, leading to positive *rb*, *and* direct fitness returns for the actor, leading to negative *c*.

Sometimes, in such cases, there may be separable causal explanations for the indirect fitness effects and the direct fitness returns. The phenomenon of worker policing in the eusocial Hymenoptera may be an example. In most species, workers are not entirely sterile: they can lay unfertilized eggs which can develop into males. However, in some colonies, around 98% of worker-laid eggs are eaten by the queen or by other workers (Ratnieks and Wenseleers, 2008). Both direct and indirect fitness considerations feature in the most plausible explanation of this behaviour. First, policing provides a direct fitness benefit, since the eggs nourish the workers or queens who eat them. Second, it yields an indirect fitness benefit for the workers, since the workers are more closely related to the offspring of the queen than to the offspring of their fellow workers. Their actions thus help the queen to reproduce at other workers' expense, leading to net positive rb (Ratnieks, 1988). In this case, the direct and indirect fitness components of the explanation cite different consequences of the behaviour: it is the nutritional value of the eggs that explains the direct fitness returns to egg-eating, whereas it is the easing of competition for resources on the queen's larvae that explains the indirect fitness benefits.

In other cases, however, the same biological process causally contributes to both rb and c. These are cases in which interactions among relatives generate 'synergistic' effects—effects that are not attributable to a single behaviour performed by a single actor, but which result from the interaction of behaviours performed by more than one actor (Queller, 1985). Consider again the stag hunt game. This game involves synergistic effects, but in the absence of any genetic assortment these effects only make a difference to c, since $rb = 0$. Now imagine, however, that the agents playing the game are genetic relatives. In this case, successfully hunting the stag yields both direct and indirect fitness returns, and it therefore makes both a negative contribution to c and a positive contribution to rb.[20]

There is a class of models, collectively known as synergy games with genetic assortment, in which both rb and c depend on a synergistic payoff obtained when both agents play a particular strategy (Queller, 1985; Gardner et al., 2007, 2011; Taylor and Maciejewski, 2012;

---

[20] Reciprocity among genetic relatives is also an important source of synergy in this sense. See the discussion of Lehmann and Keller (2006) in the next chapter.

van Veelen, 2009; van Veelen et al., 2012; Taylor, 2013, 2016; Birch, 2014b; Okasha and Martens, 2016a, b). In some games, and for some parameter values, synergy leads to the satisfaction of $rb > c$ by boosting rb and mitigating c without making it negative, in which case what is on offer is fundamentally an indirect fitness explanation of positive change. However, it can also be the case that the expected direct fitness return from a synergistic effect more than offsets the expected costs of cooperating, leading to negative c, in which case both direct and indirect fitness effects are driving the evolution of the behaviour, and the explanation on offer is a hybrid explanation.

This particular way of interpreting the effects of synergy—that is, as a factor that offsets the direct fitness costs and boosts the indirect fitness benefits of cooperating with relatives, leading to hybrid explanations—is not the only way. It is the way favoured by Gardner et al. (2007, 2011), who show precisely how the rb and c coefficients in HRG depend on the same synergistic effects in simple synergy games (for more detailed discussion of this, see Birch, 2014b and Okasha and Martens, 2016a). Queller (2011) however, despite emphasizing that his (1992a) general model does accommodate synergistic effects implicitly as effects that modulate cost and benefit, prefers to interpret the effects of synergy using an 'expanded' version of Hamilton's rule in which such effects are explicitly represented in a separate 'd' coefficient, an approach also favoured by Marshall (2011b, c, 2015). This approach is no less correct than that afforded by HRG. It simply offers a different, somewhat more fine-grained way of carving up the space of explanations—one that I will discuss further in the next chapter.

2.6.2 (Partially) non-selective explanations

If $rb \leqslant c$, then positive change in the mean of the character of interest requires an explanation that is at least partially non-selective, which is not to say that it must avoid any appeal to selection, but simply that it must advert to some other evolutionary process to explain why the selective bias against the character (or selective neutrality) has been overcome. In these cases, we need to revisit the evolutionary processes we intentionally set aside when deriving HRG: drift, mutation, migration, meiotic drive, gametic selection, and changes in the average effects of alleles (i.e. changes in the 'genic environment').

As the inclusion of 'gametic selection' (i.e. selection among gametes) in that list indicates, the term 'non-selective' here should not be read as excluding within-organism selection: it is simply intended as a shorthand for explanations that invoke a process other than natural selection acting on fitness differences between organisms. It is well known that biased transmission at the level of organisms is often explicable in terms of selective processes occurring within organisms, and selection among gametes is one example of such a process.

We should not discount non-selective explanations. One might worry that adopting HRG as an organizing framework encourages us to discount them, but I think this worry is misplaced. While it is true that HRG focuses primarily on drawing distinctions among selective explanations, it also draws our attention to the conditions under which a (partially or wholly) non-selective explanation is required.

Although wholly non-selective explanations are rare in social evolution theory, partially non-selective explanations have an important role to play. For one example, consider again the repeated prisoner's dilemma. A well-known drawback of the Tit-for-Tat strategy in this game—one that arguably undermines the idea that it can be stable in real evolving populations—is that, in a population of agents playing this strategy, Always Cooperate can invade by mutation and then increase in frequency by drift. Since populations of unconditional cooperators are vulnerable to invasion by unconditional defectors, this can destabilize cooperation altogether in the long run (Boyd and Lorberbaum, 1987).[21] Clearly, the overall explanation for the instability of reciprocal cooperation here does appeal to selection. However, the spread of unconditional cooperators through a population of reciprocators is attributable to non-selective processes. We can therefore see how the long-run stability of a strategy in this game depends on the interaction of selective and non-selective causes of change, which matter at different times.

For another example, consider the production of so-called 'public goods' in microbes, which will be the topic of Chapter 6. To foreshadow that discussion briefly, empirical work in this area has led to the remarkable discovery that the production of public goods is often caused by mobile genetic elements such as plasmids, which are able to move

---

[21] This is one of the drawbacks that allows an alternative strategy—'Win Stay, Lose Shift'—to outperform Tit-for-Tat, as shown by Nowak and Sigmund (1993).

'horizontally' between individuals. Smith (2001) argued that the mobility of the genes for public goods production might help overcome the threat of 'free-riding', since it allows producers within a group to transform 'cheaters' into fellow producers. There is a selective component to this hypothesis, because Smith proposes that gene mobility is maintained by group selection for groups that can sustain high frequencies of public goods production. However, there is also a non-selective component, because a crucial part of the hypothesis is a systematic tendency for producers to convert cheaters into producers, rather than the reverse, which is a form of biased transmission. Smith's model, and other more recent models, bring out the interplay of selection and biased horizontal transmission in microbial social evolution—this fascinating issue merits further discussion, but I will postpone that discussion until Chapter 6.

This admittedly brief survey has been, I think, adequate to establish what it was intended to establish: that there exists sufficient diversity among explanations of social evolution for an organizing framework to be desirable, and that HRG provides such a framework. This, I suggest, is the source of its explanatory value. In the next chapter, I defend HRG against several recent criticisms. These criticisms, I argue, rest on misunderstandings about the nature of HRG's explanatory role. They cut successfully against the value of HRG for other explanatory purposes, but they do not undercut its value as an organizing framework.

2.7 Summary of Chapter 2

Queller's (1992a) version of Hamilton's rule (HRG), derived from the Price equation, states that the mean breeding value for a social character increases if and only if $rb > c$, where r is the coefficient of relatedness between social partners, b is the benefit conferred on recipients, and c is the cost incurred by actors. All the variables in HRG are population statistics, not properties of individual organisms or particular social interactions.

The value of HRG lies in its ability to provide an organizing framework for social evolution theory, helping us to interpret, classify and compare more detailed models of particular scenarios. HRG does this by allowing us to classify causal explanations of positive change by their commitments regarding the sign of rb and c (Figure 2.2).

This leads to a four-part taxonomy of explanations, comprising indirect fitness explanations ($rb > 0, c \geqslant 0$), direct fitness explanations ($rb \leqslant 0, c < 0$), hybrid explanations ($rb > 0, c < 0$), and wholly or partially non-selective explanations ($rb \leqslant c$). There are plausible instances of all four categories in the natural world.

3

The Rule under Attack

Tautology, Prediction, and Causality

This chapter picks up where the last left off: with a positive account of the explanatory role of HRG in place, it is now time to confront some recent, high-profile criticisms of this version of Hamilton's rule (Nowak et al., 2010, 2011; Allen et al., 2013) and to consider some prominent challengers to its status as the best known and most widely used organizing framework for social evolution research.[1]

In the first half of the chapter, I will focus on three criticisms in particular: the criticism that HRG is an 'empty statement', or tautology (Section 3.1), the complaint that it has no predictive power (Section 3.2), and the criticism that it fails to yield causal explanations of particular evolutionary outcomes (Section 3.3). These criticisms are not without foundation, and they do undermine alternative conceptions of the explanatory role of HRG. However, I contend that they do not undermine the value of HRG as an organizing framework.

In arguing that HRG is apt to provide an organizing framework for social evolution theory, I have not argued that it is the only possible such framework. One potentially powerful line of criticism of HRG is to argue that an alternative framework is superior. There are several potential contenders, including Queller's (2011) 'expanded' version of the rule, the multi-level Price equation (Price, 1972a), and the Lehmann-Keller

---

[1] I will not address criticisms levelled at other formulations of Hamilton's rule. For example, van Veelen (2009) criticizes a formulation of the rule in which the cost and benefit coefficients are payoff parameters in a specified game-theoretic model. See Birch (2014b) and Birch and Okasha (2015) for discussion of this formulation. In a later paper, van Veelen et al. (2012) criticize a phenotypic formulation of the rule, devised by Queller (1992b), that differs from HRG in taking phenotypes, rather than breeding values, as the predictors of fitness. Birch and Marshall (2014) rebut these criticisms.

framework (Lehmann and Keller, 2006). In the second half of the chapter (Sections 3.4–3.6), I discuss how these alternatives relate to HRG, and I argue that HRG provides a more useful framework in many (although not all) explanatory contexts.

3.1 The 'Tautology Problem' Redux

The case against HRG is given its most forceful expression by Ben Allen, Martin Nowak, and Edward O. Wilson (2013). At the heart of their critique is the idea that the fairly minimal nature of the assumptions HRG requires, cited as a virtue by its defenders, is in fact a serious shortcoming. Allen et al. write:

> [The] lack of utility [of HRG] is not due to any technical oversight. Rather, it arises from the attempt to extend Hamilton's rule to every instance of natural selection. This impulse is understandable, given the intuitive appeal of Hamilton's original formulation. However, the power of a theoretical framework is derived from its assumptions, thus a theory with no assumptions cannot predict or explain anything. As Wittgenstein argued in his *Tractatus Logico-Philosophicus*, any statement that is true in all situations contains no specific information about any particular situation. (Allen et al., 2013, p. 20138)

There is some exaggeration here: it is not correct to suggest that HRG requires no assumptions at all. It does make assumptions, most notably the assumption that $E(w_i \Delta p_i) = 0$. But its assumptions are admittedly minimal in comparison to many other models (this is why Queller calls it a 'general model'). This gives rise to an understandable concern, and one need not be a Wittgensteinian to see the thrust of it. In fact, it is reminiscent of a problem philosophers of biology have engaged with since the early days of the field, namely the 'tautology problem'.

Some brief background on this problem will help to put the present debate in context. A tautology, in the ordinary sense of the word, is a phrase that is true only by virtue of saying the same thing in two different ways.[2] The original tautology problem concerned the allegedly tautologous nature of the phrase 'survival of the fittest'. Although this so-called problem stimulated important work on the nature of fitness (e.g. Mills and Beatty, 1979), in hindsight it is difficult to take seriously, since (a) fitness

---

[2] 'Tautology' also has a technical meaning in propositional logic, to which Allen et al. allude by referring to Wittgenstein, but that need not concern us here.

is not simply a matter of survival, and (b) the phrase itself plays no deep explanatory role in evolutionary theory (Lewontin, 1969; Dawkins, 1982; Waters, 1986).

However, philosophers of biology came to interpret the tautology problem more broadly, and more charitably, as a concern about the scientific value of evolutionary modelling (Sober, 1993, Section 3.4). The broader problem began with the observation that evolutionary models tend to have an *a priori* character: they start with certain assumptions about the causes of change, and then show that these assumptions mathematically imply certain consequences regarding the direction of change or the eventual equilibrium. Elliott Sober (1993) gives the example of Fisher's (1930) sex ratio argument, which moves from assumptions about the reproductive value of each sex and the parental expenditure each requires to a conclusion about the equilibrium sex ratio. The tautology problem, broadly construed, is the problem of explaining how these *a priori* arguments can illuminate real processes of evolutionary change—processes that seem to be the sort of things that call for empirical investigation.

The standard response to this broader problem, as set out by Sober (1993), is roughly the following. It is true that evolutionary modelling typically aims at uncovering mathematical truths of the form 'if these assumptions (regarding dynamics, initial conditions, and so on) obtain, then this evolutionary outcome follows (or is likely to follow)'. These conditional statements are indeed *a priori* truths rather than empirical hypotheses. However, they are scientifically valuable nonetheless, because they provide the basis for empirical projects that investigate the conditions under which the assumptions of the model are satisfied or violated in real populations. For example, Fisher's sex ratio argument shows that the equilibrium sex ratio depends on the crucial variables of parental expenditure and reproductive value, guiding empirical researchers to investigate these variables. The argument predicts a 1:1 ratio unless certain assumptions are violated, which tells researchers where to look in order to explain 'extraordinary' sex ratios (i.e. ratios other than 1:1) (Hamilton, 1967). Modelling results may not themselves be empirical hypotheses, but they help steer empirical inquiry in fruitful directions.

The recent debate about HRG adds a new twist to this story, because Nowak, Allen, van Veelen, and their supporters appear to endorse this general picture of the scientific value of modelling—and are themselves professional modellers—and yet they still dismiss the Price equation and

HRG as mere tautologies or 'empty statements' (Nowak et al., 2011; van Veelen et al., 2012; Allen et al., 2013). Their critique, therefore, is evidently not aimed at evolutionary modelling in general, but at these particular ways of representing evolutionary change. Their concern is that these representations rest on assumptions that are *so* minimal their scientific utility is undermined.

To see the source of this concern, note that the Price equation and HRG deliberately avoid making detailed dynamical assumptions of the sort one has to make in order to derive long-run evolutionary trajectories of populations.[3] For example, they assume nothing about the ploidy of the organisms or about the mating scheme. They are therefore compatible with many different evolutionary dynamics, including the replicator dynamics (which assumes asexually reproducing haploid organisms), classical population genetics for diploid organisms with random mating, and dynamics that posit more complex genetic architectures or non-random mating. It is well known, however, that the long-run trajectory of a population will depend a great deal on the dynamics. This leads to the accusation that, while the Price equation and HRG may achieve a high degree of generality by avoiding detailed assumptions about evolutionary dynamics, the very absence of such assumptions renders these principles unable to guide empirical inquiry in the way good models do.

Although I have some sympathy with this criticism, I think it ultimately rests on a misunderstanding of the explanatory role HRG is intended to play. It is true that HRG is not well suited to the role typically envisaged for detailed evolutionary models of particular ecological scenarios, but it is not intended as a substitute for such models. It is designed for a different job: that of an organizing framework. For this organizing role, the minimal assumptions of HRG are an advantage, because they ensure its compatibility with a wide range of models of particular scenarios— models that make more substantial assumptions in order to derive long-run evolutionary trajectories.

---

[3] This is sometimes expressed as the idea that the Price equation and HRG are not 'dynamically sufficient'. Defenders of these principles now tend to avoid this terminology because it has often led to misunderstandings about what the principles aim to achieve (Grafen, 2006a; Frank, 2012). They are not aspiring to dynamic sufficiency and failing: rather they are intentionally aimed at providing a description of change compatible with a plurality of underlying dynamics.

Allen and colleagues' accusation in the above quotation thus rests on an overly narrow conception of explanatory power. If the power of a theoretical framework consists in its ability to derive dynamical trajectories that lead to particular outcomes from specified initial conditions, then HRG does indeed lack power. But it does not aspire to power in this sense.

This criticism does not undermine the utility of HRG as an organizing framework, since this only depends on the relations in which it stands to other models that, by virtue of making more substantial assumptions, are dynamically richer and more predictively powerful.

Critics of HRG might reply that my conception of explanatory power is too broad—that a model is not explanatory merely because it offers a way of organizing a class of other, more detailed models. They might even draw on the philosophical literature on explanation in support of this claim, because that literature has tended to minimize the significance of organizing frameworks. An organizing framework is not, as I see it, a source of causal explanations of particular phenomena, in either the 'process' sense of Wesley Salmon (1984) or in the 'interventionist' sense of James Woodward (2003). Rather, causal explanations of particular phenomena (in Woodward's sense, or something close to it) are provided by the detailed models that the framework seeks to organize.[4] Moreover, although an organizing framework does have a 'unifying' role in an intuitive sense of the word, I have already noted that it is not 'unifying' in the technical sense of Kitcher's (1981; 1989) 'unificationist' theory of explanation, since it does not provide an 'argument pattern' that can be used to derive particular evolutionary outcomes.[5]

---

[4] This is not to say that HRG is irrelevant to causal explanation. On the contrary, by organizing models of particular scenarios in ways that reveal a unity in the evolutionary consequences of very different processes, HRG deepens our understanding of the causes of social evolution (see Section 3.3, below).

Here I part ways with Woodward (2014) who, immediately following the passage quoted in Chapter 2, footnote 13, remarks that these kinds of unification (i.e. the construction of classificatory schemes and common mathematical frameworks) do not 'have much intuitively to do with explanation, at least if we think of explanation as involving the citing of causal relationships.' I see this as a mistake: it fails to recognize that classificatory schemes and common mathematical frameworks can serve to organize our thinking about causes in a way that deepens our understanding of those causes, as the case of HRG illustrates.

[5] By way of comparison, the Taylor-Frank method (Taylor and Frank, 1996; Frank, 1998), mentioned briefly in Section 3.2, does provide an 'argument pattern' for deriving evolutionarily stable strategies in models of social evolution, and so might be said to be unifying in Kitcher's sense, but this cannot be said of HRG.

However, I take this to be a failure of Kitcher's theory to capture the sort of explanatory unification HRG affords, rather than a reason to regard the sort of unification afforded by HRG as non-explanatory. It would be non-explanatory only if it added nothing of value to our understanding of social evolution, and I claim that, in sorting causal explanations of particular phenomena into biologically meaningful classes, it does aid understanding. For example (and to reiterate a point made earlier), when one comes to see that kin discrimination, limited dispersal, recognition of phenotypic markers, shared habitat preference, and horizontal gene transfer are all potential sources of positive genetic assortment between social partners—and are all, for that reason, processes that potentially enable the evolution of altruism—one comes to understand something about social evolution one did not understand before. One sees a unity in the effects of these diverse processes—one sees something evolutionarily significant that they have in common. It is not my task here to provide a detailed theory of understanding, and I do not think one is needed for my purposes.[6] Rather, I claim that the onus is on those who would deny that HRG provides understanding to explain why revealing a significant unity in the evolutionary consequences of a diverse class of processes does not qualify.

3.2 The Predictive Limitations of HRG

With this general line of response in mind, we can now turn to two other, closely related criticisms Allen et al. (2013) level against HRG. One is the criticism that HRG is unable to predict the direction of selection. At first sight, HRG appears to offer a recipe for prediction: simply measure rb and c, and you can predict the sign of $\Delta \bar{p}$. Allen et al. (2013) object that this recipe is worthless, because if one had the data that would be required in order to calculate rb and c accurately—namely, data about the genotype and reproductive success of each individual in the ancestral

---

[6] Though see De Regt and Dieks (2005) for a theory of understanding well suited to my aims. De Regt and Dieks suggest that understanding a phenomenon consists in constructing an intelligible theory of it, where a theory is 'intelligible' to a scientist just in case the scientist can recognize 'qualitatively characteristic consequences' of the theory. HRG helps us to see 'qualitatively characteristic consequences' of classes of evolutionary models. For example, it allows us to see that altruism (in the sense of Chapter 1) will evolve by natural selection only if there is positive r, and spite will evolve by natural selection only if there is negative r.

population—then one would be able to calculate $\Delta \bar{p}$ directly using the same data. They add that:

It is logically impossible to predict the outcome of a process without making prior assumptions about its behavior. In the absence of any modeling assumptions, all that can be done is to rewrite the given data in a different form.

(Allen et al., 2013, p. 20137)

I should again emphasize that HRG does make some modelling assumptions. Recall in particular the assumption that $E(w_i \Delta p_i) = 0$. The direction of change implied by the sign of $rb - c$ might differ from the sign of the total change if this assumption is violated, so there is enough of a logical gap between the sign of $rb - c$ and the direction of total change to make talk of 'prediction' intelligible.

Even so, Allen et al. are correct to suggest that HRG is not very useful for prediction. There are two main reasons for this. One is that, for the vast majority of evolving populations, we lack the sort of fine-grained data about genotypes and fitness that would be required in order to calculate its coefficients accurately. The other is that, as emphasized earlier, HRG does not specify the dynamics of change—on the contrary, it deliberately abstracts away from them to provide a statistical truth compatible with a wide range of underlying dynamics—and therefore cannot be used to derive predictions about long-run evolutionary trajectories.

There is a danger here of conflating HRG with other formulations of Hamilton's rule that are more apt for predictive purposes. If we aim to predict evolutionarily stable strategies, a 'marginal' formulation of Hamilton's rule in which the partial regression coefficients in HRG are approximated by partial derivatives of a fitness function is particularly valuable. The general idea is that, to predict the mean value of the phenotype of interest at equilibrium, we express b and c as partial derivatives and solve the partial differential equation $rb - c = 0$ (Taylor and Frank, 1996; Frank, 1998; Lehmann and Rousset, 2014a, b). I have previously called this the 'approximate version of Hamilton's rule', or 'HRA' (Birch and Okasha, 2015). This version of the rule is commonly used by social evolution researchers and has enjoyed notable predictive successes (Wenseleers et al., 2010).[7]

---

[7] For example, (Wenseleers et al. 2004a, 2004b) used a version of HRA to predict a negative correlation between the frequency of egg-laying workers and the strength of policing

In comparison with HRG, HRA buys its predictive utility at the cost of its utility as an organizing framework. This is because an assumption of weak selection must be invoked in order to justify the approximation of regression coefficients by partial derivatives (Frank, 1998; Wild and Traulsen, 2007). If selection is strong, such that non-first-order fitness effects become non-negligible, the approximation is no longer accurate. An organizing framework, recall, should not make any assumptions that are not made by all the models it seeks to organize. The implication is that HRG can serve as an organizing framework for models with any strength of selection, whereas HRA cannot.[8]

The key here is to distinguish HRA from HRG, and to understand the different theoretical functions they serve. HRG provides a superior organizing framework but an inferior predictive tool; for HRA, the reverse is true. The defender of HRG should therefore concede the point that HRG has serious predictive limitations but should not see this as grounds for concern, because the role of the principle in the theory is not predictive. While Allen and colleagues' discussion shows clearly why it would be a mistake to put HRG to work as a tool for prediction, it does not undermine the value of HRG as an organizing framework.

3.3 The Causal Interpretation of Cost and Benefit

A third line of criticism is that HRG does not yield causal explanations of social evolution, because its regression coefficients are purely statistical notions that do not admit of a causal interpretation. Allen et al. (2013, p. 20137) write, for example, that 'the claim that the regression method [HRG] identifies the causes of allele frequency change cannot be correct, because regression can only identify correlation, and correlation does not imply causation.'

The status of this criticism depends on what exactly is meant by 'a causal interpretation' of a regression coefficient. Here is one way of thinking about causal interpretability: a regression coefficient admits of a causal

---

in social insect species, and also a negative correlation between the frequency of egg-laying workers and the relatedness between workers, which were confimed by empirical studies (Wenseleers and Ratnieks, 2006).

[8] See Chapter 5 for further discussion of weak selection.

interpretation if and only if it accurately quantifies the expected change in the dependent variable that would result from an intervention on the predictor (i.e. regressor) variable so as to change its value by one unit. If a regression coefficient is causally intepretable in this sense, let us say it is interpretable as a measure of 'direct causal influence'. This is plainly not normally true of r, because r does not normally (setting aside some of the interesting cases discussed in Chapter 6) quantify the direct causal influence of one's social partners' average genotype ($\hat{p}_i$) on one's own genotype (p_i). Rather, r captures a statistical association between these genotypes that typically arises because they are effects of a common cause, namely a common ancestral genotype.

In some circumstances, however, c and b may be interpretable as measures of direct causal influence. That is to say they may be interpreted as quantifying, respectively, the direct causal influence of one's own genotype (p_i) and one's social partners' average genotype ($\hat{p}_i$) on one's individual fitness (w_i). This will be the case if the correct causal model of fitness has the same linear structure as the two-predictor linear regression model in equation 2.3. In other words, it will be the case if w_i really is, causally speaking, a linear function of p_i and $\hat{p}_i$ and no other variables.

The problem is that the causal structure of the relationship between genotype and fitness is rarely so simple. In many models—not to mention real ecological scenarios—the causal structure of this relationship is far more complex than the structure of a two-predictor linear regression model. For example, as noted in 'Hybrid explanations' earlier, there will often be synergistic effects that depend on the product of p_i and $\hat{p}_i$. Central to the utility of HRG as an organizing framework is that c and b are still well-defined in models with synergy, and HRG still captures a statistical truth about the direction of change in these models. This is because, as Queller (1992a, 2011); Gardner et al. (2007, 2011), and Marshall (2015) have all emphasized, c and b implicitly take synergistic effects into account. However, the precise way in which c and b take synergistic effects into account undermines the interpretation of c and b as measures of direct causal influence. In a careful recent treatment of this issue, Samir Okasha and Johannes Martens (2016a) show that, in games with synergy, c and b cannot be interpreted as measuring the expected change in w_i that would be caused by an intervention on p_i or $\hat{p}_i$ (respectively) so as to change its value by one unit. I will not recount the technical details here; I will simply note that synergy is one source of trouble for the interpretation of c and b as measures of direct causal influence.[9] Another potential source of trouble, highlighted by Allen et al. (2013), is assortment that involves discrimination on the basis of expected reproductive success. This can lead to situations in which associations between $\hat{p}_i$ and w_i arise not due to the causal influence of the former on the latter, but rather as an effect of one's expected fitness on the composition of one's social neighbourhood. They give three toy examples, the general flavour of which can be gleaned from the first:

In the first hypothetical scenario, a 'hanger-on' trait leads its bearers to seek out and interact with individuals of high fitness. We suppose that these interactions do not affect fitness. However, this seeking-out behavior leads fitness to become positively correlated with having a hanger-on as a partner; thus the regression method yields [$b > 0$]. According to the proposed interpretation, hangers-on should be understood as cooperative, bestowing high fitness on their partners. However, of course this gets causality backward—the high fitness causes the interaction, not the other way around.   (Allen et al., 2013, p. 20137)[10]

To be clear, I have not argued that we can simply read off the correct classification of a behaviour (e.g. as cooperative) from the sign of c and b. I prefer to define the categories of Hamilton's schema (including 'cooperation') in explicitly causal terms, and in terms of past selection history (see Chapter 1). So I am not the opponent Allen et al. are targeting in this passage. Moreover, the example is not a counterexample to HRG (and they do not claim it to be one). In their hanger-on model, rb equals c, implying, correctly, that there is no net selection gradient on the

---

[9] One way to evade this problem is to expand Hamilton's rule, adding an extra term to the regression model that explicitly represents synergistic effects (Queller, 1992b, 2011; Smith et al., 2010; Marshall, 2011b, 2015). This leads to a principle sometimes known as 'Queller's rule', which states that the change in the population mean of the breeding value for the character of interest is positive if and only if $rb - c + sd > 0$, where 'sd' captures the synergistic effects and their association with breeding value. I discuss this expanded partition of change in Section 3.4.

[10] The interpretation that 'the high fitness causes the interaction' seems to suggest that reproduction has already occurred before the interaction takes place, but I do not think this is what Allen et al. have in mind. I take them to be envisaging a situation in which one's reproductive success and the composition of one's social neighbourhood are joint effects of a common cause, to wit, some phenotypic indicator of high expected fitness that a 'hanger-on' can recognize.

character.[11] However, the example does pose a further problem for the idea that the cost and benefit coefficients in HRG can be interpreted as measures of direct causal influence.

The overall message from these cases is that regression coefficients are not always interpretable as measures of direct causal influence (Spirtes et al., 2000; Birch, 2014b; Birch and Okasha, 2015). I take the view that, just as we should be candid about HRG's lack of predictive utility, we should also be candid about the problems with interpreting c and b in this way. Put simply, correlation is not causation, and c and b track the former, not the latter. I regard synergy as a more serious problem than preferential assortment with high- or low-fitness social partners, because the strength of evidence for the biological importance of the former strikes me as overwhelming, and the same cannot be said of the latter. Yet even someone minded to dismiss both phenomena as biologically unimportant should still acknowledge the conceptual point that c and b, as purely statistical notions, cannot be relied upon to measure causal influence.

Because of this, I prefer to conceive of c and b in strictly statistical terms, as population statistics that quantify the overall extent to which an organism's reproductive success is predicted by its breeding value and that of its social partners. I do not, however, think this undermines the value of HRG as an organizing framework. This is because, although the use of HRG as an organizing framework does involve using its coefficients to classify causal explanations of particular scenarios, it does not require us to interpret its coefficients as measures of direct causal influence. This is easiest to see with respect to r. We have already seen that r is plainly not a measure of the causal influence of $\hat{p}_i$ on p_i. However, this is compatible with there being a distinctive and biologically significant class of causes (kin discrimination, limited dispersal, etc.) that are relevant to the direction of natural selection by virtue of being causes of non-zero r. This latter claim is what makes r a useful concept to have in an organizing framework.

---

[11] There is negative relatedness ($r < 0$) in the model, since hangers-on differentially assort with organisms who are not themselves hangers-on. Thus $rb < 0$, and this negative rb is exactly cancelled out by negative c. In general, Allen and colleagues' examples lead to somewhat counterintuitive values of b and c, but they do not lead us to misclassify causal explanations of change (e.g. they do not lead us to mistake an indirect fitness explanation for a direct fitness explanation).

A similar point can be made in relation to c and b. These are useful concepts to have in an organizing framework because there is a distinctive class of causal explanations of change that are united by their commitment to positive rb (i.e. indirect fitness explanations) and a distinctive class of causal explanations of change that are united by their commitment to negative c (i.e. direct fitness explanations), as well as a third class that combines both commitments (i.e. hybrid explanations).

As with r, the aptness of c and b for this organizing role depends not on their interpretability as measures of direct causal influence, but on their interpretability as evolutionarily significant *effects* that facilitate a useful, though fairly coarse-grained, classification of causal explanations (Figure 2.2).

The lesson here, and one that may be of more general interest to philosophers of science, is that a regression model, when used to obtain a statistical decomposition of change, can aid our understanding of causes even if its coefficients are not interpretable as measures of direct causal influence, and even if its structure is far simpler than the true causal structure of the relationship between the predictors and the dependent variable. To be clear, HRG is no substitute for constructing detailed causal models of particular scenarios—models that do attempt to represent the causal structure of the relationship between genotype and fitness. Rather, HRG complements such models by generating a framework in which they may be compared, classified, and interpreted. By organizing our thinking about causes, HRG deepens our understanding of the causes of social evolution, but in a more subtle way than would be suggested by a reading of its cost and benefit coefficients as measures of direct causal influence.

How does this bear on the complaint that HRG does not yield 'causal explanations'? This depends on how narrowly we construe the term 'causal explanation'. Causal explanations in the sense of Woodward (2003) are provided by the models of particular scenarios HRG serves to organize, not by HRG itself. It is to these detailed models that we should turn to find causal relationships that are 'invariant under interventions', in Woodward's sense. The regression equation (2.3), being too simple to capture the causal structure of fitness in most cases, would often fail to be invariant under interventions. In other words, intervening on the genotype of a particular individual, or that of its social partners, would often fail to produce the change in that individual's fitness predicted by the regression model.[12] But this should not worry the defender of HRG, since HRG does not aspire to yield causal explanations in this Woodwardian sense.

In a more liberal sense of the term, however, HRG does aid causal explanation, in so far as it deepens our understanding of the causes of social evolution. As noted in Section 3.1, it does this by revealing an evolutionarily significant unity in the effects of what initially seem to be very heterogeneous causes. We have two options here. One is to reserve the term 'causal explanation' for a particular way of generating understanding of causes—a way that proceeds by constructing detailed models of particular scenarios and citing relationships that are invariant under interventions. If we take this route, then HRG does not provide causal explanations— that is not its job—but it nevertheless generates understanding of causes by providing a framework for comparing, classifying, and interpreting such explanations. The other option is to understand 'causal explanation' more broadly, as encompassing any principle or framework that deepens our understanding of causes. If we take this route, HRG can be said to explain causally, albeit in an unusual and interesting way.

I have no strong opinion on how narrowly or broadly the term 'causal explanation' should be construed. The key philosophical point, which is independent of our semantic choices, is that an organizing framework based on a regression model can aid our understanding of causes even if that model intentionally abstracts away from causal detail, with the result that it is not invariant under interventions on the predictor variables.[13]

3.4 Coarser- and Finer-Grained Partitions of Change

A very different way of objecting to HRG is to grant its ability to play an organizing role in social evolution theory, but to argue that an alternative way of decomposing change is better suited to this role. There are several serious alternative candidates.

[12] See Okasha and Martens (2016a) for more on how this plays out in games with synergy.
[13] There are some interesting (though tangential) connections here with the debate between proponents of 'statisticalist' and 'causalist' interpretations of evolutionary theory in the philosophy of biology. I will reflect on some of these connections in the conclusion of the book.

One is the Price equation itself. This is even more minimal in its assumptions than HRG. However, it compresses all pathways from genes to reproductive success into a single covariance term—an example of what Elliott Sober and David Sloan Wilson (1998) have called the 'averaging fallacy.'[14] This is not particularly helpful when our aim is to understand the causes of social evolution, because we want to be able to draw distinctions among different causal explanations for covariance between p_i and w_i. By contrast, by partitioning the selective change into two components, HRG allows a more fine-grained, and for that reason more useful, partition of the space of explanations.

However, this line of thought leads naturally to a concern. HRG, in partitioning selective change into just two components, provides a partition that is very coarse-grained. Finer-grained partitions, which carve up the space of explanations more finely, are clearly possible (Queller, 2011; Marshall, 2011b, 2015). So why aren't they more useful?

Consider, for example, Queller's (1985; 2011) 'expanded' version of Hamilton's rule in which synergistic effects are explicitly represented in a separate term.[15] We start with a regression model that adds to equation (2.3) a further predictor of fitness, $p_i\hat{p}_i$, the product of one's breeding value and the average breeding value of one's social partners. We can substitute this into the Price equation, rearrange, and re-label (by a procedure that closely parallels that in Chapter 2, Section 2.1; I will not recount the details here) to obtain the following expanded rule, sometimes known as 'Queller's rule':

$$\Delta\bar{p} > 0 \iff rb - c + sd > 0, \text{ provided Var}(p_i) \neq 0 \quad \text{(Queller's rule)}$$

Here, d labels the partial regression of w_i on the new predictor $p_i\hat{p}_i$, and s is a 'coefficient of synergism' defined as the simple regression of $p_i\hat{p}_i$ on p_i. To be clear, this version of the rule is neither more nor less accurate than HRG: all it does it represent explicitly what HRG takes into account

---

[14] The same can be said in relation to the principle I have elsewhere called 'Robertson's rule' (in Birch, 2014b, after Robertson, 1966), a corollary of the Price equation which states that a character undergoes positive selective change if and only if the simple regression of w_i on p_i is positive, assuming Var(p_i) $\neq$ 0.

[15] Queller (2011) also provides an expansion for effects that rely on phenotypic correlations, which he calls 'kith selection'. I do not discuss this expansion here, but since it is another way of partitioning change at a finer grain of analysis, the issues it raises are essentially the same.

implicitly. In HRG, synergistic effects are shared between the c and b coefficients in a ratio that depends on the details of the case; in Queller's rule, synergistic effects go into the d coefficient.

Queller's rule is an important result that is useful for certain empirical applications, especially in microbes (Smith et al., 2010). My objection to its use as an organizing framework is simply that it is more fine-grained than is usually optimal for that role. Like HRG, Queller's rule can be conceived as defining and partitioning a space of explanations. In this case, the space (analogous to that in Figure 2.2) has three dimensions: rb, c and sd. The plane $rb - c + sd = 0$ slices through the space, separating selective explanations of positive change from partially or wholly non-selective explanations. In the selective region, there are seven sub-regions.[16] In effect, we carve up each category in Figure 2.2 into two sub-categories, one of which involves a boost from positive synergy and one of which involves overcoming negative synergy, and we add a seventh category in which positive synergy is the only driver of positive change. In relation to the intuitive four-category taxonomy provided by HRG, this eight-category taxonomy is cumbersome: it becomes a much more difficult task to locate a particular explanation in the space, and the additional understanding one would gain from this exercise is questionable.

The moral here is that, given the cognitive role an organizing framework is intended to play in generating understanding of causes, the optimal grain of analysis for such a framework is fairly coarse-grained. Although the Price equation is too coarse-grained, Queller's rule is already too fine-grained. The attraction of HRG for social evolution researchers is that it gets the grain of analysis just right for most purposes (though see Section 3.6 for a qualification).

3.5 The Multi-Level Price Equation

There is, however, another potential organizing framework that decomposes change at the same grain of analysis as HRG, but in a quite different way. This is the multi-level Price equation (MLS), which partitions the covariance term of the standard Price equation (see Chapter 2,

---

[16] These correspond to $(rb > 0, c > 0, sd > 0)$; $(rb > 0, c > 0, sd < 0)$; $(rb > 0, c < 0, sd > 0)$; $(rb > 0, c < 0, sd < 0)$; $(rb < 0, c < 0, sd > 0)$; $(rb < 0, c < 0, sd < 0)$; and $(rb < 0, c > 0, sd > 0)$.

Section 2.1) into a 'between-group' component and a 'within-group' component (Price, 1972a):

$$\overline{w}\Delta\overline{p} = \text{Cov}(W_i, P_i) + \text{E}\left[\text{Cov}_i(w_{ij}, p_{ij})\right] \qquad \text{(MLS)}$$

Here W_i represents the mean fitness of the ith group, P_i represents the frequency of the allele in that group, and w_{ij} and p_{ij} represent (respectively) the individual fitness and individual gene frequency of the jth member of the ith group. $\text{Cov}(W_i, P_i)$ therefore captures the covariance in the whole population between the mean fitness and gene frequency of a group, while $\text{Cov}_i(w_{ij}, p_{ij})$ captures the local covariance between individual fitness and individual gene frequency within the ith group.[17]

The MLS partition implies a corresponding rule for positive change, which we might aptly call 'Price's rule':

$$\Delta\overline{p} > 0 \iff \text{Cov}(W_i, P_i) + \text{E}\left[\text{Cov}_i(w_{ij}, p_{ij})\right] > 0 \qquad \text{(Price's rule)}$$

Informally, in the case of an altruistic trait that is positively selected between groups and negatively selected within groups, the population mean for the trait increases if and only if between-group selection in its favour is stronger than the within-group selection against it.

This too provides a framework in which detailed models of particular scenarios can be classified, compared, and interpreted (Sober and Wilson, 1998; Okasha, 2006). In particular, it draws our attention to a three-way distinction between 'individual selection' explanations for positive change that cite positive selection within groups and zero or negative selection between groups, 'group selection' explanations that cite positive selection between groups and zero or negative selection within groups, and hybrid explanations that cite positive selection at both levels. Like HRG, this partitions the space of explanations at the right grain of analysis to provide a useful and intuitive organizing framework. The case for organizing our thinking about the causes of social evolution in this way is made powerfully by Sober and Wilson (1998).

However, I maintain that HRG provides the more useful organizing framework of the two. The reason is that the domain of applicability of MLS is more limited than that of HRG, since the former applies

---

[17] This formulation assumes that groups are equal in size; if they vary in size, the MLS partition is still possible, but we must use 'size-weighted' covariances and expectations, as defined by Price (1972a).

only to group-structured populations (Okasha, 2006; Godfrey-Smith, 2006, 2008; Birch and Okasha, 2015). Not all populations are group-structured. For a simple example of one that is not (from Godfrey-Smith, 2006), imagine a population with the spatial structure of a square lattice. Each organism occupies one node on the lattice, no node is unoccupied, and each organism interacts with the organisms on the four adjacent nodes (i.e. its 'von Neumann neighbours'). In this model, my neighbours' neighbours are not my neighbours. There is social interaction, but there is no non-arbitrary way to partition the population into discrete social groups: social neighbourhoods blur continuously into each other. Godfrey-Smith (2006, 2008) describes such populations as 'neighbour-structured' (see Chapter 4 for more on this notion). In models of neighbour-structured populations, HRG still applies, but MLS does not, unless we assign organisms to groups arbitrarily. This move, however, would deprive MLS of any biological meaning: its value as an organizing framework relies on the 'groups' it describes being biologically real.

Here I should state an important qualification, which foreshadows the discussion of Chapter 4. I am claiming here that HRG provides a more versatile organizing framework than MLS, primarily because it assumes less about the population structure. Traditionally, the HRG partition of the Price equation has been associated with the idea of 'kin selection' (as in Queller, 1992a) and the MLS partition of the Price equation has been closely associated with the idea of 'group selection' (as in Sober and Wilson, 1998). However, I do not think the concepts of kin and group selection should be tied to specific statistical formalisms in this way. In the next chapter, I will argue that we should break that association and think of kin and group selection in explicitly causal terms, as distinctive kinds of causal process, both of which can contribute to indirect fitness explanations of change. Hence, in claiming that HRG provides the better organizing framework for social evolution research, I do not intend to imply that the process of group selection is rare or unimportant.

3.6 The Lehmann-Keller Framework

Although I cannot discuss all possible alternative organizing frameworks here, one more alternative merits discussion, namely that of Laurent Lehmann and Laurent Keller (2006). This is another example of a framework that is more fine-grained than HRG. I will not recount the formal details, since the framework is quite complicated (the glossary of symbols has thirty-five entries). In short, Lehmann and Keller explicitly represent the effects of reciprocity by partitioning the c and b coefficients in HRG into an 'immediate returns' component and a 'returns from reciprocation' component. In other words, they express c as a sum of (i) the immediate net fitness consequences of your behaviour and (ii) the expected net fitness returns you accrue from your social partner's reciprocation of your behaviour, and they express b as a sum of (i) the immediate net fitness consequences of your social partner's behaviour and (ii) the expected benefits that accrue to you in the long run from reciprocating their behaviour.

The Lehmann-Keller framework is illuminating for various reasons: perhaps most notably, by explicitly separating out the effects of reciprocity, it shows how, in games of reciprocal interaction among relatives, c and b depend on the same model parameters (e.g. the probability of interacting again with the same individual), but in different ways. This is another way of saying that reciprocation among relatives is an important source of synergistic effects (see Chapter 2, Section 2.6).

However, as Grafen (2006c) points out in a commentary on Lehmann and Keller's article, their proliferation of parameters sometimes obfuscates rather than clarifies. For example, it is not clear why they separate the immediate cost to the actor of cooperating ('C') from the immediate benefit to the actor ('$\zeta B'$'), rather than simply talking of the immediate net cost: the biological rationale for the separation here is not clear.

The comparative value of Queller's general model (HRG) and the Lehmann-Keller framework is not easy to assess: it ultimately turns on the gains and losses, in terms of overall understanding, that are achieved by formally separating immediate effects from the longer term effects of reciprocity. I see it as a particularly helpful feature of HRG that it makes plain that, fundamentally, immediate returns and reciprocity among non-relatives both contribute to direct fitness explanations, which is to say they are causes of negative c. But HRG does not make it clear that reciprocity among relatives is different, because it also makes a difference to rb. The virtue of the Lehmann-Keller framework is that it does make this clear, at the cost of a significant amount of additional formal complexity.

We do not have to choose between these frameworks: they are wholly compatible and indeed complementary, since the Lehmann-Keller framework simply provides a finer-grained partitioning of the coefficients in HRG.[18] The comparison, however, brings out the need to qualify my earlier remarks about the 'optimal' grain of analysis for an organizing framework. To some extent, the optimal grain of analysis is a context-dependent matter. For many purposes, a coarse-grained partitioning of the space of explanations, as provided by HRG, is what we want. But for some purposes, a finer formal subdivision of those categories may be useful, and this is what the Lehmann-Keller framework offers.

3.7 Summary of Chapter 3

HRG has been criticized for being an 'empty statement' or tautology, for failing to yield predictions of change, and for failing to yield causal explanations of change. There is some justification for all of these charges, but I have argued that they do not undermine the use of HRG as an organizing framework.

In response to the 'tautology' complaint, we should admit that HRG is indeed tautology-like. It says, in effect, that the change under one description is positive if and only if the change under another description (a description that partitions it into an rb and $-c$ component) is also positive. It thereby avoids making detailed dynamical assumptions about the processes responsible for the change it describes. But, although the absence of dynamical assumptions would be a disadvantage in a detailed model of a particular evolutionary scenario, it is an advantage in an organizing framework, because it makes the framework compatible with a wide range of more detailed models.

In response to the 'prediction' complaint, we should concede that HRG, by virtue of its tautology-like character, is not very useful for prediction. But the role of an organizing framework is not a predictive role: predictions are generated by detailed models of particular scenarios.

To respond to the 'causal explanation' complaint, we need to understand the subtle relationship of HRG to causality. I have argued that, by organizing our thinking about the causes of social evolution, HRG generates understanding of causes. But it does this without attempting

---

[18] This marks a contrast with Queller's rule, which redistributes a portion of the change from rb and c to a different term, and with MLS, which partitions the change in quite a different way.

to represent the causal structure of the relationship between fitness and its genetic basis. For this reason, HRG does not provide (and does not attempt to provide) causal explanations of particular evolutionary outcomes in the sense of Woodward (2003). Causal explanations in this sense are provided by the detailed models of particular scenarios that HRG serves to organize. Yet, to the extent that HRG generates understanding of causes, it might still be said to 'explain causally' in a more liberal sense of the term.

HRG is not the only possible organizing framework: alternatives include the Price equation itself, an expanded version of Hamilton's rule known as 'Queller's rule', the multi-level Price equation (MLS), and the Lehmann-Keller framework. Comparing HRG with MLS highlights an important virtue of HRG: its compatibility with any population structure. MLS applies only to populations with a special sort of population structure, namely group-structure. We will revisit this idea in the next chapter, which discusses the relationship between kin and group selection.

Comparing HRG with the Price equation, Queller's rule and the Lehmann-Keller framework raises the question of the optimal grain of analysis for an organizing framework. I have argued that HRG gets the grain of analysis right in most contexts, making it preferable to frameworks that carve up change at a finer or coarser grain. Sometimes, however, we may want a finer-grained partition of the c and b coefficients in HRG, and this is what the Lehmann-Keller framework provides.

4

Kin Selection and Group Selection

The relationship between kin and group selection is a longstanding source of controversy in the social evolution literature. In earlier debates, biologists tended to regard kin and group selection as rival empirical hypotheses (Maynard Smith, 1964, 1976; Dawkins, 1978, 1982). But many biologists now regard them as 'formally equivalent' approaches, and see this formal equivalence as implying that they are not competing empirical hypotheses after all (e.g. Marshall, 2011a).[1] Although there are high-profile dissenters from this equivalence claim[2], including Nowak et al. (2010), the majority of social evolution theorists appear to endorse it.[3]

Yet the debate has long been hampered by insufficient attention to the distinction between statistics and causality (Birch and Okasha, 2015; Okasha, 2016). It is crucial to distinguish between the formal equivalence of two statistical descriptions of change and the identity (or otherwise) of two types of causal process responsible for change. The former does not imply the latter. Indeed, my claim in this chapter is that, although

---

[1] Here, and throughout the chapter, the type of group selection I have in mind is 'MLS1' in the terminology of Heisler and Damuth (1987). In other words, it is group selection in which the fitness of a group is defined as the average fitness of its members, rather than the number of offspring groups it produces. I use the term 'group selection' in preference to 'multi-level selection' because I see both kin and group selection as processes that can occur at multiple levels of organization, as I explain in Section 4.6.

[2] For example, Hölldobler and Wilson (2009); van Veelen (2009); Traulsen (2010); Nowak et al. (2010); van Veelen et al. (2012), and Wilson (2012) depart from this view in various ways. Sober and Wilson (1998) depart from this view by regarding kin selection as a special case of group selection. This view, though not widespread among social evolution theorists, remains influential among philosophers of biology. As will become clear in due course, I do not regard either process as a special case of the other.

[3] For example, Queller (1992b); West et al. (2008); Wenseleers et al. (2010); Gardner et al. (2011); Marshall (2015).

there is an important sense in which kin and group selection are formally equivalent when conceived as statistical descriptions of change, there is a real and useful—but not sharp—distinction to be drawn between kin and group selection conceived as causal processes responsible for change. The differences lie in their commitments regarding population structure.

Here is the chapter in outline. In the first section, I consider the 'formal equivalence' results mentioned earlier, explaining why these results are compatible with there being a worthwhile causal distinction to be drawn between kin and group selection. In Section 4.2, I set out two ways of making sense of this distinction. One approach, developed recently by Okasha (2016), locates the difference in the causal path at the individual level between an organism's genotype and its fitness. I highlight some problems with Okasha's approach that, although not fatal, motivate the development of an alternative. My favoured alternative, which I call the 'population-centred' approach, locates the difference in the structural features of populations responsible for generating indirect fitness effects.

The rest of the chapter pursues the population-centred approach. In Section 4.3, I draw inspiration from two sources: Hamilton's (1975) own views on the relationship between kin and group selection, and Peter Godfrey-Smith's (2006; 2008) recent work on the varieties of population structure. Section 4.4 combines these influences into a positive proposal. The intuitive idea is that kin selection occurs in populations that are structured such that relatives tend to interact differentially, while group selection occurs in populations in which there are stable, sharply bounded, and well-integrated social groups at the relevant grain of analysis. Some populations have both features, but it is possible for one to occur without the other. Since these structural features are matters of degree, a spatial metaphor ('K-G space') is useful for thinking about the distinction.

The account also requires that $rb \neq 0$ as a precondition for both kin and group selection; in Section 4.5, I explain and defend this requirement. In Section 4.6, I discuss the relationship between kin/group selection distinction and levels of biological organization, arguing that both types of selection process can occur at multiple levels. Finally, in Section 4.7, I close by setting out the key substantive questions at stake, by the lights of my account, when we investigate whether a process is one of kin selection or group selection.

4.1 Equivalence Results and Their Limitations

The best-known argument for the formal equivalence of kin and group selection involves comparing Queller's generalized version of Hamilton's rule (HRG) with 'Price's rule', the condition for positive change implied by the multi-level version of the Price equation (MLS), and noting the very minimal assumptions that both rules require.[4] Both are derived from the Price equation (Price, 1970). The assumptions required for the derivation of HRG from the Price equation are that $\mathrm{Var}(p_i) \neq 0$, that p_i and $\hat{p}_i$ are not collinear (so that the c and b coefficients are well-defined), and that $\mathrm{E}(w_i \Delta p_i) = 0$. The assumptions required for the derivation of Price's rule from the Price equation are that the population is group-structured and (again) that $\mathrm{E}(w_i \Delta p_i) = 0$. Hence, in all group-structured populations in which $\mathrm{E}(w_i \Delta p_i) = 0$, $\mathrm{Var}(p_i) \neq 0$, and p_i and $\hat{p}_i$ are not collinear, the assumptions required for both rules obtain and the following equivalence holds (Marshall, 2011a; Frank, 2013; Birch and Okasha, 2015):[5]

$$\Delta \bar{p} > 0 \iff rb > c \iff \mathrm{Cov}(W_i, P_i) + \mathrm{E}\left[\mathrm{Cov}_i(w_{ij}, p_{ij})\right] > 0$$
(4.1)

To understand the intuitive rationale for this equivalence, imagine the typical circumstances under which each condition would be satisfied with respect to an altruistic trait. First, consider what is required for $rb > c$. It must be that bearers of the genes for altruism cluster together, so that the benefits of altruism fall differentially on bearers of those genes. Second, consider what is required for the selection against the trait within groups to be outweighed by selection for the trait between groups. It must be that bearers of the genes for altruism cluster together, so that the genetic variation within groups is suppressed and the genetic variation between groups is boosted. Both approaches can thus be seen as alternative ways of capturing the fundamental requirement that bearers of the genes for altruism cluster together and interact differentially with each other.

The result in (4.1) is plainly an equivalence result of a sort. But we should be clear about what it does and does not show. Four main limitations are worth spelling out. Firstly, the result holds only in populations with a particular type of structure: that is, *group-structured* populations.

---

[4] HRG was introduced in Chapter 2; MLS and Price's rule were introduced in Chapter 3.

[5] It is important here that the 'Cov' in $\mathrm{Cov}_i(w_{ij}, p_{ij})$ and the 'E' in $\mathrm{E}\left[\mathrm{Cov}_i(w_{ij}, p_{ij})\right]$ are interpreted as 'size-weighted' functions in the sense of Price (1972a); otherwise we need the further assumption that all groups are equal in size (cf. Chapter 2, footnote 17).

As I emphasized in the previous chapter, not all populations are group-structured, and the multi-level Price equation can be applied in the absence of group-structure only by assigning organisms to groups arbitrarily, which deprives it of biological significance. I think the importance of this qualification has been understated in the literature (Godfrey-Smith 2006, 2008 is an important exception, which I will discuss in Section 4.3). As will soon become clear, I also think this provides a clue as to where we should look when drawing a causal distinction between kin and group selection processes.

Secondly, the result involves comparing maximally general and purely genetic formulations of kin selection and group selection theory, ignoring the complications that arise when we want to apply one of these approaches to analyse change in a particular ecological scenario. For example, in both the kin selectionist and multi-level modelling traditions, theorists use phenotypic rather than genetic predictors of fitness when they have empirical applications in mind, since hypotheses about phenotypic selection gradients are easier to test empirically (Grafen, 1984; Queller, 1992b, 2011; Frank, 1998; Goodnight and Stevens, 1997; McGlothlin et al., 2014). In fact, formal equivalence results can still be derived in relation to phenotypic versions of the two approaches, provided like is compared with like (Queller, 1992b; Birch and Marshall, 2014). The resounding moral from this literature is that, as long as the same assumptions go into the construction of the kin selection and group selection models being compared, the same predictions will come out regarding the direction of change (Queller, 1992b; Godfrey-Smith and Kerr, 2002; Lehmann et al., 2007; Birch and Marshall, 2014).

Thirdly, not all group selection theorists accept that the multi-level Price equation (MLS) succeeds in separating the effects of selection at the group and individual levels. There is a prominent alternative—contextual analysis—advanced by Lorraine Heisler and John Damuth (Heisler and Damuth, 1987; Damuth and Heisler, 1988) and by Charles Goodnight and colleagues (Goodnight et al., 1992; Goodnight and Stevens, 1997; Goodnight, 2013). The clash between contextual analysis and the multi-level Price equation is long-running, and I do not aim to weigh into that debate here.[6] For current purposes, it is sufficient to note that contextual

---

[6] See Okasha (2006) for an overview of the issues, see Sober (2011) for a commentary on Okasha, and see the disagreement between Gardner (2015) and Goodnight (2015) for a recent instalment.

analysis involves decomposing change in a very similar way to the generalized version of Hamilton's rule: here too we decompose fitness using a regression model, but rather than taking the average genotype of the focal individual's social partners as a predictor, we take properties of the focal individual's social group (Heisler and Damuth, 1987). Thus the formal relationship between kin selectionist and multi-level methodologies would be even closer if we were to take contextual analysis as our flagship example of a multi-level approach, and it would become even clearer that the methodological differences between these traditions reflect divergent modelling preferences and explanatory interests rather than divergent empirical commitments (Okasha, 2016, p. 440).[7]

Fourthly, and most fundamentally, neither HRG nor Price's rule should be seen as embodying a substantive set of commitments about the causes of change. Like the Price equation itself, these rules are highly abstract, highly general, statistical results, compatible with a wide range of underlying causal explanations of change. As I emphasized in Chapter 2, there are many different causal explanations for the satisfaction of HRG, and the role of HRG is to provide an organizing framework within which we can interpret, compare, and classify more detailed explanations. The same goes for Price's rule: it provides a different way of carving up the change in gene frequency, and a different organizing framework, but it too abstracts far away from causal detail. It would therefore be a mistake to infer the identity of kin and group selection, conceived as causal processes responsible for change, from an equivalence result that merely concerns the relationship between two statistical conditions for change.

Of course, if we were to stipulate that by the term 'kin selection' we mean HRG and by the term 'group selection' we mean Price's rule, evading the issue of causality, then there would be little to add to the equivalence result in (4.1). But I doubt whether this is the most useful way to employ

---

[7] Goodnight (2013) suggests two ways in which the explanatory interests of the kin selectionist and contextual analysis traditions diverge: contextual analysis focusses on phenotypes whereas kin selectionist approaches tend to focus on genotypes (although many models in the kin selectionist tradition also focus on phenotypes, e.g. Queller, 1992b, 2011; Frank, 1998; Lehmann and Rousset, 2014a, and McGlothlin et al., 2014); and contextual analysis focusses on away-from-equilibrium change whereas kin selectionist approaches tend to focus on finding equilibria (although many models in the kin selectionist tradition also focus on away-from-equilibrium change, see e.g. Hamilton, 1964; Queller, 1992b; Grafen, 2006a). These differences indicate different modelling preferences and explanatory interests, not deep disagreements about the causes of evolution.

these terms. After all, these terms intuitively refer to kinds of causal process—to things that actually happen in natural populations, and that feature in causal explanations—and not to formal methods, modelling traditions, or statistical conditions for change. I think we should hold on to that intuition. I contend that the right moral to draw from the formal equivalence of HRG and Price's rule, and other similar equivalence results, is not that kin and group selection are identical causal processes, but rather that purely statistical formalisms lack the resources to capture the causal distinction between them.[8]

4.2 Individual- and Population-Centred Approaches

Broadly speaking, there are two approaches one can take to capturing this causal distinction. One is an individual-centred approach that explicates the distinction in terms of differences in the causal path that runs from a focal individual's genes to its fitness. The other, which I will develop in this chapter, is a population-centred approach that explicates the distinction in terms of structural properties of populations. To provide a rationale for pursuing the second approach, I should comment briefly on the first.

Okasha (2016) has recently pursued the first approach, drawing on the notion of a causal graph (see Spirtes et al., 2000; Pearl, 2009). Okasha suggests that, in paradigm cases of group selection, a causal path runs 'upwards' from the individual gene frequency of a focal individual (p_i) to the local group's gene frequency (P_i), then through the group gene frequency to the group mean fitness (W_i), and finally 'downwards' from group mean fitness and an 'allocation mechanism' to the focal individual's fitness (w_i) (see Figures 8 and 9 in Okasha, 2016). In paradigm cases of kin selection, by contrast, there is no causal path running via the group means and no allocation mechanism. Instead, we have a causal path running directly, at the individual level, from the genes of one individual, via its own behaviour, to the fitness of another individual, and the fitness of the group is determined by the individual fitness of its members (see Figure 6 in Okasha, 2016). Figure 4.1, reprinted from Okasha (2016), depicts the

---

[8] A point also stressed by Birch and Okasha (2015); Okasha (2016); and Lehtonen (2016).

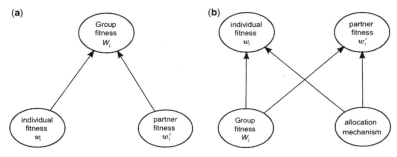

Figure 4.1 An illustration of the causal graphs approach. Case (a) is a paradigm case of kin selection; case (b) is a paradigm case of group selection. The mathematical relation between group fitness (W_i) and individual fitness (w_i) is the same in both cases: W_i is the group mean of w_i. However, in case (a) the individual fitness values metaphysically determine the group mean; whereas in case (b) the group mean, in conjunction with an allocation mechanism, metaphysically determines the individual fitness values (Figure reprinted from Okasha, 2016, Figure 4).

relations between individual and group fitness in the two cases, without including genotypes (see Okasha, 2016, for more detailed figures).

Okasha's graphs for paradigm cases of group selection posit 'bottom-up' causal relationships between individual gene frequencies and the group gene frequency and 'top-down' causal relationships between the group mean fitness and individual fitness values. I am uneasy with this aspect of the proposal, because I do not see the relationship between a set of individual properties and the group mean of those properties as one of causation. It strikes me as more accurate to describe this as a relationship of supervenience, because two groups cannot differ in their mean value of some property unless there is at least one difference between their respective sets of individual values.

Foreseeing this problem, Okasha argues that, although these relationships would not normally be considered causal, they 'can be depicted as if [they] were causal without violating the principles of causal modelling' (Okasha, 2016, p. 449). However, this 'as if' move leads to a concern about whether the direction of these arrows is adequately constrained by the causal facts. In all cases, W_i supervenes on the set of w_i values. In some cases, Okasha draws a causal arrow from w_i to W_i; in other cases, he draws a causal arrow from W_i to w_i. Why is the same relationship of supervenience to be represented in some cases by a top-down causal arrow and in other cases by a bottom-up causal arrow, and what constrains this choice?

Okasha's view is that the choice depends on the 'direction of metaphysical determination' between w_i and W_i, which may be ascertained using 'modal intuitions, empirical knowledge of the system being modelled, or both' (p. 451). For example, Okasha suggests that, if w_i depends on the sharing of a group payoff, such as a large animal carcass, then it accords with intuition to say that the individual fitness values are metaphysically determined by the group mean fitness; whereas, if w_i depends only on payoffs obtained separately by individuals, such as smaller animals they have hunted individually, then it accords with intuition to say that the group mean fitness is metaphysically determined by the individual fitness values.

I do not share these intuitions: my intuition, for what it's worth, is that a group mean is always metaphysically determined by the individual values over which it averages, and that this remains the case even when the individual fitness values are causally explained by the sharing of a group resource. If this is right, then the arrow between w_i and W_i should always be a bottom-up arrow, and never a top-down arrow. However, I take it that intuitions on this question will differ, as will opinions regarding the evidential weight such intuitions merit. The deeper concern here is that Okasha's approach makes the classification of a process as one of kin or group selection dependent on such intuitions. This, I suggest, motivates the development of an alternative approach that can classify a process on the basis of its empirically observable features, without relying on intuitions about the direction of metaphysical determination that are subject to interpersonal variation.

A related but subtly different problem for Okasha's graphs concerns the arrow at the group level that runs from P_i to W_i. If we accept that the true relationship between a set of individual properties and the group mean of those properties is one of supervenience rather than causation, we run into traditional philosophical concerns about the causal efficacy of supervenient properties. Can group means cause other group means, or can the appearance of a causal relationship between two group means be explained away as a by-product (i.e. an 'epiphenomenon') of causation at the level of individual properties? So-called 'causal exclusion' arguments, a staple of the philosophy of mind for several decades, seem to have some purchase here (Kim, 1998, 2005).

This is not the place for a lengthy discussion of such arguments, or of the numerous responses to them (for a review of this area, see Robb and Heil, 2014). Okasha is right, I think, to set this issue to one side for his purposes. However, the way in which he does so leads to a problem. After acknowledging that the question of causal exclusion is a 'controversial metaphysical issue that is better not to prejudge' (p. 450), Okasha aims to sidestep the question by explicating the meaning of causal arrows between group variables in terms of hypothetical interventions on the supervenient property *and its lower-level supervenience base*:

> [T]he following convention is adopted here: in a causal graph in which one variable supervenes on others, when we consider hypothetically intervening on the supervenient variable we do not hold fixed the variables on which it supervenes, but rather alter them to preserve consistency. Modulo this convention, causal arrows going out of supervenient variables, if any, can be understood in the usual way. (Okasha, 2016, p. 450)

Thus, we are to interpret a causal arrow running from P_i to W_i as implying that a counterfactual intervention on P_i and the individual *gene frequencies over which it averages* would lead to a change in W_i. This renders such arrows neutral regarding the causal exclusion problem, since even a sceptic about full-blooded causation between group means should not object to the metaphysically thin relations of counterfactual dependence Okasha takes the group-level arrows in his graphs to imply. The trouble with this manoeuvre is that this thin sort of counterfactual dependence holds even in cases in which there is intuitively no group selection at work.

Consider G. C. Williams's (1966) famous example of a population of deer, structured into herds. Herds containing faster deer are more successful than those containing slower deer, but only because faster individuals are more successful at evading predators than slower individuals. This is usually considered a case in which there is no genuine group selection—only covariance between a group's mean running speed and its mean fitness caused by natural selection acting on individuals (Okasha, 2006, Ch. 3). Yet if one were to intervene on the mean running speed of a herd of deer, *altering the individual running speeds of the group members to preserve consistency*, this would make a difference to the group mean fitness. Okasha cannot consistently omit a causal arrow from P_i to W_i in such cases (as in Figure 5 in Okasha, 2016), given his apparent interpretation of the meaning of such an arrow.

I do not see these as fatal objections to the individual-centred approach Okasha pursues, but they are enough to motivate the development of an alternative. There are two key ideas at the heart of my approach that mark important departures from Okasha's. First, I see the causal differences between kin selection and group selection as differences of degree, not all-or-nothing differences explicable in terms of the presence or absence of certain causal relationships. Second, I take it that the degree to which a selection process resembles a paradigm case of kin selection or group selection depends primarily on the structure of the population. Okasha's graphs implicitly make assumptions about population structure (e.g. a graph containing a 'group gene frequency' variable implicitly assumes the existence of groups), but they do not give population structure a central role. I favour an approach that explicitly accounts for the differences between kin and group selection in terms of the structural features of populations, bringing the role of population structure to the fore.

4.3 Two Influences: Hamilton and Godfrey-Smith

Before setting out the details of my proposal, I want to acknowledge (and highlight the insights of) two important influences. First, here are Hamilton's (1975) own views on the relationship between kin and group selection:

If we insist that group selection is different from kin selection the term should be restricted to situations of assortation definitely not involving kin. But it seems on the whole preferable to retain a more flexible use of terms; to use group selection when groups are clearly in evidence and to qualify with mention of 'kin' (as in the 'kin group' selection referred to by Brown), 'relatedness' or 'low migration' (which is often the cause of relatedness in groups), or else 'assortation', as appropriate. The term 'kin selection' appeals most where pedigrees tend to be unbounded and interwoven, as is so often the case with humans.   (Hamilton, 1975, p. 337)

This passage is a little confusing: Hamilton initially sounds sceptical of there being any useful distinction to be drawn between kin and group selection, but he then proceeds to set out a nuanced way of thinking about that distinction. As I read it, the point he is making is that the terminology of 'kin selection' and 'group selection' does track real and biologically important differences, but the differences that matter are differences of degree in aspects of population structure. The degree to which groups are 'clearly in evidence' matters, as does the degree to which assortment is explained by kinship. But the distinction is not clean or neat; it is not a dichotomy.

A second inspiration is Godfrey-Smith's (2006; 2008) work on the varieties of population structure, which we first encountered in Chapter 3, Section 3.5. Godfrey-Smith contrasts group-structured populations with what he terms 'neighbour-structured' populations. In the former, social interactions are contained within sharply bounded, well-integrated groups in which everyone interacts with everyone else. In the latter, every individual interacts with its nearest neighbours, but there are no well-defined groups: there are only continuously overlapping networks centred on individuals. As Godfrey-Smith notes, we can conceptualize this difference in terms of the transitivity (or otherwise) of the social network. In the paradigm case of a group-structured network, the relation of fitness-affecting interaction is perfectly transitive (if A affects the fitness of B, and B affects the fitness of C, then A affects the fitness of C). By contrast, in the paradigm case of a neighbour-structured network—one in which each individual interacts with its four adjacent 'von Neumann neighbours' on a square lattice—the relation is perfectly intransitive: if A affects the fitness of B, and B affects the fitness of C, then A does not affect the fitness of C, assuming $A \neq C$. These should be seen as extreme cases: real social networks are likely to be neither perfectly transitive nor perfectly intransitive, but will instead have some intermediate level of transitivity.

The mathematical literature on network analysis gives us some formal tools with which to quantify the extent to which a network approximates these extreme cases. Network analysis has grown rapidly in recent years, and a great deal of work in this area has concentrated on the problem of identifying communities within networks (reviewed in Fortunato, 2010). The starting point for any approach to this problem is to represent the whole-population social network as a graph ($\mathcal{G}$) in which the individuals are the vertices (or nodes) and social interactions are the edges (or connections) between the vertices. Social neighbourhoods of focal individuals can then be represented as subgraphs. The vertices to which a focal vertex (v_i) is directly connected by an edge are known as its adjacent vertices. The subgraph $\mathcal{N}[v_i]$, comprising v_i and all vertices adjacent to v_i, is known as the closed neighbourhood of v_i. The subgraph $\mathcal{N}(v_i)$, comprising all vertices adjacent to v_i but not v_i itself, is known as the open neighbourhood of v_i. This gives us the basic framework we need to start thinking more formally about the structure of social neighbourhoods.

One formal tool that may be of use for our purposes is the *clustering coefficient*, which provides a quantitative measure of the transitivity of a neighbourhood (Watts and Strogatz, 1998). The (local) clustering coefficient of v_i is the ratio of the number of edges in $\mathcal{N}(v_i)$ to the maximum possible number of such edges. Informally, this quantifies the extent to which the neighbours of v_i are directly connected to each other. So, in a network in which each individual interacts with its four von Neumann neighbours on a square lattice, the clustering coefficient at all vertices is 0, because one's neighbours are never directly connected to each other. In a group-structured network in which all members of a social group interact with each other, the neighbourhood of a focal individual will be maximally 'joined-up', implying a clustering coefficient of 1. An intermediate case is a square lattice in which each individual interacts with its eight 'Moore neighbours' (including, in addition to its four von Neumann neighbours on each side, the four neighbours on the corners between these sides). In this network, each of the focal individual's neighbours is connected to either two or four of its other neighbours out of a possible seven, with an average of three, so the clustering coefficient is 3/7.

We can also think of the difference between neighbour-structure and group-structure in terms of the *relative density* of social neighbourhoods. This is a more subtle notion, but arguably a more useful one for our purposes. Formally, the relative density is defined in terms of two other concepts: the internal and total degree of a subgraph. Consider the subgraph $\mathcal{N}[v_i]$, representing the closed neighbourhood of a focal vertex. The internal degree of a vertex v_j in $\mathcal{N}[v_i]$ is the number of edges directly linking v_j to other vertices within $\mathcal{N}[v_i]$; the external degree of v_j is the number of edges directly linking it to vertices outside $\mathcal{N}[v_i]$; and the total degree of v_j is the sum of its internal and external degrees. The internal degree of the subgraph $\mathcal{N}[v_i]$ is then defined as the sum of the internal degrees of its vertices, and the external and total degrees of the subgraph are likewise defined as the sum of the external and total degrees (respectively) of its vertices. The relative density of $\mathcal{N}[v_i]$ is the ratio of its internal degree to its total degree (Fortunato, 2010, p. 85).

Informally, then, relative density compares the number of 'inner' connections joining up the members of a social neighbourhood to the number of 'outer' connections linking the members to other organisms outside the neighbourhood. In Godfrey-Smith's paradigmatic neighbour-structured population, in which each organism interacts with its four von Neumann neighbours on a square lattice, the subgraph defined by a focal individual and its von Neumann neighbourhood has a relative density of 2/5 (0.4): the internal degree is 8 and the total degree is 20. By contrast, the subgraph defined by an hermetically sealed social group, with no outward connections, has a relative density of 1. A focal individual interacting with its eight Moore neighbours is again an intermediate case, but one much closer to the former than the latter: the internal degree is 40 and the total degree is 72, implying a relative density of 5/9 (0.55).[9]

These concepts differ in that the clustering coefficient considers only how internally 'joined-up' a subgraph is, without considering the extent to which it is isolated from the rest of the network. A subgraph consisting of a focal individual and its four von Neumann neighbours will always have a clustering coefficient of 0, regardless of how this neighbourhood joins up with the rest of the graph. It will therefore be 0 even if the neighbourhood is completely cut off from the rest of the population, intuitively forming a distinct social group. By contrast, the relative density is very sensitive to isolation—a subgraph with some internal connections and no outward connections will always have a relative density of 1, no matter how poorly integrated it is[10]—but, for any subgraph with some outward connections, it is also sensitive to the extent to which the subgraph is internally joined-up. This, I suggest, gives us the toolkit we need to make precise the extent to which groups are 'clearly in evidence' in a population.

---

[9] A social neighbourhood cannot have a relative density of 0, because there must be at least one internal connection in a subgraph to justify interpreting it as a social neighbourhood. However, we can imagine social neighbourhoods with relative densities of approximately 0. Think here of a social outcast who interacts with only one individual, and suppose this other individual has ninety-eight connections to the rest of the population. The subgraph comprising the outcast and its social partner would have a relative density of 0.02.

[10] But note that, if a group is isolated but poorly connected internally, this will tend to show up in lower relative densities for the social neighbourhoods of individuals at the periphery of the group. For example, imagine a subgraph comprising a central individual and its four von Neumann neighbours that has no outward connections to the rest of the population. The central individual's social neighbourhood has a relative density of 1, but, for the four peripheral individuals, the relative density of their social neighbourhood is 0.4. The average relative density over all neighbourhoods will therefore tend to be quite low when groups are poorly integrated internally; this matters for the discussion of G in the next section.

4.4 K and G

My positive proposal, in short, is that we conceptualize the distinction between kin and group selection in terms of gradated differences in two key structural properties of populations. I will label these properties as K (for 'kin-structure') and G (for 'group-structure').[11] Kin selection, roughly speaking, is selection on indirect fitness differences ($rb \neq 0$) in a high-K population (i.e. a population with a high degree of kin-structure); whereas group selection, roughly speaking, is selection on indirect fitness differences ($rb \neq 0$) in a high-G population (i.e. a population with a high degree of group-structure).

To forestall any misunderstandings, let me be clear that this proposal is not intended to capture current usage of the terms 'kin selection' and 'group selection'. Rather, it is a proposal about how these concepts should be used, if we want them to mark a real and evolutionarily significant distinction among selection processes. It is to some extent a revisionary proposal, although, as I have been emphasizing, I see it as well-aligned with Hamilton's own views on how the distinction should be drawn.

Before explaining K and G, let me stress the condition that, for either kin or group selection to occur, it must be the case that $rb \neq 0$ in the population as a whole. In other words, kin and group selection are processes that contribute to indirect fitness explanations and hybrid explanations of change, but not to direct fitness explanations (in the sense of Chapter 2). If $rb = 0$, then the selection process at work relies on direct fitness effects alone, and I claim that to count such a process as one of kin or group selection unhelpfully obscures this fact. If what is on offer is a direct fitness explanation, we should not invoke these concepts. While this may sound uncontroversial, many authors in fact allow that group selection can occur when $rb = 0$, so I will comment further on this issue below (in Section 4.5).

4.4.1 K

K, the degree of kin-structure in a population, is intended to capture the overall extent to which genealogical relatives interact differentially with respect to the character of interest. Accordingly, I will refer to populations

---

[11] This form of labelling is inspired by that of Godfrey-Smith (2009b), who labels the key properties that determine the Darwinian character of a population in a similar way.

in which there is a high degree of differential interaction between relatives as 'high-K' populations; and I will refer to populations in which there is no tendency for relatives to interact differentially as 'zero-K' populations. I do not intend to commit to a single quantitative measure of K, firstly because I want to allow that different measures may be appropriate in different contexts, and secondly because I do not need to commit to a measure in order to use K to make qualitative comparisons among populations (cf. Godfrey-Smith, 2009b; Queller and Strassmann, 2009). However, for the purpose of fixing ideas, it may be helpful to think of K as the counterfactual correlation between social partner breeding values (with respect to the character of interest) that would obtain in the absence of any kinship-independent sources of such correlation, such as greenbeard effects.[12]

How high does the degree of differential interaction between relatives have to be before we have a case of kin selection? Because we are dealing with a continuum of cases here, any cut-off will be a pragmatic choice, and it is arguably best to avoid any such cut-off. Following Godfrey-Smith (2009b), I prefer to talk of 'marginal' and 'paradigm' cases. Paradigm cases of kin selection occur in high-K populations. When we have non-zero rb but very low K, either because r is very low or because it is largely generated by kinship-independent mechanisms, we have at best a marginal case of kin selection, and such a selection process is probably more aptly described in other terms. Human evolution may be an example of a marginal case, since estimates based on studies of modern hunter-gatherers suggest a value of genetic relatedness of around 0.05 in such societies (Hill et al., 2011; Bowles and Gintis, 2011; see Chapter 8 for more discussion of this issue).

One might ask: why does K matter? Why is this a structural property worth estimating at all? Why are comparisons among populations, in regard to their degree of K, worth making? My answer is that kin-structure has a special role to play in generating the conditions for the evolution of stable altruistic or spiteful behaviour. Genetic correlations can arise without kinship, as greenbeard phenomena demonstrate. But recall the concern about greenbeard effects raised in Chapter 2: altruism

---

[12] In cases where kinship-independent sources are actually absent, this is related to r but not identical to it, since r is a regression coefficient rather than a correlation coefficient. Correlations are more useful for my purposes because they take values between 0 and 1.

that relies on greenbeard effects will be stable only if, for some reason, the expression of the altruistic behaviour cannot be suppressed without also suppressing the marker that attracts benefits from others. If this selective suppression is possible, then it will pay to be a 'falsebeard': an organism who expresses the marker without expressing the altruism. By contrast, genetic correlations generated by kinship-dependent mechanisms are not so easy to subvert, because kinship generates genetic correlation at every locus in the genome (Ridley and Grafen, 1981; Okasha, 2002; West and Gardner, 2010).

4.4.2 G

G, the degree of group-structure in a population, is intended to capture the overall extent to which a population contains well-defined social groups, at the right grain of analysis for generating non-zero rb, that are stable over the course of the life cycle. A 'high-G' population is one in which groups are well-integrated, highly stable, and effectively insulated from other groups, with no room for ambiguity regarding group membership. Maynard Smith's (1964) haystacks model, in which we imagine social interaction and reproduction occurring in isolated subpopulations (envisioned as haystacks inhabited by mice), with occasional mixing events, is a good example of this.[13] A 'low-G' population is one in which, although interaction is locally structured to some extent, there are no discrete, well-defined social groups to speak of, because—as in the von Neumann neighbour-structured populations of Godfrey-Smith (2008)—social neighbourhoods blur continuously into one another. A 'zero-G' population is one in which we do not even have neighbour-structure: individuals interact with social partners drawn from the population as a whole, with no regard to their spatial location.

The qualification 'at the right grain of analysis for generating non-zero rb' merits emphasis. For example, one might worry that all populations of multicellular animals are ultimately high-G populations: after all, there is always group-structure if one looks at a fine enough grain of analysis, because one can always describe individual animals as groups of cells.

---

[13] The place of a haystacks model on the K-axis depends on the parameter values specifically, the size of the founding population, the assortativity of group formation, and the time of isolation. With small founding populations, assortative grouping and/or long isolation periods, the population is likely to be high-K.

However, if our goal is to explain an organism-level phenotype, groups of cells are groups at the wrong grain of analysis. The right grain of analysis is that of the organism-level social network defined by fitness-affecting interactions with respect to the phenotypic character of interest. The population is 'high-G' if that network can be subdivided into sharp and stable social groups.

As with K, I do not intend to commit to a single quantitative measure of G. I suspect there is no perfect measure, and that the most appropriate measure will depend on the context, because the relative importance of the different properties that contribute to G—that is, internal integration, external isolation, and stability over time—will depend on the context. But again, for the purpose of fixing ideas, it may be helpful to have a possible measure in mind. One possible measure with attractive features is the average, taken over all individuals in the population and over an appropriate time period, of the relative density of a focal individual's social neighbourhood. This ranges between 0 and 1, and (as noted earlier) places von Neumann neighbour-structure at 0.4, Moore neighbour-structure at 0.55, and perfectly integrated, hermetically sealed groups at 1. The range 0 to 0.4 is occupied by social structures in which the average social neighbourhood has a greater external degree than we see in a von Neumann neighbour-structured population, without displaying significantly more internal integration.[14] The range 0.55 to 1 is occupied by social structures that display less internal integration and/or external isolation than in the idealized extreme case, but more internal integration and/or external isolation than we see in a Moore neighbourhood.

The relative density is well suited to measuring internal integration and external isolation of social neighbourhoods, but less well suited to measuring their stability, underlining the point that there is probably no single perfect measure of G. However, the time-average of the relative density over an extended time period will convey something about the stability of groups over that time period: if well-defined groups are ephemeral and dissolve soon after forming, the relative density will be high while they exist but lower once they have dissolved, resulting in a lower time-average than in a population with more stable group-structure. So, while

---

[14] For example, imagine a structure in which every individual has five social partners drawn at random from a very large population. This is likely to result in social neighbourhoods with relative densities of around 1/3.

the relative density is not intended as a measure of group stability, time-averages of the relative density may sometimes be useful for that purpose. As with K, one might ask: why does G matter? Why is this a structural property worth measuring? Why are comparisons among populations, in regard to their degree of G, worth making? My answer to this question is to point to the special role of high-G populations in evolutionary transitions in individuality (the topic of Chapter 7). A population that is high-G contains identifiable higher-level entities—namely, social groups—formed of collections of lower-level entities. These groups are not automatically higher-level individuals. I take it that higher-level individuality requires some process of collective reproduction (see Godfrey-Smith, 2009b), as well as the presence of mechanisms that suppress selection within (or, in Godfrey-Smith's memorable terminology, 'de-Darwinize') the groups (Michod, 1999; Godfrey-Smith, 2009b; Queller and Strassmann, 2009; Clarke, 2013). Nevertheless, group-structure is clearly an important precondition for the evolution of higher-level individuals. When we identify a population as high-G, we cannot conclude that a transition is underway, but we can conclude that an important precondition for such a transition has been met.

4.4.3 K-G space

K and G can be imagined as the axes of a two-dimensional space, and we can think of kin selection and group selection as large, overlapping regions of that space. Paradigm cases of kin selection occur in high-K populations: they are cases in which we find selection on indirect fitness differences in a population with a fairly high degree of relatedness between social partners, and with kinship-dependent mechanisms serving as the main source of this relatedness. Paradigm instances of group selection occur in high-G populations: they are cases in which we find selection on indirect fitness differences in a population in which social interaction is structured by stable, well-integrated, and sharply bounded groups. The distinction here is not sharp, but nor is it merely arbitrary or conventional.

Figure 4.2 provides a visualization of the proposal, illustrated with some notable cases. The placement of the points is not exact and is open to debate: the aim is simply to provide an intuitive visualization. In the bottom-left corner, we have populations that are low-K and low-G—populations with neither kin-structure nor group-structure.

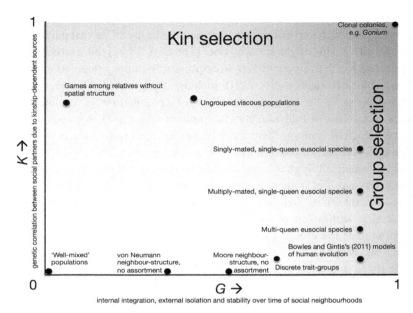

Figure 4.2 *K-G* space. Kin selection and group selection can be conceptualized as overlapping regions of a 2D space defined by the variables *K* and *G*. Locations of points are approximate and for illustration only (see the main text for commentary on some of the points).

An important class of examples are so-called 'well-mixed' populations in which individuals interact at random such that no pair of invividuals is any more likely to interact than any other. These are populations in which neither kin nor group selection can be said to occur, since the required structural features are entirely lacking.

As we move up the *K*-axis, we come to populations in which organisms still interact with sets of individuals drawn from the whole population with no regard to their spatial location, rather than interacting in structured local neighbourhoods, but in which there is some greater-than-chance probability of interacting with a relative (e.g. a sibling). Models of this sort have a long history in social evolution theory and continue to be studied (e.g. Grafen, 1979; Maynard Smith, 1982; Queller, 1984; Allen and Nowak, 2015). These are aptly described as cases of kin selection, but, since interactions are not contained within localized social groups, they are not aptly described as cases of group selection.

As we move along the G-axis, we come to Godfrey-Smith's neighbour-structured populations, in which there are discernible local neighbourhoods that structure interaction, but nothing yet resembling well-defined social groups. A square lattice in which organisms interact with their von Neumann neighbours and are assigned to vertices at random, with no limited dispersal, is a zero-K version of this. As we go up the K-axis here, introducing differential interaction between kin due to limited dispersal, we arrive at populations that are high-K but still fairly low-G. Models of so-called ungrouped viscous populations that make use of von Neumann neighbourhoods and similar structures, such as the models of D. S. Wilson et al. (1992), belong in this area; their precise position will depend on the parameter values. In models of haploid organisms, very high levels of relatedness can be attained due to limited dispersal from the birth site (in one of the simulations discussed by Wilson et al. 1992, $r = 0.59$), and this is reflected in the figure in the value of K. Moving further along the G-axis, we arrive at the discrete 'trait-groups' of D. S. Wilson (1975), which are externally isolated and fairly well integrated (at least with respect to the trait of interest) while they exist, but which are not stable for long periods and are typically outlived by their members. These can be anywhere on the K-axis depending on the role of kinship in generating assortative grouping, but for illustrative purposes I have put them at low-K.

In the bottom-right corner, there are populations that are low-K and high-G. Here, groups are 'clearly in evidence' but groups are not composed of close kin. Bowles and Gintis's (2011) models of human evolution belong in this region. Bowles and Gintis assume that early human populations were structured into well-defined, stable groups with low relatedness. Finally, as we go up the K-axis to the top-right, we arrive at populations that are high in both K and G. These are the cases for which Hamilton favoured the term 'kin-group selection'. In these populations, there is sharp and stable group-structure *and* a high degree of genetic correlation between social partners due to kinship-dependent mechanisms.

The evolution of multicellularity is a source of extreme cases in this corner (see Chapter 7, and Maynard Smith and Szathmáry, 1995; Michod, 1999; Queller, 2000). Consider colonial algae such as *Gonium*: the colonies are clonal, implying high K, and the group-structure is sharp and stable over the course of the life cycle, implying high G. There is little to be gained by arguing over whether the selection processes that operate in these populations are cases of kin or group selection, because they have the core structural features of both. The term 'kin-group selection' removes the misleading appearance of competing hypotheses.

4.5 The $rb \neq 0$ Requirement

The proposal I have advanced includes the requirement that, for either kin or group selection to occur, it must be the case that $rb \neq 0$. I noted earlier that this requirement, traditionally associated with kin selection, might prove controversial as a requirement on group selection, and it is now time to elaborate further on the consequences of, and justification for, this requirement.

Let us first consider some of its implications. One is that not all processes of natural selection occurring in populations that intuitively contain groups will qualify as cases of group selection. Consider again G. C. Williams's scenario in which a group containing fast-running deer outperforms a group containing slower-running deer because the faster deer, as individuals, evade predators more easily. This is not group selection on my account, because the trait's advantage arises entirely from its direct fitness effects (Okasha, 2006). The intuitive motivation for excluding these cases is that, although a form of group-structure is present, it plays no role in explaining the selection for fast running. Similarly, processes of natural selection that involve interactions among relatives do not qualify as kin selection if the interactions fail to generate non-zero rb, perhaps because the interactions are not fitness-affecting, or because social partners, though related, are not differentially related relative to the population average (see Chapter 2, Section 2.2).

Awkward cases arise when, although $rb = 0$, intergroup conflict plays an essential role in the generation of a direct fitness benefit. Sterelny's (2013b) hypothesis regarding the evolution of hierarchy in early Holocene human societies provides an interesting example. In broad terms, Sterelny proposes that ruling elites were tolerated by the majority because the intense and frequent intergroup warfare of the early Holocene put a fitness premium on strong and centralized military leadership. Groups with strong leaders were more successful in warfare, causing traits associated with hierarchy to spread. Is this a group selection hypothesis? In one sense it is, because the advantage of acquiescing to the demands of an elite depends on the existence of intergroup conflict. But on my proposal, it is not, because the explanation on offer is a direct fitness explanation. Norms of acquiescence evolve because, at an individual level, it pays in direct fitness terms to adopt them; there is no requirement that $rb > 0$ (Birch, 2014d). Not a lot hangs on how we classify these cases. I propose that we resist the urge to describe them as cases of group selection. In so doing, however, we should take care not to forget that direct fitness explanations can still appeal to intergroup conflict as a source of direct fitness benefit.

If $rb \neq 0$, is one or other of kin and group selection at work? Not necessarily: the requirement is intended as a necessary condition but not a sufficient condition. Consider greenbeard effects. Populations in which the only genetic correlations between social partners are owed to greenbeard phenomena belong in the bottom-left quadrant of Figure 4.2. They do not require group-structure, provided we assume that bearers of the greenbeard marker can still seek each other out successfully in a non-group-structured population. But nor do they rely on differential interaction between genealogical kin, since bearers of the greenbeard gene need not be kin in this sense.

Gardner et al. (2011) propose regarding greenbeard effects as a form of kin selection, broadly construed. But although we could go this way, I advise against it. It is important to distinguish clearly between processes that rely on shared ancestry and processes that rely on genetic similarity generated by others means, and I suggest we mark that distinction by reserving the term 'kin selection' for the former. As we noted earlier, gene mobility provides another mechanism for generating positive r without genealogical kinship (see Chapter 6 for a more detailed discussion). Rankin et al. (2011a) suggest that this too can be regarded as a form of kin selection, but I regard it as a marginal case. Note that, in some cases, these kinship-independent mechanisms may operate in conjunction with kinship-dependent mechanisms, such that both contribute to the value of r. We therefore have a continuum here—not a dichotomy—ranging from cases of socal evolution in which shared ancestry is wholly unimportant to cases in which it is essential.

The main reason I anticipate resistance to the idea that group selection requires $rb \neq 0$ is that $rb \neq 0$ is neither necessary nor sufficient for there to be variation in fitness between groups, and many group selection theorists consider this a hallmark of group selection. Non-zero rb is unnecessary because, as in the aforementioned cases of Williams's fast-running deer and Sterelny's explanation for acquiescence to hierarchies, there can be fitness variation between groups even though direct fitness effects fully account for this variation. It is insufficient due to the possibility of soft selection with local population regulation, as discussed by Heisler and Damuth (1987); Goodnight et al. (1992), and Okasha (2006). In such cases, we have a group-structured population, but each group makes the same, fixed contribution to the next generation, and all fitness variation occurs within groups. Yet grouping is assortative—altruists interact differentially with other altruists—leading to non-zero rb. This population is high-G, suggesting a paradigm case of group selection by the lights of my account, but there is no variation in fitness between groups.

If one takes variation in fitness between groups to be the mark of group selection, then one should take $Cov(W_i, P_i) \neq 0$, not $rb \neq 0$, as the minimal statistical requirement all cases of group selection must satisfy. This adds an extra layer of complexity to the account, since kin and group selection would then differ in their minimal statistical requirements as well as their commitments regarding population structure. However, I resist this amendment, because I do not see a compelling case for regarding variation in group fitness as necessary for group selection. If well-defined group-structure is implicated in generating non-zero rb, I take the view that the selection process can be aptly described as one of group selection, even if groups do not vary in mean fitness.[15]

Why insist that group selection must require fitness variation between groups? I see two main motivations. One is a desire that the conditions for group selection should be directly analogous to the conditions for natural selection in a population of individuals, but with 'groups' substituted

---

[15] My position is well-aligned with what Okasha (2006) calls the 'neighbour approach' of Nunney (1985), which diagnoses group selection in a group-structured population whenever there is positive rb. This is closely related to, although not identical to, the 'contextual approach' of Heisler and Damuth (1987). Both approaches decompose change using regression models of fitness. The difference is that the contextual approach uses regression models that take group characters (e.g. group gene frequencies) as predictors, whereas the neighbour approach uses neighbourhood characters (e.g. the average gene frequency of the focal individual's social partners). The latter corresponds to the partition of change represented in HRG.

for 'individuals'. The conditions for natural selection include fitness variation among individuals, so group selection must require fitness variation among groups for a direct analogy to hold.

I reply that, although a direct analogy between the conditions for individual and group selection would be elegant, it does not deserve high priority. It is helpful here to invoke Heisler and Damuth's (1987) MLS1/MLS2 distinction, and to recall that the type of group selection at issue in this article is the MLS1 type. In MLS2, groups are higher-level individuals or proto-individuals, reproducing in their own right. In this context, a direct analogy between the conditions for individual and group selection seems important, because 'group selection' in this sense is simply a higher-level form of individual selection. In MLS1, by contrast, groups structure interaction at the lower-level but do not reproduce in their own right, making the need for a direct analogy seem less pressing (Okasha, 2006). The priority, in my view, is that the category of group selection demarcates (albeit not sharply) a real and evolutionarily significant class of selection processes—a class that is worth distinguishing from the class of kin selection processes. On my account, it does this: the distinction between kin and group selection highlights real and evolutionarily significant differences in population structure within the class of indirect fitness explanations of change.

A second motivation is that group selection should be apt to generate group adaptation, and there can be no group adaptation without fitness variation between groups (Gardner and Grafen, 2009). I reply that, although the connection between group selection and group adaptation is clearly important, especially in the context of evolutionary transitions, there should be no requirement that group selection must be apt to generate group adaptation in all cases. It is enough that this can happen under some further conditions—conditions that will include variation in fitness between groups. To insist that group selection must require variation in fitness between groups is, I think, to insist on too close a link between group selection and group adaptation.

4.6 Levels of Organization

One final clarifying remark deserves special emphasis, owing to its particular relevance for later chapters. Both kin-structured (high-K) and group-structured (high-G) populations can occur at multiple levels of biological organization. If we take a group-structured population of base-level entities and 'frameshift' (i.e. change perspective) up a level to consider the population of groups, this higher-level population will itself have a position in K-G space.

The population of groups may have higher-order group-structure: there may be well-defined meta-groups, or groups of groups, defined by patterns of social interaction. This may lead to higher-level group selection. For example, there might be higher-level group selection for genes that promote cooperation among members of the same meta-group who are located in different first-order groups.

The population of groups may also be kin-structured. This will be the case if groups form well-defined lineages, and if groups that are closely related genealogically are more likely to interact with each other than groups that are not. This may lead to a higher-level form of kin selection. For example, if nearby groups tend to be 'offspring' groups of the same 'parent' group, there might be higher-level kin selection for genes that promote cooperation among nearby groups. This may occur even if the population of groups is simply a viscous population, with no well-defined meta-groups.

These ideas may sound strange at first hearing, but they are simply unusual ways of describing something familiar. From the point of view of social evolution theory, multicellular organisms can be regarded as particularly well-integrated social groups of cells (see Chapter 7). From this perspective, populations of animals are populations of groups of lower-level entities, and standard cases of kin selection and group selection occur in such populations.

This should alert us to the possibility of kin and group selection occurring at higher levels of biological organization than we usually envisage: that is, in kin- or group-structured populations of groups of organisms. For example, in many ant species we find 'supercolonies', each consisting of multiple distinct nests. This leads to the idea that supercolonies may be created and maintained by group selection acting on groups of nests—a possibility discussed by Kennedy et al. (2014). Moreover, dispersal of offspring nests from parental nests is limited within supercolonies, raising the possibility that, within a supercolony, kin selection at the level of the nest favours cooperation between adjacent nests—a possibility discussed by Chapuisat et al. (1997).

4.7 The Key Substantive Questions

Debates surrounding kin and group selection are easily derailed by semantic confusion. This, combined with the plethora of 'equivalence results' described in Section 4.1, gives rise to the suspicion that there are no worthwhile debates to be had here at all: that all the disputes on these issues are merely verbal disputes. But I think this suspicion is misplaced. By identifying kin and group selection with overlapping regions of K-G space, we make room for worthwhile debates about the resemblance of a given selection process (e.g. early human evolution, or social evolution in microbes, or the evolution of eusociality in insects) to a paradigm case of kin or group selection. These debates can be usefully recast as debates about the position of the population in that space. A population's position in K-G space will depend on the answers to the following questions:

1. How high is K in the population? That is, how strong are the genetic correlations between social partners, and how important are kinship-dependent sources, as opposed to greenbeard effects and other kinship-independent sources, in generating those correlations?
2. How high is G in the population? In other words, how internally integrated, sharply bounded, and stable is the group-structure at the relevant grain of analysis?

These are substantive, empirical questions: they are the sort of questions it takes serious empirical inquiry, not just stable semantic conventions, to settle. So, although the distinction between kin and group selection is not sharp, these concepts can still provide a useful way of framing meaningful debates about the importance of kin-structure and group-structure in real processes of social evolution. There can be no universal answers to these questions, and hence no universal answer to the question of whether social evolution proceeds by kin selection or group selection: the answers depend on the details of the case at hand. Kin and group selection correspond to large, overlapping regions of a space of population structures, and real populations can be found throughout both of these regions.

4.8 Summary of Chapter 4

In group-structured populations in which some other assumptions are satisfied, HRG (the generalized version of Hamilton's rule) and Price's rule (the corresponding condition for change entailed by the multi-level Price equation) provide formally equivalent conditions for change. However, this result and others like it merely show an equivalence between two statistical descriptions of change; they do not show that there is no useful distinction to be drawn between kin and group selection, conceived as causal processes responsible for change.

One can distinguish two broad ways of drawing such a distinction. An 'individual-centred' approach locates the crucial differences in the causal path at the individual level between a focal organism's genotype and its fitness. A 'population-centred' approach, inspired by Hamilton (1975) and Godfrey-Smith (2006, 2008), locates the crucial differences in the structural features of populations responsible for generating indirect fitness effects.

Here I have pursued a population-centred approach, identifying kin and group selection with large, overlapping regions of a space defined in terms of two key structural features of populations: K, the overall degree to which genealogical kin interact differentially, and G, the overall degree to which the population contains stable, internally integrated, and externally isolated social groups.

The significance of K lies in the fact that high-K populations may support the evolution of stable altruistic and spiteful behaviour—behaviour that is not suppressed by modifier alleles at other genomic loci. The significance of G lies in the fact that high-G populations meet a basic precondition for an evolutionary transition in individuality. Populations at any level of biological organization can be given a position in K-G space.

This way of thinking about the distinction allows us to see that, in some cases, there is no worthwhile debate to be had about whether a process is one of kin or group selection, because the population has the paradigmatic structural features of both. These cases are aptly described as 'kin-group selection'. However, the overlap is not total, and the question of where a particular population lies in K-G space is a substantive question that requires empirical investigation to settle.

5

Two Conceptions of Social Fitness

On the way to deriving the original version of Hamilton's rule, Hamilton (1964) described two alternative ways of thinking about the fitness of an organism in the context of social evolution. He called them inclusive fitness and neighbour-modulated fitness (Hamilton, 1964, pp. 5–6). Hamilton chose to focus on developing the inclusive fitness concept, and this continues to be the better known of the two. However, by the mid-1990s, the neighbour-modulated fitness concept—often going under the name of 'direct' or 'personal' fitness—had inconspicuously grown into a full-fledged alternative modelling approach.[1] In recent years its popularity has grown steadily, to the point where it is now the preferred methodology of many social evolution researchers (Taylor et al., 2007; Wenseleers et al., 2010; Frank, 2013).

Unsurprisingly, this has led to considerable discussion of the relationship between Hamilton's two fitness concepts. The key questions are: When are the two fitness concepts equivalent for the purposes of calculating gene frequency change? When do they come apart? And when the choice between them is not forced by considerations of accuracy, which fitness concept is preferable? I will argue that, although the neighbour-modulated fitness concept requires fewer assumptions than the inclusive fitness concept, the latter retains important advantages when its assumptions are at least approximately met. This is because inclusive fitness, in contrast to neighbour-modulated fitness, provides a criterion for improvement and a standard for optimality in a process of cumulative adaptation.

---

[1] Landmarks in this literature include Orlove (1975, 1979); Cavalli-Sforza and Feldman (1978); Grafen (1979); Queller (1985); Taylor and Frank (1996); Frank (1998).

Here is a more detailed outline. In Section 5.1, I set out the conceptual contrast between neighbour-modulated and inclusive fitness. I explain how the two fitness concepts embody different perspectives on the role of relatedness in social evolution, leading them to make different choices regarding the assignment of descendants to ancestors. Roughly, the former assigns descendants to ancestors according to considerations of parenthood, whereas the latter assigns descendants to ancestors according to considerations of social causation. I then turn to the question of their formal equivalence, briefly surveying existing views on this issue. In Section 5.2, I reconstruct Hamilton's (1970) argument for the formal equivalence of the two concepts, highlighting two crucial assumptions on which the argument rests: actor's control and additivity. In Section 5.3, I consider what it takes for these assumptions to hold, arguing that they are rarely, if ever, exactly true if interpreted as claims about total effects.

In Section 5.4, I explain why social evolution theorists typically invoke a certain kind of 'weak selection' to justify both assumptions as approximations concerning marginal effects. I explain that this move, although it may seem *ad hoc* at first glance, emerges naturally from a gradualist picture of the origins of complex adaptation. In Section 5.5, I argue that, in the context of a process of cumulative adaptation driven by weak selection, inclusive fitness has a special role as the criterion for improvement and the standard for optimality. In Section 5.6, I argue against the related but more ambitious claim, which remains popular in social evolution research, that we should expect inclusive fitness to be at least approximately optimized in nature.

5.1 The Conceptual Contrast

To understand the difference between the two fitness concepts, consider two perspectives on what happens when a social trait evolves because of positive relatedness between social partners (Box 5.1). From one perspective, we can view genetic relatedness as the underlying source of *phenotypic correlation*: when r is high, bearers of the genes for altruism are differentially likely to interact with other bearers, so they are differentially likely to receive the benefits of other agents' altruistic behaviour. Thus high r means that bearers of the genes for altruism may have greater reproductive output, on average, than non-bearers.

Box 5.1 Two ways to conceptualize the role of relatedness

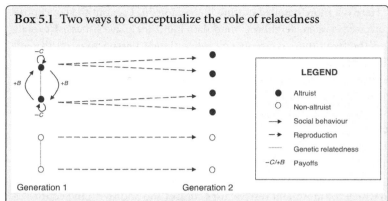

Generation 1   Generation 2

Picture 5.1 Genetic relatedness leads to phenotypic correlation. Two altruists (black) confer a fitness benefit (*B*) on each other at a cost (*C*) to themselves. As a result, they are fitter overall than two nearby non-altruists (white). Genetic relatedness can give rise to such patterns of correlated interaction in a population, making altruists fitter (on average) than non-altruists.

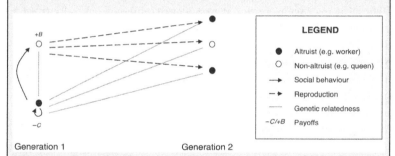

Generation 1   Generation 2

Picture 5.2 Genetic relatedness leads to indirect reproduction. An altruist (black) confers a fitness benefit (*B*) on a related recipient (white) at a cost (*C*) to itself. The recipient does not express the altruistic phenotype. However, it possesses the genes for altruism, which it transmits to some of its offspring (as indicated by the dotted lines, which show the genetic similarity between the actor and the recipient's offspring). The recipient thereby provides the actor with a means of 'indirect reproduction'—that is, an indirect route to genetic representation in the next generation.

From another perspective, we can view genetic relatedness as providing opportunities for *indirect reproduction*: when r is high, recipients provide actors with an indirect means of securing genetic representation in the next generation. Thus genes for altruism may spread, if the genetic representation an altruist secures indirectly through conferring greater reproductive output on its relatives exceeds the genetic representation it loses through sacrificing a portion of its own reproduction success.[2]

These contrasting perspectives on the role of r push us towards contrasting ways of thinking about social fitness. If we think of relatedness as a source of phenotypic correlation, then we can continue to think of fitness as (roughly speaking) a measure of an individual organism's direct reproductive success, but we will need to pay special attention to the ways in which this quantity is affected by correlated interactions with neighbours. If, however, we think of relatedness as a source of indirect reproduction, then we are pushed towards a more 'inclusive' conception of fitness—a conception that counts an individual's success in reproducing indirectly through relatives in addition to its own personal offspring.

The first perspective is captured formally in Hamilton's concept of neighbour-modulated fitness (Figure 5.1), which analyses the correlations between an individual's genotype and its social neighbourhood, and helps predict when these correlations will give bearers of the genes for altruism greater personal fitness, on average, than non-bearers (Hamilton, 1964; Taylor and Frank, 1996; Frank, 1998, 2013). The second perspective is captured formally in Hamilton's concept of inclusive fitness (Figure 5.2), which adds up all the fitness effects causally attributable to a social actor—weighting each component by the relatedness between actor and recipient—in order to calculate the net effect of a social behaviour on the actor's overall genetic representation in the next generation (Hamilton, 1964; Frank, 1998, 2013; Grafen, 2006a).

Both fitness concepts are often misunderstood. To pre-empt some common misunderstandings, I need to note explicitly what these fitness concepts are *not*. First, neighbour-modulated fitness is not simply a new name for classical individual fitness, even though both are measured in terms of direct reproductive success. The qualifier 'neighbour-modulated' is introduced in order to make explicit some additional assumptions

---

[2] This dual theoretical role for the coefficient of relatedness—r as capturing the underlying source of phenotypic correlation between actor and recipient, and r as capturing the value of a recipient to an actor for the purposes of indirect reproduction—is discussed by Frank (1997b, a, 1998), who suggests we should define relatedness slightly differently for each theoretical purpose. See Birch (2013b, Ch. 5) for further discussion of this idea.

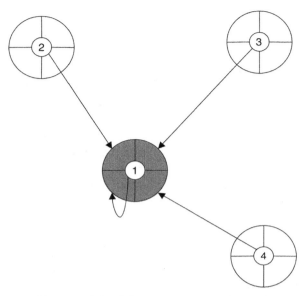

Figure 5.1 Neighbour-modulated fitness. An organism's neighbour-modulated fitness is an unweighted sum of effects on its own reproductive success. In this illustration, organism 1's reproductive success is affected by the behaviour of four organisms, including itself. The organisms are labelled 1, 2, 3, and 4, and the arrows indicate causal influence of behaviour on reproductive success. 1's neighbour-modulated fitness is a sum of these effects, plus a baseline non-social component.

that are being brought into play. As Figure 5.1 indicates, the concept of neighbour-modulated fitness assumes that an individual's reproductive success can be decomposed into a sum of components, each of which is causally attributable to a particular neighbourhood phenotype, plus a 'baseline' component that is independent of what these neighbours do. Since the classical Darwinian fitness concept does not make any such assumption about the causal structure of fitness, it would be incorrect to simply equate the two (Marshall, 2015, pp. 57–8).

Second, inclusive fitness is not simply an organism's classical individual fitness plus the classical individual fitness of its relatives, with the latter quantities weighed by relatedness coefficients. Hamilton never defined inclusive fitness in this way, because it leads to serious problems. As Grafen (1982, 1984) emphasizes, it is a constraint on any fitness concept that if bearers of one allele are, on average, fitter than bearers of an alternative allele, then the former should be favoured by selection at the expense of

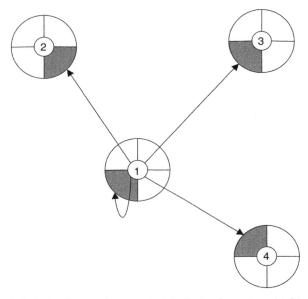

Figure 5.2 Inclusive fitness. An organism's inclusive fitness is a weighted sum of its effects on the reproductive success of others. In this illustration, organism 1's behaviour affects the fitness of itself and of organisms 2, 3, and 4 (as shown by the arrows; the shaded regions represent components of fitness caused by the behaviour of organism 1). Organism 1's inclusive fitness consists of a baseline non-social component, plus the effect on its own reproductive success caused by its own behaviour, plus its effects on organisms 2, 3, and 4, weighted in each case by the relevant coefficient of relatedness. In a population without class-structure, the coefficient of relatedness will be the same for every effect and will correspond to the r coefficient in HRG (for discussion of more complex cases in which class-structure is present, see Taylor, 1990, 1992; Frank, 1998; Grafen, 2006a; Wenseleers et al., 2010; Birch, 2013b).

the latter. A simple weighted sum of classical individual fitnesses violates this constraint. This is essentially because it allows any given descendant to be counted multiple times, once in computing the fitness of its parents, and again (and again, and again . . .) in computing the fitness of any collateral relatives. This multiple-counting has the consequence that organisms with 'bushier' family trees can end up much fitter than organisms with more sparse family trees, even though the bushiness of one's family tree makes no difference in itself to the future representation of one's genes in a population (Box 5.2).

What Hamilton (1964) saw from the outset is that, if the notion is to make sense at all, inclusive fitness must be defined in a way that avoids multiple-counting. His solution was to assume (as illustrated in Figure 5.2) that every organism's reproductive output can be written as a sum of components, each attributable to the behaviour of a specific social actor. Given this assumption, we can make sure that each component is counted once—and only once—by insisting that each component counts only towards the fitness of the actor who was causally responsible for it. As Hamilton (1964) himself put it:

Inclusive fitness may be imagined as the personal fitness which an individual actually expresses in its production of adult offspring as it becomes after it has been stripped and augmented in a certain way. It is stripped of all components which can be considered as due to the individual's social environment, leaving the fitness he would express if not exposed to any of the harms or benefits of that environment. This quantity is then augmented by certain fractions of the quantities of harm and benefit which the individual himself causes to the fitness of his neighbours. The fractions in question are simply the coefficients of relationship.

(Hamilton, 1964, p. 8)

Thus inclusive fitness is an inherently causal notion: a weighted sum of the fitness components for which a given social actor is causally responsible, where the weights are coefficients of relatedness. This weighted sum can be interpreted as a measure of the net genetic representation an actor gains in future generations by means of its social actions. The core conceptual contrast with neighbour-modulated fitness is that, while the neighbour-modulated fitness concept assigns descendants to ancestors in the traditional way—according to direct genealogical descent—the inclusive fitness concept assigns descendants to ancestors according to considerations of social causation (Frank, 1998; Queller, 2011).

Box 5.2 The trouble with a simple weighted sum

Consider a population containing two types of organisms: squares and circles. The initial generation contains one square and one circle. The initial circle has three offspring while the initial square has only one. But in the second generation, the square produces two offspring while each circle produces only one. The situation is depicted in the figure below (the first generation is the top row, the second generation is the middle row, and the third generation is the bottom row; arrows represent parent-offspring relationships).

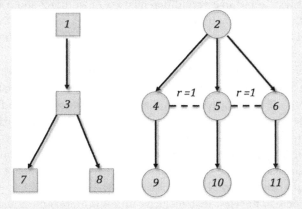

If individual fitness (w_i) is measured by personal reproductive output, then organism 3 (for which $w = 2$) is fitter than organisms 4, 5, or 6 (for which $w = 1$). If individual fitness is measured by a simple weighted sum, with relatedness providing the weights, then organism 3 (for which $w = 2$) is less fit than organisms 4, 5, or 6 (for which $w = 3$).

Now consider the question: what do these fitness concepts predict about the change in the relative frequencies of squares and circles between the second and third generations? If fitness is personal reproductive output, then squares in the second generation are fitter on average than circles, so we predict that squares increase in relative frequency. But if fitness is a simple weighted sum, then circles are fitter on average than squares, so we predict that circles increase in relative frequency. The correct answer is that squares increase in relative frequency: personal reproductive output gets the prediction right, whereas a simple weighted sum gets it wrong.

The simple weighted sum gets the direction of change wrong because it counts the same offspring three times over, simply because the parents happen to be (clonally) related. The moral is that an adequate formulation of inclusive fitness must avoid counting the same offspring multiple times over, and must therefore be something more subtle than a simple weighted sum.

On the face of it, phenotypic correlation and indirect reproduction sound like very different phenomena, and neighbour-modulated and inclusive fitness sound like very different ways of thinking about fitness. Despite this, the two approaches are often considered 'formally equivalent', in the sense that they reliably yield identical results about the direction of gene frequency change.[3] Yet there have always been dissenters from the consensus. For example, Maynard Smith (1983) contrasted 'the exact "neighbour-modulated fitness" approach' with 'the more intuitive "inclusive fitness" method' (1983, p. 315). He advocated inclusive fitness on the grounds that he considered it easier to apply, but he thought it less accurate. Another advocate of neighbour-modulated fitness is Frank, who has written of the 'mistaken conclusion that direct [i.e. neighbour-modulated] and inclusive fitness models are the same process described in different ways' (1997b, p. 1719) and has come to the view that 'inclusive fitness is more limited and more likely to cause confusion' (2013, p. 1172). In recent years, Jeffrey A. Fletcher and Michael Doebeli (2006; 2009; 2010) have defended a somewhat similar position, arguing that only a neighbour-modulated (or 'direct') fitness approach has the resources to provide 'a simple and general explanation for the evolution of altruism'.

To achieve a degree of clarity on this issue, I suggest that Hamilton's own work provides an excellent starting point. Hamilton (1964) asserted that gene frequency change can be calculated using either fitness concept, but he provided no formal argument for their equivalence. He did, however, include such an argument in his (1970) paper on selfishness and spite. Within a new, elegant formalism drawing on the work of Price (1970), Hamilton articulated clearly and concisely the basic insights he had presented in a rather dense way in earlier work. But perhaps the argument is a little *too* concise. As I will show, it leaves important assumptions unarticulated.

---

[3] See, for example, Dawkins (1982); Rousset (2004); Taylor et al. (2007); West et al. (2007c); Gardner and Foster (2008); Wenseleers et al. (2010); Gardner et al. (2011); Queller (2011); Marshall (2015). Taylor et al. (2007) qualify their endorsement of the equivalence thesis by noting that it holds when selection is weak in a specific sense, but might not hold when selection is strong. This chapter eventually arrives at a similar view by a different route (see Section 5.4).

5.2 Hamilton's Argument Reconsidered

Here I reconstruct the argument I take Hamilton to have given for the formal equivalence of neighbour-modulated and inclusive fitness.[4] In doing so, I want to draw attention to two assumptions Hamilton left implicit, since they point to interesting limitations of this equivalence.[5]

Consider a finite population of N numbered individuals. Let W_i^{tot} represent the total reproductive success of the ith individual ('the recipient'), and let s_{ij} represent the additive effect of the social behaviour of the jth individual ('the actor') on the reproductive success of the ith individual. We should pause here to consider the meaning of s_{ij}. Hamilton (1970) simply glosses the s_{ij} as 'additive effects'. However, I suggest that, to do justice to Hamilton's explicitly causal conception of social fitness, we should interpret s_{ij} in explicitly *causal* terms, as the *causal* effect the jth individual has on the reproductive success of the ith individual by means of expressing the social character of interest. In keeping with Hamilton's own verbal descriptions, this idea can be explicated in terms of counterfactuals: we can interpret the quantity ($W_i^{tot} - s_{ij}$) as the reproductive success that the ith individual *would* have achieved, if it had never been affected by the trait-value of the jth individual.[6]

Note the contrast here with HRG (Chapter 2). In the context of HRG, I argued that b and c should be understood as aggregate population statistics that are causally interpretable only in special cases. The difference arises because, in deriving HRG, we deliberately abstracted away from all detail regarding the individual-level causal paths linking genotype to fitness in order to arrive at a statistical decomposition of high generality. Here, however, we are putting some of that detail about individual-level causal paths back in, so as to capture Hamilton's causal conception of

---

[4] Frank (1998) also reconstructs and discusses Hamilton's model, though without drawing attention to its assumptions.

[5] Readers wishing to avoid mathematical details may skip this section—but please note the two key assumptions stated verbally at the end of it.

[6] This explication assumes a relatively simple relationship between causation and counterfactuals. As Lewis (1973), Woodward (2003), Paul and Hall (2013), and many other philosophers have argued, the true relationship is far more complicated, but we can bracket these complications for current purposes. To be clear, the s_{ij} are defined in terms of causation, and I am merely invoking counterfactuals to provide an intuitive gloss on what 'causation' amounts to.

social fitness, conceived not as a population statistic but as a property of an individual organism.

We can now return to the model. Let r_{ij} represent the coefficient of relatedness: a regression prediction of the recipient's genotype on the basis of that of the actor, calculated by averaging over interacting pairs of actors and recipients. More precisely, let (i, j) label a possible recipient-actor pair, where i labels the recipient and j labels the actor. Let A denote the subset of all possible recipient-actor pairs that actually interact socially. Let $r_{ij} = \text{Cov}_A(p_i, p_j)/\text{Var}_A(p_j)$, where p_i is the recipient's genic value for a particular allele, p_j is the actor's genic value, and the covariance and variance are computed by summing over the set of all interacting pairs, A.[7]

We can express an individual's reproductive success, with full generality, as a sum of additive effects attributable to distinct social actors, plus a term representing the individual's baseline non-social fitness (α_i), plus a term representing the deviation from fitness additivity (ϵ_{W_i}):

$$W_i^{\text{tot}} = \alpha_i + \sum_j s_{ij} + \epsilon_{W_i} \tag{5.1}$$

There are many biological reasons why an individual's reproductive success might deviate from additivity in the real world; see in particular the discussion of task-structured cooperation in Chapter 1 and synergistic effects in Chapter 2 (see also Queller, 1985, 1992b). Hamilton (1970) simply assumes deviations from additivity to be absent (for reasons discussed in Sections 5.3 and 5.4 of this chapter). However, I want to represent them explicitly in the model, in order to state precisely the nature of the assumption we must make about them (see the NMF equation below).

---

[7] This is closely related to the the regression definition of relatedness from Chapter 2 that features in HRG. There is a difference: here we are using actor genotypes as predictors of recipient genotypes, whereas HRG involves using recipient genotypes as predictors of actor genotypes. However, reversing the direction of the regression in this way makes no difference to the value of r if we assume, as we are assuming here, that there is no class-structure in the population. For discussion of the complications introduced by class-structure, see Frank (1998); Taylor et al. (2007); Birch (2013b).

Let us now follow Hamilton (1970) in defining the neighbour-modulated fitness of the ith individual as the sum of all additive effects on its reproductive success, plus the baseline non-social component:

$$W_i^{\text{NMF}} = \alpha_i + \sum_j s_{ij} \qquad \text{(NMF)}$$

If the deviations from additivity are zero for all individuals (i.e. $\epsilon_{W_i} = 0$ for all i), then an individual's neighbour-modulated fitness can be equated with its total reproductive success. If $\epsilon_{W_i} \neq 0$, then neighbour-modulated fitness can still be used to calculate gene frequency change accurately, provided the deviations from additivity do not co-vary with the gene of interest. However, in cases in which deviations from additivity do co-vary with the gene, neighbour-modulated fitness may mislead. This is the point at which a substantive assumption of 'additivity' is required, and the nature of this assumption is now clear: we must assume that deviations from fitness additivity (ϵ_{W_i}), if present, do not co-vary with the gene of interest, and so are irrelevant to the direction and magnitude of gene frequency change.

Now let us define the inclusive fitness of the jth individual as its baseline, non-social fitness (α_j) plus the sum of all the additive fitness effects (s_{ij}) for which it is causally responsible, weighted in each case by the coefficient of relatedness r_{ij}:

$$W_j^{\text{IF}} = \alpha_j + \sum_i s_{ij} r_{ij} \qquad \text{(IF)}$$

We can see immediately that if there is no social interaction at all (i.e. if $s_{ij} = 0$ for all i, j such that $i \neq j$), then our two fitness concepts are identical. Unsurprisingly, both yield the result that an individual's fitness is simply equal to its baseline, non-social fitness α. When social interaction occurs, however, the two concepts are non-identical. Neighbour-modulated fitness assigns the s_{ij} to recipients, whereas inclusive fitness assigns them to actors, weighting them by relatedness.

We can now ask: under what conditions does $\text{Cov}(W_i^{\text{NMF}}, p_i)$ equal $\text{Cov}(W_j^{\text{IF}}, p_j)$? This is the crucial question as regards the 'formal equivalence' of the two fitness concepts for the purpose of calculating gene frequency change. In fact, it turns out that, given one further important assumption, these quantities are equal.

First, we can use our definitions of neighbour-modulated and inclusive fitness to split each covariance into a non-social and social component:

$$\text{Cov}(W_i^{\text{NMF}}, p_i) = \overbrace{\text{Cov}(\alpha_i, p_i)}^{\text{non-social}} + \overbrace{\text{Cov}\left(\sum_j s_{ij}, p_i\right)}^{\text{social}} \tag{5.2}$$

$$\text{Cov}(W_j^{\text{IF}}, p_j) = \overbrace{\text{Cov}(\alpha_j, p_j)}^{\text{non-social}} + \overbrace{\text{Cov}\left(\sum_i s_{ij} r_{ij}, p_j\right)}^{\text{social}} \tag{5.3}$$

The non-social component is the same in both cases: the only difference is the indices, and since both i and j are being used to label elements of the same set, this difference is merely notational. Hence it is only the equivalence of the two social components that needs to be established. Following Hamilton, let us call these social components (respectively) the 'neighbour-modulated fitness effect' and the 'inclusive fitness effect'. Hamilton further simplifies matters by assuming α to be a constant (of value 1), so that the non-social component is zero in both cases; but this assumption is dispensable to the argument.

The neighbour-modulated fitness effect can be usefully rewritten as

$$\text{Cov}\left(\sum_j s_{ij}, p_i\right) = \sum_j \left\{\frac{1}{N}\sum_i (p_i - \overline{p})s_{ij}\right\} \tag{5.4}$$

Now note that, from the definition of relatedness as a regression prediction of the recipient's genotype on the basis of that of the actor, it follows that

$$p_i - \overline{p} = r_{ij}(p_j - \overline{p}) + \epsilon_{p_i} \tag{5.5}$$

where ϵ_{p_i} denotes the extent to which the recipient's actual genotype deviates from the regression prediction. Assume now that

$$\text{Cov}\left(\sum_j s_{ij}, \epsilon_{p_i}\right) = 0 \tag{5.6}$$

This key assumption, which Hamilton (1970) makes implicitly, amounts to assuming that the recipient's personal gene frequency predicts its social fitness only via correlations with actors, and not via any other pathway (e.g. via conferring an ability on the recipient to make better use of the help it receives). This entitles us to substitute $r_{ij}(p_j - \bar{p})$ for $(p_i - \bar{p})$ in equation 5.4, yielding

$$\text{Cov}\left(\sum_j s_{ij}, p_i\right) = \sum_i \left\{ \frac{1}{N} \sum_j (p_j - \bar{p}) r_{ij} s_{ij}) \right\} \quad (5.7)$$

The right-hand side of (5.7) can now be rewritten once again as a covariance:

$$\text{Cov}\left(\sum_j s_{ij}, p_i\right) = \text{Cov}\left(\sum_i s_{ij} r_{ij}, p_j\right) \quad (5.8)$$

Comparing this result to (5.2) and (5.3), we see that

$$\text{Cov}(W_i^{\text{NMF}}, p_i) = \text{Cov}(W_j^{\text{IF}}, p_j) \quad (5.9)$$

as we hoped to prove.

We can now see that Hamilton's (1970) argument for the formal equivalence of neighbour-modulated and inclusive fitness relies on two pivotal assumptions, both of which amount to assumptions of uncorrelated residuals:

- *Additivity*: Deviations from fitness additivity (ϵ_{W_i}), if present, do not co-vary with the gene of interest, and so are irrelevant to the direction and magnitude of gene frequency change.
- *Actor's control*: The recipient's genotype predicts its social fitness only via its correlation with actor genotypes, and not via any other pathway (e.g. by enabling it to make better use of the help it receives).

Reliance on these assumptions is by no means an idiosyncratic feature of Hamilton's (1970) model. More recently, Grafen (2006a, pp. 543–9) has provided an argument for formal equivalence that improves on Hamilton's in various respects: in particular, it accommodates uncertainty, and it accommodates the various different social 'roles' an actor can occupy.[8] Nevertheless, for all its additional sophistication, Grafen's argument still relies crucially on the assumptions of additivity and actor's control. The only difference is that, while Hamilton left these assumptions implicit, Grafen notes them explicitly.[9]

5.3 Hamilton's Assumptions: Actor's Control and Additivity

Actor's control points to one important qualification we need to add to Hamilton's equivalence result. If the recipient's genotype correlates with the fitness effects it receives in ways that are *not* fully explained by correlations with actor genotypes, the result will be a situation in which $\mathrm{Cov}(\sum_j s_{ij}, \epsilon_{p_i}) \neq 0$. This is a situation in which inclusive fitness could lead to errors. Essentially, this is because inclusive fitness involves substituting the actual value of the recipient's genotype with a regression prediction based on the actor's genotype. If this substitution can be achieved without losing a portion of the covariance between the recipient's genotype and its reproductive success (something guaranteed by actor's control) then there is no problem; but if a portion of the covariance goes missing, there is a problem.

Such a situation may seem intuitively hard to visualize. But all it needs is for there to be some genotype that, in addition to disposing an organism to express a social behaviour, also affects its ability to receive the benefit of that behaviour when expressed in others. Consider, for example, a genotype that disposes its bearer to produce an alarm call. In so doing, it reveals the organism's location to nearby predators, adversely affecting its ability to benefit from the alarm calls of others. In this scenario, the benefit of receiving an alarm call for a recipient does not just depend on the genotype of the actor. It also depends on a fact about the recipient (i.e. whether or not the recipient has also produced an alarm call) that

---

[8]   Grafen (2006a) goes on to argue (controversially) that there is a sense in which inclusive fitness is 'optimized' in evolution. We will discuss this idea later in the chapter.

[9]   Frank (1998) also derives a qualified equivalence result that holds under broadly similar assumptions in a framework that explicitly incorporates class structure. See Birch (2013b) for discussion of Frank's formalism.

will be correlated with its genotype (see Section 5.4 for further discussion of this example).[10] When actor's control is violated, neighbour-modulated and inclusive fitness are no longer equivalent, and only the former is valid. Neighbour-modulated fitness does not require the actor's control assumption, because it does not rely on substituting the recipient's genotype with a regression prediction based on the actor's genotype. Instead, it simply looks at the overall covariance between the recipient's genotype and the fitness effects it receives, implicitly allowing for cases in which the value of a social fitness effect depends on the genotype of the recipient as well as that of the actor.

Let us now turn to additivity. This assumption enters Hamilton's argument at an early stage, as a prerequisite for the formulation of both neighbour-modulated and inclusive fitness. Hamilton defines both fitness concepts in terms of an additive causal model of reproductive success, and assumes that deviations from that model are irrelevant to the direction of change. Consequently, if this assumption turns out to be widely violated in nature, this will not undermine the claim that the two fitness concepts are equivalent, but it will pose a threat to the utility of both concepts.

Is the additivity assumption widely violated? We should distinguish here between strong and weak varieties of additivity. If the deviation from the additive causal model, ϵ_W, is zero for all individuals, then we can say that the structure of social interaction is *strongly additive*. If ϵ_W is non-zero for some individuals but makes no difference to gene frequency change, we can say that the structure of social interaction is *weakly additive*. Strong additivity implies weak additivity, but the converse is not true, and Hamilton's fitness concepts require only weak additivity. Either way, we are talking about a property of the causal structure of social interaction in a population, not a property of any particular organism or gene.

It is clear that social interactions in the natural world frequently violate strong additivity. Strong additivity requires that an individual's social

---

[10] The assumption of 'equal gains from switching', which is often invoked in evolutionary game theory, can be seen as a way of securing actor's control in a class of simple evolutionary games (van Veelen, 2009; Nowak et al., 2010; Birch, 2014b). As critics of inclusive fitness have often noted, synergistic payoffs, such as those found in alarm call scenarios, imply a violation of equal gains from switching.

fitness can be written, without remainder, as a sum of causal components, each of which reflects the amount of reproductive success a recipient would lose if it had never been affected by the trait-value of a particular social actor. Compare this to paradigm cases of task-structured cooperation, such as those discussed in Chapter 1: fruiting body formation in social amoebae, bubble-net feeding in humpback whales, fungus cultivation in leafcutter ants, and so on. Such task structures tend to create situations in which the effect on the recipient cannot be expressed as a sum of components, each corresponding to the difference made by a single actor's contribution (Birch, 2012). Or imagine jumping into a river to save a drowning child. If your action saves the child's life, then any future occasions on which the child's life is saved are only possible because of your action, so the effects of your action and these later actions will not combine additively.

Weak additivity, however, is compatible with substantial deviations from the additive causal model. Its tenability in any particular case depends on whether these deviations co-vary with the gene of interest. This makes the empirical status of weak additivity difficult to assess. We are often in a position to know empirically that a social interaction violates strong additivity, since this depends only on the causal structure of the interaction, but we are less often in a position to know whether the deviations from strong additivity co-vary with any genes. I will not try to settle this empirical question here. Note, however, that failures of weak additivity are clearly possible in principle whenever there are deviations from strong additivity. We should therefore be cautious about assuming weak additivity when strong additivity is violated.

These considerations lend weight to the view that, as Grafen puts it, 'the assumption of additivity . . . is not in general a realistic assumption. In many applications, non-additivity is an important part of the problem' (Grafen, 2006a, p. 543; see also Queller, 1985, 2011; Marshall, 2015). What does this mean for our two conceptions of social fitness and for the relationship between them?

The immediate challenge is not to the formal equivalence of the two fitness concepts but rather to the generality of both. Hamilton formulated both fitness concepts in terms of an additive causal model. If the model is inappropriate in some biological scenario, then both fitness concepts as Hamilton originally conceived them are inappropriate in that scenario.

Yet it would be wrong to conclude that the two fitness concepts are on a par when it comes to accommodating deviations from additivity.

A key difference is that neighbour-modulated fitness, because it does not assume actor's control, has more leeway for accommodating effects that depend on the behaviour of multiple actors. Neighbour-modulated fitness requires that an individual's fitness can be expressed as a sum of effects attributable to properties of its social neighbourhood, but it does not require that each property is controlled by a single actor. This means that, as Queller (1985, 2011) has shown, we can augment the basic additive causal model with 'synergistic effects' that depend in complex ways on the phenotypes of multiple actors (see also Smith et al., 2010 and Marshall, 2015, pp. 66–7).

By contrast, the inclusive fitness concept relies fundamentally on the assumption that each fitness effect can be attributed to a single controlling actor, whose inclusive fitness it counts towards. Since synergistic effects are not controlled by any single actor, there is no principled answer to the question of whose inclusive fitness they promote. In these contexts, inclusive fitness, as Hamilton conceived it, is no longer a well-defined property of an individual organism.

Thus, the two fitness concepts are threatened in different ways by failures of weak additivity. Put simply: for neighbour-modulated fitness, the problem is a technical one that can often be surmounted by expanding the causal model of fitness. For inclusive fitness, however, the problem runs deeper, for it is a problem of a conceptual nature. The reassignment of fitness components to controlling actors that Hamilton envisaged is no longer possible when the additive causal model fails.

5.4 Weak Selection and Fisher's Microscope

So far, then, things look bad for both fitness concepts as formulated by Hamilton, since both assume an empirically questionable form of additivity. Things look doubly bad for inclusive fitness, since this also relies on an empirically questionable assumption of actor's control, and this extra assumption blocks the extension of the concept to accommodate synergistic effects. Critics of inclusive fitness are likely to feel that the discussion should end here: since both neighbour-modulated and inclusive fitness demand restrictive assumptions, we should concentrate on modelling approaches that simply use reproductive success as a fitness measure, without neglecting or reassigning any of its causal components. This, roughly, is the line advocated by Nowak et al. (2010) and Allen et al. (2013). But I do not think the discussion should end here. I take the view that, for all their strong underlying assumptions, a good case can be made for the theoretical value of both fitness concepts, and of inclusive fitness in particular.

Defenders of inclusive fitness (e.g. Grafen, 1985, 2006a) have long noted that both of its main assumptions can be justified as approximations if we assume a specific form of weak selection, now usually known as δ-weak selection (Wild and Traulsen, 2007). To assume δ-weak selection is to assume that the character of interest is a quantitative character, and that the alternatives competing in the population are a wild type and a mutant that differs only very slightly from the wild type. For example, in a strategic interaction with two discrete pure strategies, such as a prisoner's dilemma or a hawk-dove game, a δ-weak selection model would pit a mixed-strategy wild type that chooses one strategy with probability q and the other with probability $1 - q$ against a mixed-strategy mutant that chooses the first strategy with probability $q + \delta$ and the other strategy with probability $1 - q - \delta$, where δ is a very small increment such that $\delta^2 \approx 0$ (Wild and Traulsen, 2007). To give a more vivid example, if we wanted to construct a δ-weak selection model of the evolution of jumping into rivers to save drowning children, we might compare the strategy of jumping with probability q to the strategy of jumping with probability $q + \delta$.[11]

With this idea in hand, we can go back to Hamilton's model and reinterpret the s_{ij} parameters. Instead of thinking of s_{ij} as the *total* causal effect of the jth actor's behaviour on the ith recipient's reproductive output (i.e., roughly, the total amount by which the recipient's reproductive output would have been lower, had it never interacted with the actor), we can now think of s_{ij} as the *marginal* (or *differential*) causal effect of the jth actor's behaviour on i^{th} recipient's reproductive output in comparison with a default scenario in which the actor expresses the wild type behaviour. All effects common to the mutant and wild type are now folded into the 'baseline' component of fitness. Non-zero values of s_{ij} occur only when the actor expresses the mutant.

In this reinterpreted model, the key assumptions of the inclusive fitness concept can be reinterpreted as assumptions about marginal rather than total causal effects: what is required is that the marginal causal effects of

---

[11] See Grafen (1985, Section 6) for a more detailed discussion of the options for modelling such phenomena.

the mutant phenotype, relative to the wild type, are weakly additive and actor controlled. Under these conditions, a gene for the mutant phenotype is positively selected if and only if the mutant has a positive inclusive fitness effect relative to the wild type. The difference is that, with δ-weak selection assumed, the assumptions that initially seemed too strong are now reasonable as approximations, even in cases in which they would be violated if defined in relation to total causal effects.

To see the intuitive rationale for this, consider again the alarm call example. The problem here was that making an alarm call reduces the benefit an organism receives from an alarm call expressed in others, leading to a violation of actor's control. But now consider the *marginal* causal effect of making an alarm call with probability $q + \delta$ rather than probability q. This will have a first-order negative effect on one's own fitness and a first-order positive effect on the fitness of nearby recipients. It will also have a second-order effect on the benefit one receives from a very small increase in the probability with which another nearby individual makes an alarm call. However, this second-order effect, which is the source of the trouble for the actor's control assumption, is precisely the kind of effect that the assumption of δ-weak selection entitles us to regard as approximately zero, since it relies on the product of two tiny phenotypic differences.[12]

The upshot is that there is a class of models—models of δ-weak selection—in which both of Hamilton's original fitness concepts are valid and require no extension. Moreover, because δ-weak selection secures both weak additivity and actor's control (as first-order approximations) in one fell swoop, inclusive fitness does not end up with a more limited domain of application within this class of models by virtue of assuming actor's control. So, although the actor's control assumption does necessitate a qualification to Hamilton's equivalence claim—it is something formally assumed by inclusive fitness but not neighbour-modulated fitness—this qualification turns out to be less significant than one might have supposed.

To critics of inclusive fitness, the appeal to δ-weak selection will seem *ad hoc* and perhaps even a little desperate: to justify two empirically questionable assumptions, we invoke another assumption that appears to be no less questionable. Why think that selection is normally δ-weak?

---

[12] The 'jumping into the river' case can be handled in a similar way (Grafen, 1985).

Indeed, why think it is ever δ-weak? However, it would be not be fair to characterize this assumption as an *ad hoc* move intended to immunize inclusive fitness against empirical challenges. It is fairer, I think, to see δ-weak selection as an assumption that is reasonable given some important empirical and methodological background commitments that inclusive fitness theorists hold. These are commitments which can be traced back to Hamilton, but which critics of inclusive fitness do not necessarily share.

At the heart of the inclusive fitness paradigm is a version of methodological adaptationism that takes complex adaptation—or 'organism design'—to be the field's main explanatory target (Gardner, 2009; Grafen, 2014). This is combined with an empirical commitment to a Fisherian 'micromutationist' picture of how complex adaptation arises. Fisher (1930) took complex adaptation to result from the gradual accumulation of mutations with tiny effects on the phenotype.[13] He posited small-effect mutations on the grounds that large-effect mutations are much less likely to constitute adaptive improvements. In support of this claim, he offered two iconic arguments: one involving an informal analogy with a microscope, the other involving a more formal geometric model.

To paraphrase (and simplify) the informal argument, suppose you are attempting to focus a microscope by turning an adjustment knob. Knowing nothing of microscopes, you have no idea which way to turn the knob, so you turn it in a random direction. If the adjustment is very small, there is a 50% chance it will improve the focus, because any very small adjustment in the right direction will help. But the larger the adjustment gets, the lower the probability it will be an improvement, because it becomes ever more likely that an adjustment, even if it happens to be in the right direction, will overshoot the target.

Using a geometric model in which a population is displaced from the optimum in phenotypic space and must find its way back to the optimum

---

[13] Darwin (1859) was also a gradualist about complex adaptation: there is a passage in the *Origin* in which Darwin clearly envisages 'organs of extreme perfection' arising through the accumulation of tiny improvements (Birch, 2014c). However, it would be tendentious to project on to Darwin the whole package of Fisher's views about the typical strength of selection and the typical effect size of adaptive substitutions. Darwin, knowing little about the mechanisms of inheritance, at times appears to invoke very strong selection as a way of cancelling out the effects of blending inheritance (Lewens, 2010a).

through random gene substitutions, Fisher showed that the probability of an improvement, which falls off with the size of the adjustment even in the one-dimensional case, falls off more rapidly in the case of an adjustment in two dimensions, and falls off very rapidly indeed when we are adjusting at random in many dimensions, as in the case of a mutation that affects many aspects of the phenotype. The chance of improvement is greatest—at 50%—for a mutation that affects the phenotype by an infinitesimal amount. Fisher's argument has not been without its critics. Notably, Motoo Kimura (1983) argued that, in finite populations, mutants with larger effects on the phenotype have a greater chance of going to fixation, because mutants with small effects are prone to drifting out of existence. In a seminal analysis, H. Allen Orr (1998) showed that both Fisher and Kimura could be partially vindicated in relation to different stages of the process of cumulative adaptive evolution: the typical effect size of a mutation fixed at an early stage in the process, when the phenotype is far from the optimum, is much larger than Fisher thought; but, as the phenotype gets closer to optimality, Fisher's concern about 'overshooting' becomes increasingly salient and the typical effect size of a fixed mutation becomes progressively smaller.

Although Fisher's argument remains a source of on-going debate (see e.g. Waxman and Welch 2005; Martin and Lenormand 2006), what matters for current purposes is that the micromutationist picture remains the received wisdom in behavioural ecology, and certainly among inclusive fitness theorists. It was, notably, central to Hamilton's own thinking on these issues. In an autobiographical note included in his (1996) collected papers, he wrote:

I was and still am a Darwinian gradualist for most of the issues of evolutionary change. Most change comes, I believe, through selected alleles that make small modifications to existing structure and behaviour. If one could understand just this case in social situations, who cared much what might happen in the rare cases where the gene changes were great and happened not to be disastrous? Whether under social or classical selection, defeat and disappearance would, as always, be the usual outcome of genes that cause large changes. I think that a lot of the objection to so-called 'reductionism' and 'bean-bag reasoning' directed at Neodarwinist theory comes from people who, whether through inscrutable private agendas or ignorance, are not gradualists, being instead inhabitants of some imagined world of super-fast progress. Big changes, strong interlocus interactions, hopeful monsters, mutations so abundant and so hopeful that several may be under selection at one time—these have to be the stuff of their dreams if their criticisms are to make sense.   (Hamilton, 1996, pp. 27–8)

This allows us to see why an assumption of δ-weak selection is not *ad hoc*, but rather stems directly from the core commitments of Hamilton's program. This assumption is at the heart of the micromutationist picture Hamilton advocated, on which selection assembles complex adaptations cumulatively by acting on tiny phenotypic differences. The subset of selection processes for which inclusive fitness is a valid predictor of gene frequency change is thus the same subset that inclusive fitness theorists, on independent grounds, take to be responsible for the generation of cumulative adaptation.

5.5 Inclusive Fitness as a Criterion for Improvement

However, the connection between inclusive fitness and cumulative adaptation runs deeper than this. The fact that inclusive fitness can be used to calculate short-term gene frequency change under δ-weak selection does not give it any advantage over neighbour-modulated fitness, since this too can be used to calculate short-term gene frequency change under δ-weak selection. But, in the context of explaining adaptation, there is a different sort of theoretical role for a fitness concept with respect to which inclusive fitness is superior: that of providing a stable criterion for phenotypic improvement over the evolutionary medium term.

Before explaining why inclusive fitness is apt for this role, let me explain what I mean by the 'evolutionary medium term'. A number of authors (e.g. Eshel and Feldman, 1984, 2001; Neander, 1995; Hammerstein, 1996; Eshel et al., 1998; Godfrey-Smith and Wilkins, 2009; Metz, 2011) have noted the disconnect between the 'microevolutionary' timescale of most population genetics models and the longer timescale over which complex adaptations are cumulatively assembled. Most population genetics models focus on relatively short-term changes in allele frequency, leading to equilibria that are stable given the alleles currently competing in the population, but that may be destabilized by the appearance of new mutants. By contrast, cumulative adaptation occurs over many successive episodes of short-term allele frequency change, as one new mutant responsible for a small improvement spreads through the population, eventually followed by another, and another, and so on, in a process memorably described by Dawkins (1996) as 'climbing Mount Improbable'. This is clearly a longer timescale than that of short-term microevolution, but nor are we talking here about the timescale of 'macroevolution' (in the sense of, e.g., Gould, 2002; Sterelny, 2007), since these changes are typically still occurring within a single species. Metz (2011) and Godfrey-Smith (2012) have suggested the term 'mesoevolution' for the timescale of cumulative adaptation. This is what I mean by 'medium term' evolution.

Consider, then, a picture of cumulative adaptation arising from the gradual accumulation of tiny improvements to the phenotype over a mesoevolutionary timescale. In this context, I suggest that we want more from a fitness measure than accurate calculations of short-term gene frequency change and short-term equilibria. We also want a fitness measure that can serve as a stable criterion, throughout the whole process, for what constitutes an 'improvement' to the phenotype. In other words, fitness must be a property of an organism, X, such that new mutants are systematically favoured over the wild type if and only if they make a positive marginal contribution (in contrast with the wild type) to X. The distinctive advantage of inclusive fitness is that it is a very good candidate for property X.

Neighbour-modulated fitness is not a good candidate. To see why, imagine a process of cumulative adaptation in which natural selection gradually 'shapes' various different aspects of a complex behavioural strategy. Suppose the strategy is initially shaped by selection for marginal direct benefits to the actor, then goes through a stage in which it is shaped by selection for marginal indirect benefits conferred on a relative at a direct cost to the actor, and then finally goes through a 'streamlining' stage in which the direct cost to the actor is gradually reduced.

At all stages in this hypothetical process, the actor's inclusive fitness provides a consistent criterion for improvement: all and only those mutants which differentially promote the inclusive fitness of the actor are favoured. Yet the same cannot be said of the actor's neighbour-modulated fitness, since mutants that detract from this quantity are favoured during the middle stage; and nor can it be said of the recipient's neighbour-modulated fitness, since mutants that are neutral with respect to the recipient's neighbour-modulated fitness are favoured in the initial and final stages.

It is true that, at any given stage in this process, one can point to a neighbour-modulated fitness property—that of the actor in the first and third stages, and that of the recipient in the second stage—and say that the trait's marginal effects on that property are driving the evolution of the trait. But this does not lead to a *stable* criterion of improvement, because the relevant property changes over time: selection sometimes favours mutants that promote the neighbour-modulated fitness of the recipient and sometimes favours mutants that promote the neighbour-modulated fitness of the actor. Only the inclusive fitness of the actor provides a stable criterion for improvement throughout the whole process, as natural selection 'shapes' different aspects of the phenotype.

This distinctive role for inclusive fitness as a criterion for phenotypic improvement points to a close relationship between inclusive fitness and the concept of optimality, because a criterion for improvement implies a standard with respect to which the optimality (or suboptimality) of a phenotype can be judged. For social evolution researchers thinking about cumulative adaptation over mesoevolutionary timescales, it makes sense to conceptualize a locally 'optimal' trait, within a specified set of alternatives, as one that leaves no room for further cumulative improvement under δ-weak selection; and it makes sense to conceptualize a 'suboptimal' trait as one that does leave room for such improvement. Since, as I have argued, inclusive fitness provides the appropriate criterion for what constitutes an improvement, it also provides the appropriate standard for optimality. An optimal trait, within a set of alternatives, is one that at least locally maximizes inclusive fitness; a suboptimal trait is one that does not.

5.6 Should We Expect Inclusive Fitness to be Optimized?

On all the points so far discussed, I take my view to be well aligned with those of Grafen (2014); Gardner (2009), and West and Gardner (2013), all of whom emphasize the special role of inclusive fitness in explaining 'organism design'. I want to stress, however, that in calling inclusive fitness the criterion for improvement and the standard for optimality in a process of cumulative adaptation, I am not making any empirical claim that we should expect cumulative improvement to occur in any particular case, and nor am I suggesting that we should expect optimality, approximate optimality, or anything remotely close to optimality, to be reliably achieved by natural evolutionary processes.

After all, there are numerous well-known obstacles to cumulative improvement: if there is too much dominance or epistasis, if there is too much drift, if the environment changes too rapidly, or if the mutation rate is too high or too low, cumulative adaptation can stall or fail to get off the ground at all.[14] There can be no theoretical guarantee that these obstacles will ever be overcome in nature. When we find a phenotype that is approximately locally optimal among a range of variants, this provides some inductive evidence that the conditions under which the trait evolved were favourable to cumulative optimization (although tests of this sort should be performed and interpreted carefully; see Orzack and Sober, 1994, 2001). But there can be no deductive proof that the optimization of inclusive fitness is widespread, likely, or indeed ever instantiated in the natural world.

Here I suspect I part ways with Grafen, who writes, for example, that the theoretical results of his 'Formal Darwinism' project support 'a very general expectation of something close to [inclusive] fitness maximization, which will convert into [inclusive] fitness maximization unless there are particular kinds of circumstances' (Grafen, 2014, p. 166). It is not easy to tease out the empirical commitments of such a hedged claim; but I take it that Grafen, like many other social evolution researchers, regards cumulative optimization as a process that, on theoretical grounds, we should expect to occur frequently in natural populations, leading in many cases to at least approximately optimal outcomes.

To explain why I am sceptical of this claim, a brief comment on Grafen's 'Formal Darwinism' project is needed. The aim of the project is to derive mathematical links between a formal representation of natural selection (a version of the Price equation), and a formal representation of phenotypic optimality that uses the apparatus (borrowed from economics) of

---

[14] Many of these obstacles are discussed by Godfrey-Smith (2009b), who characterizes a 'paradigm' Darwinian population as one in which cumulative adaptation is apt to occur, and a 'marginal' Darwinian population as one that departs from a paradigm Darwinian population in one or more ways. The conditions for cumulative adaptation highlighted by Godfrey-Smith (2009b) include the fidelity of transmission, the smoothness of the fitness landscape, and the strength of selection in relation to drift. It is worth noting here that selection can be strong in relation to drift even if selection is δ-weak, although the prospect of advantageous mutations drifting to extinction is particularly concerning under δ-weak selection, as noted by Kimura and discussed briefly earlier in the chapter.

optimization programs. I find the project admirable but do not think it has proved—or could prove—the above claim, or any empirical claim about the regularity with which cumulative optimization of phenotypes occurs in nature.

I have discussed the Formal Darwinism project in detail on several occasions and I will not repeat these discussions here, although two concerns do merit repeating (Birch, 2014c, 2016a, b).[15] First, Grafen's framework involves an assumption of 'perfect transmission, that is, no mutation, no gametic selection, fair meiosis, and that all contributing loci have the same mode of inheritance' (Grafen, 2002, p. 77). The assuming away of mutation implies that his model is one in which no cumulative adaptation can occur, so his formal links between gene frequency change and phenotypic optimality are results that are proven to hold only in a world in which no cumulative adaptation is possible (Birch, 2014c, 2016b). Second, Grafen's framework avoids making any assumptions about the genetic architecture underlying phenotypic traits, such as the absence of dominance and epistasis. It follows that his formal results would hold even in a world in which dominance and epistasis were ubiquitous, imposing severe genetic constraints on optimization (Okasha and Paternotte, 2014a; Birch, 2014c). These two observations should lead us to question whether these formal results can be said to support a 'general expectation of something close to inclusive fitness maximization', even in a highly qualified sense. In fact, they do not imply that inclusive fitness maximization will ever occur.

There is a broader point to be made here: we should not overstate the ability of purely theoretical arguments to support empirical generalizations, no matter how hedged, about natural populations.[16] We can say that if a particular social adaptation has originated by means of the process Fisher envisaged—that is, via the gradual accumulation of small-effect mutations under δ-weak selection—then inclusive fitness provides the appropriate criterion for improvement and the appropriate standard for optimality with respect to that adaptation. This points to an important and distinctive theoretical role for the concept of inclusive fitness: one

---

[15] For other perspectives on Formal Darwinism, see the commentaries collected in Okasha and Paternotte (2014b).

[16] Orzack's (2014) commentary on Formal Darwinism provides a particularly forceful statement of this point.

to which neighbour-modulated fitness, although equally valid for the purpose of calculating short-term gene frequency change under δ-weak selection, is not well suited. But we should add the qualification that, in such a case, the distance from optimality of the end product will depend on many different variables, including how readily small mutations arise, how reliably they are inherited, how constant they are in their average effects on the phenotype, how effective selection is at retaining them in the face of drift and other evolutionary processes, and how long the whole process of cumulative improvement has been able to operate in a sufficiently stable environment. All of these are empirical matters that no amount of theoretical work can settle.

5.7 Summary of Chapter 5

Hamilton (1964) introduced two alternative conceptions of social fitness, which he termed neighbour-modulated fitness and inclusive fitness. The core conceptual contrast is that the former assigns descendants to ancestors according to considerations of parenthood, whereas the latter assigns descendants to ancestors according to considerations of social causation.

In subsequent work, Hamilton (1970) offered a simple formal argument that the two frameworks provide equivalent ways of calculating gene frequency change. This argument, like Grafen's (2006a) updated version, relies on two key assumptions: actor's control and additivity. Additivity is required by both fitness concepts, whereas actor's control is an additional assumption required by inclusive fitness.

Both assumptions are empirically questionable if interpreted as exact claims about total effects. However, both can be justified as first-order approximations regarding marginal effects under δ-weak selection, which is to say selection on tiny differences between the mutant and the wild type. An assumption of δ-weak selection is not *ad hoc*: it stems from a methodological stance that takes complex, cumulative adaptation to be the main explanatory target of social evolution research, together with an empirical commitment to a gradualist picture on which such adaptation arises through the accumulation of small improvements.

In the context of a process of cumulative adaptation by δ-weak selection for small improvements to the phenotype, short-term gene frequency change can be calculated using either neighbour-modulated or inclusive fitness, but inclusive fitness has a special role to play as the criterion for improvement and the standard for optimality. This is not to say that optimal or even approximately optimal phenotypes are regularly achieved in natural populations, or that cumulative improvement reliably occurs. Given the number of potential obstacles to optimization, the question of how often cumulative improvement occurs and the question of how often optimality is approximately achieved are empirical questions that cannot be answered by theory alone.

PART II

Extensions

6

Gene Mobility and the Concept of Relatedness

6.1 Sociality in the Microbial World

The most celebrated examples of cooperation in the natural world involve multicellular animals. We marvel at the elaborate nests of ants, bees, wasps, and termites; at the hunting strategies of lions, orcas, and wolves; and at the complex social hierarchies of baboons and chimpanzees. Yet this stock of familiar examples provides only a meagre sample of the full range of cooperative phenomena in nature. Moreover, it is a biased sample: many of nature's most spectacular social phenomena go largely unnoticed by human eyes, for they are too small for the unaided eye to see.

In Chapter 1, we met the social amoeba *Dictyostelium discoideum*, with its mobile slug (or 'grex') and its fruiting bodies (Bonner, 1959; Strassmann et al., 2000; Strassmann and Queller, 2011). We also met the social bacterium *Myxococcus xanthus*, with its 'pack hunting' in synchronized ripples (Berleman and Kirby, 2009). Such impressive feats of collective action should convince us that cooperation in microbes is no mere sideshow: it is no less sophisticated, no less spectacular, and no less central to the life cycles of the organisms involved than cooperation in the macroscopic world.

But these headline-grabbing examples are only the tip of the iceberg. The moral from the past few decades of research in microbiology is that sociality is pervasive in microbial populations (Crespi, 2001; West et al., 2007a). We now realize that what looked like a blob on a Petri dish is in reality a dynamic social network: a community in which vast numbers of microorganisms—often including members of several different species—interact with each other in complex and evolutionarily significant ways. Perhaps the most frequent type of social interaction involves the production and consumption of so-called 'public goods'. These goods include enzymes, surfactants, antibiotics, toxins, adhesive polymers, ammonia, and other useful organic molecules: what they have in common is that, when emitted by a producer into the external environment, they confer a fitness benefit on at least some other nearby microorganisms (in some cases indirectly, by harming their competitors). In recent years, many instances of public goods production have been documented across otherwise highly disparate microbial taxa (West et al., 2007a).

Economic metaphors such as 'collective action' and 'public goods production' do more than simply point to a superficial resemblance between microbial sociality and our own feats of cooperation. They also draw our attention to a distinctive explanatory puzzle these behaviours present, a puzzle of a kind we also encounter in economics. For it is a truism, in both economics and evolutionary biology, that collective action and the production of public goods are often destabilized by free riding (Olson, 1965; Hardin, 1982; Kagel and Roth, 1995). Cooperative actions are often costly, free riders reap the profits of their neighbours' cooperative actions without paying that cost, and so one intuitively expects such free riders to do better, in the long run, than cooperators.

There is no reason to think that microbial cooperation is immune to this threat. In microbes, the production of public goods usually imposes a metabolic cost (and hence, all else being equal, a fitness cost) on the producer, and so one would intuitively expect organisms that consume the goods without producing them to prosper at the producers' expense. So the puzzle we face is this: why does natural selection appear, in so many cases, to have favoured collective action and public goods production in microbes? Why are these behaviours not destabilized by free-riding? This is the 'problem of cooperation' in microbes (West et al., 2006, 2007a), and understanding how the problem is solved in nature is one of the central tasks of the emerging program of 'sociomicrobiology' (Parsek and Greenberg, 2005).

Of course, as we saw in Part I, the problem of stabilizing cooperation has been studied for over half a century in mainstream behavioural ecology, where theorists have developed a variety of modelling approaches that show how natural selection can, under certain conditions, favour costly cooperative behaviour among multicellular animals. Ideally, then, we would simply import our off-the-shelf solutions to the problem of animal cooperation to a microbial context. Matters, however, are not quite so simple. Complications arise from the fact that our traditional approaches to the problem were developed with multicellular animals in mind. Applying them to microbial populations is often far from straightforward, because social evolution in microbes has a number of distinctive features that traditional approaches were never intended to accommodate. As a result, we often find that standard formal methods require various extensions and amendments before they can be put to work in a microbial setting (Smith et al., 2010; Cornforth et al., 2012). Hamilton's rule is an important case in point. As we saw in Part I, this provides an organizing framework for social evolution research in which the concept of relatedness plays a crucial role. In populations of multicellular animals, the concept of relatedness is fairly (though not wholly) unproblematic: roughly speaking, the degree of relatedness between two organisms can be estimated by looking at the degree to which they have ancestors in common. This leaves room for disagreement about the best quantitative measure of relatedness, and in recent decades traditional pedigree-based measures have increasingly given way to generalized, statistical measures of genetic (and, in some cases, phenotypic) similarity of the sort introduced in Chapter 2. But as long as multicellular animals are the explanatory target, the differences between these measures can often be ignored in practice, and the intuitive notion of relatedness as genealogical kinship remains adequate for many purposes.

This is far from the case in microbial populations. The source of the trouble is the propensity of microbes to exchange genes horizontally, bypassing the parent-offspring channel. A growing body of evidence points to the importance of this process to social evolution in microbes (Smith, 2001; West et al., 2007a; Nogueira et al., 2009; Rankin et al., 2011a, b; Mc Ginty et al., 2011, 2013; West and Gardner, 2013; Dimitriu et al., 2014, 2015). In this chapter, I will argue that even generalized statistical measures of relatedness do not fully account for the impact of gene mobility, forcing a further revision to the concept.[1]

---

[1] I am by no means the first author to stress the radical consequences gene mobility holds for the conceptual foundations of evolutionary theory. Other authors have rightly emphasized the ways in which mobile genetic elements (particularly when they cross species boundaries) challenge traditional conceptions of the tree of life, biodiversity, individuality, and other aspects of biological ontology (see, in particular, the articles collected in O'Malley, 2010, 2013; Dupré, 2012, as well as O'Malley, 2014). This chapter can be seen as a contribution to this growing body of work.

6.2 Gene Mobility as a Source of Genetic Similarity

Since the 1940s, microbiologists have known that prokaryotes are able to transfer genes 'horizontally' within a single generation, bypassing the parent-offspring channel (Lederberg and Tatum, 1946; Zinder and Lederberg, 1952). This horizontal gene transfer occurs most readily among conspecifics. Occasionally, genes cross species boundaries, and these events, though relatively rare, have profound implications for the notion of a 'tree of life' (O'Malley, 2010; O'Malley and Boucher, 2011). Here, I intend to focus mainly on within-species gene mobility, and on the implications it holds for our understanding of social evolution.

It is already known that gene transfer among conspecifics affects the course of evolution by facilitating recombination: mobile genetic elements, although themselves separate from the chromosomal DNA, can 'transfer large sections of the chromosome, along with parts of the conjugative element, into a recipient cell' (Frost et al., 2005, p. 725), altering the chromosomal DNA so that new gene combinations are created. But more recent literature has highlighted another way in which gene transfer among conspecifics has consequences for microbial evolution (Nogueira et al., 2009; Rankin et al., 2011a, b; Mc Ginty et al., 2011; Mc Ginty and Rankin, 2012; Mc Ginty et al., 2013; West and Gardner, 2013; Dimitriu et al., 2014, 2015). These consequences arise not from its role as a source of recombination, but from its role as a source of genetic similarity between nearby organisms.

I do not intend to discuss *all* forms of gene mobility in this chapter. 'Horizontal gene transfer' and 'gene mobility' are in fact umbrella terms for a plurality of different mechanisms (Bushman, 2002; Thomas and Nielsen, 2005). Similarly, 'mobile genetic element' is an umbrella term for various types of genetic entity that can be transferred in this way, including transposable elements, bacteriophages, and plasmids (Frost et al., 2005). My focus here will be on the evolutionary consequences of one particular mechanism, namely plasmid transfer by bacterial conjugation.

The process of conjugation, because of its role in recombination, is sometimes likened to microbial sex. It is not, however, a mode of reproduction: no cell division takes place. Instead, nearby cells come into contact via tubular protusions known as pili. Plasmids—packets of extra-chromosomal DNA—are copied from one cell to another via these pili.

The mechanistic details need not concern us here. The crucial point about plasmid transfer by conjugation, for our purposes, is that it is a *replicative* process: the plasmid does not move from one cell to another, but is copied. The result is that, after conjugating, two nearby organisms may share genetic elements that they did not share before. We can therefore see how, in principle at least, plasmid conjugation can be a source of genetic similarity between social partners.

For a simple example, imagine a population sorted randomly into large groups of size M, in which some individuals carry a rare plasmid X. Because the process of group formation is random, there is initially no tendency for X-bearers to cluster together. Suppose, however, that at a particular point in the life cycle, each individual conjugates with a randomly picked member of its local group. Further suppose that, if a bearer conjugates with a non-bearer during this conjugation phase, the plasmid will infect the non-bearer with probability λ. After transfer, groups that had no plasmid bearers prior to the transfer phase will still have no plasmid bearers, but groups that had N plasmid bearers before the transfer phase are now expected to have approximately $N + \lambda N$ bearers.[2] The distribution of plasmid bearers in the population is now non-random: plasmid bearers now cluster together in a way they did not before.

This genetic similarity can lead to positive r at the mobile genetic locus. To see why, it is crucial here to recall that, on the modern, regression-based definition of r given in Chapter 2, r quantifies the overall statistical association in a population between actor and recipient genotypes, with respect to a specified locus or set of loci. Kinship-dependent mechanisms, based on kin recognition or limited dispersal, are one source of positive r, but not the only source. We noted in Chapter 2 that kinship-independent mechanisms, such as greenbeard effects, can also be important. The case of gene mobility is another illustration of this point. With respect to genes carried on mobile genetic elements, conjugation is a source of positive genetic correlation between interacting organisms.

However, a sceptical worry arises here: is conjugation really a *significant* source of genetic similarity from the point of view of social evolution

---

[2] This approximation relies on our assumptions that the plasmid is rare and that groups are large. If we do not make these assumptions, the frequency of plasmid bearers after conjugation is $N + \lambda N(M - N)/(M - 1)$. This quantity is approximated by $N + \lambda N$ when $M >> N$ (the plasmid is rare) and $M >> 1$ (groups are large).

theory? In other words, is it ever likely to make a significant difference to the value of r at loci relevant to social traits? In fact, recent empirical work suggests that social evolution researchers often cannot afford to ignore mobile genetic elements, because these entities are indeed implicated in producing social behaviour in microbes—and more often than one might imagine. A study by Teresa Nogueira et al. (2009), which examined twenty-one *Escherichia coli* genomes, concluded that 'genes coding for secreted proteins—the secretome—are very frequently lost and gained and are associated with mobile elements' (2009, p. 1683). Daniel Rankin et al. (2011b) synthesize diverse sources of evidence in support of the hypothesis that mobile genetic elements are 'drivers of bacterial sociality' (2011b, p. 5).

More recently, an ingenious experimental study by Tatiana Dimitriu et al. (2014) found direct evidence that gene mobility promotes cooperation in laboratory conditions. Their experimental setup uses a specially modified plasmid that can enable the horizontal transfer of other plasmids without also transferring itself. This allowed them to compare a situation in which a public-goods-producing plasmid was mobile (i.e. subject to horizontal as well vertical transmission between bacteria) with a situation in which the same plasmid was immobile (i.e. unable to transfer horizontally).

To be precise, Dimitriu et al. created a population containing two distinct subpopulations (or demes) containing differing initial proportions of a public-good-producing 'P^+' plasmid and a non-public-good-producing 'P^-' plasmid. They then investigated the change over time in the ratio of P^+ to P^-, both within subpopulations and in the global population, under a setup in which the plasmids were mobile and a setup in which they were immobile. In the immobile setup, individuals with P^+ were selected against within groups, as one would intuitively expect. Dimitriu et al. then asked: how does introducing gene mobility alter the situation?

They found that introducing gene mobility did not increase the *local* ratio of P^+ to P^- within each subpopulation, in comparison with the immobile scenario, because both types of plasmid were equally mobile. However, it did increase the *global* ratio of P^+ to P^-, because the subpopulation with a higher initial density of P^+ grew more quickly than the subpopulation with a lower initial density, and this difference in growth rates was greater than it was when the plasmids were immobile. In other words, gene mobility increased the power of between-group selection for P^+. This was due to gene mobility differentially increasing the density of P^+ bearers in the subpopulation with the higher initial density, as in the abstract 'simple example' described earlier. This introduced a degree of positive assortment among bearers of P^+, leading to a greater differential growth rate between the two subpopulations than in the setup with immobile plasmids.

The remarkable result can be naturally interpreted in terms of group selection (in the sense of Chapter 4): gene mobility boosted between-group genetic variance, increasing the power of group selection in relation to individual selection. It can also be interpreted within the framework of Hamilton's rule as evidence of gene mobility causing positive genetic relatedness at the plasmid locus, leading to stronger positive selection for P^+. However, I will argue in the next section that, to capture fully the effects gene mobility may have on relatedness, we need to change the way we think about relatedness.

6.3 A Diachronic Conception of Relatedness

The role of gene mobility in microbial social evolution is ultimately an empirical question; and, although the available evidence is suggestive of a strong role, it remains an open question. I do not intend to settle it here. Instead, I want to take a step back from this empirical question to focus on a conceptual question. Suppose that gene mobility is indeed an important source of genetic similarity in microbial populations. *What follows for the concept of relatedness?*

If relatedness were defined in terms of kinship in the ordinary sense of the word, then gene mobility would clearly call for a revision of the concept, since it provides an empirically important, kinship-independent source of genetic similarity. However, we saw in Chapter 2 that relatedness in contemporary social evolution theory is *not* defined in terms of kinship: it is a measure of the statistical association between the genotypes of social partners at relevant loci. One might infer from this that social evolution theory is 'preadapted' for gene mobility—that the regression-based definition of r already implicitly takes its effects into account. However, this would be too hasty. I contend that even the regression definition of relatedness requires revision in order to fully accommodate the effects of mobile genetic elements. The source of all the trouble is a simple observation about gene mobility. The regression definition of relatedness takes it for granted that each organism in the population of interest has a determinate individual gene frequency, or genic value, for the gene of interest. But note that, when organisms are horizontally exchanging genes for social phenotypes at a non-negligible rate, we can no longer even talk of an organism's genic value *simpliciter*. This property may be altered by a plasmid transfer event, and may therefore vary diachronically (i.e. over time) during the course of the organism's life cycle. Strictly speaking, we can only talk of an organism's genic value *at a particular time in the life cycle*.[3] I contend that this has consequences for the concept of relatedness that go beyond mere technicalities. It should change the way we think about the relationship between relatedness and time, in a way that holds meaningful implications for empirical work.[4,5]

6.3.1 An idealized life cycle

To think formally about the question of how to define relatedness in the presence of horizontal transmission, it will help here to introduce an idealized life cycle in which social interaction (i.e. public goods production), horizontal transmission, population regulation, reproduction, and dispersal all occur as separate stages, rather than all occurring concurrently. Sorcha Mc Ginty et al. (2013) make the same move, and I will consider the same life cycle they do, with one exception (explained later). I will consider a 'patch-structured' population, in which microbes live

---

[3] This is also the case for organisms with complex life cycles that may (for example) include a diploid phase and an extended haploid phase (Godfrey-Smith, 2016a, b). Some of the considerations regarding relatedness discussed in this chapter might also arise in these cases, but I do not explore that possibility here.

[4] Readers wishing to avoid mathematical details can skip the rest of this section—but note the key result labelled 'HRM'.

[5] Even without gene mobility, there is a sense in which the average genotype of a social *neighbourhood* may be time-dependent, if the composition of this social neighbourhood changes during the life cycle; and this too can introduce a form of time-dependence to measures of relatedness. Time-dependence of this sort (and its consequences for r) is discussed in (Úbeda and Gardner, 2012). My claim here is that diachronic variation in the focal individual's genic value during its life cycle introduces a yet more radical sort of time-dependence.

in discrete, isolated patches.[6] The stages of the idealized life cycle are as follows:

- *Founding*: Each patch is populated with N founder cells, sampled at random from a well-mixed population of potential founders. These founders divide many times to produce a large group (no selection takes place during this time). If a founder carries the plasmid of interest, then this plasmid is transmitted vertically to its descendants, although not necessarily with perfect fidelity, since plasmids can be lost during cell division.

- *Horizontal transmission 1*: Descendants of the founders then have an opportunity to conjugate and transfer plasmids horizontally to other organisms within their local patch. The genic value of individual i prior to this stage is denoted by p_i ($p_i = 1$ if i initially carries the plasmid of interest , and $p_i = 0$ if it does not). The (potentially modified) genic value of i after this stage is denoted by p_i^*. The average initial and post-transfer genic values of i's social partners are denoted, respectively, by $\hat{p}_i$ and $\hat{p}_i^*$.

- *Public goods production*: Organisms with the plasmid of interest (i.e. individuals for whom $p_i^* = 1$) produce a public good, incurring a net cost to their own viability but conferring a net benefit on all other organisms in the patch.

- *Horizontal transmission 2*: Organisms have a second opportunity to conjugate and transfer plasmids horizontally to other organisms in the patch. The genic value of i after this stage is denoted by p_i^{**}.

- *Global competition*: Organisms in all patches are killed off with a probability proportional to the total payoff they received in the public goods production stage.

- *Dispersal*: All surviving cells disperse to form a well-mixed population of potential founders, and the life cycle begins again. The average initial genic value of the descendants of i, prior to horizontal transmission, is denoted p_i'.

---

[6] These patches (which are akin to 'haystacks' in Maynard Smith's 1964 haystacks model) could be interpreted as large animal hosts; however, as is the convention in the microbiological literature, I call them 'patches' rather than 'hosts' because the microbes themselves are 'hosts' to plasmids.

The difference from the life cycle of Mc Ginty et al. (2013) is the addition of a second horizontal transmission stage; Mc Ginty et al. only include one horizontal transmission stage. I have included this additional stage in order to argue (in due course) that horizontal transmission can still make a difference to the direction of selection on a social trait even if it occurs *after* the expression of that trait.

6.3.2 A modified Price equation

Recall (from Chapter 2, Section 2.1) the standard version of the Price equation:

$$\Delta \bar{p} = \frac{1}{w} \left[\text{Cov}(w_i, p_i) + \text{E}(w_i \Delta p_i) \right] \qquad (6.1)$$

where w_i is the fitness of the ith individual, conceptualized (in a discrete generations model) as its total number of descendants in the next generation; p_i is its genic value; and Δp_i is the change between the genic value i and the average genic value of its descendants. The term $\text{Cov}(w_i, p_i)$ is usually interpreted as capturing the part of the change in gene frequency attributable to natural selection, whereas $\text{E}(w_i \Delta p_i)$ is usually interpreted as capturing the part of the change attributable to transmission bias.

Two problems arise for the standard Price equation when the gene in question is mobile during the life cycle. One (noted earlier) is that the equation assumes each organism to have a single, unambiguous genic value that does not change over time. When genic values can and do change, we must time-index them to a particular point in the life cycle. In the notation introduced in the description of the life cycle, p_i specifically denotes the ith individual's *initial* genic value, *prior* to the first horizontal transmission stage. Correspondingly, we can interpret Δp_i as $p_i' - p_i$, the difference between the ith individual's *initial* genic value and the average *initial* genic value of its descendants in the next iteration of the life cycle.

The standard Price equation is still mathematically valid with p_i and Δp_i interpreted in this way. However, the interpretation of $\text{Cov}(w_i, p_i)$ as fully capturing the selective change in the gene frequency is now questionable—and this is the second problem. For why should we think selective change requires covariance between an organism's fitness and its genic value at the *beginning* of its life cycle, *prior* to horizontal transmission, public goods production or global competition? Shouldn't covariance between fitness and genic values at later time points also count? If genic values change significantly during the life cycle, there is a risk that this version of the Price equation will misleadingly interpret a substantial part of the effect of natural selection as an effect of transmission bias alone.

The abstract possibility of this problem has been noted by various authors in other contexts. Frank (1997a, b, 1998); Okasha (2006, 2011), and Godfrey-Smith (2007a) have all observed that the so-called 'transmission bias' term in the standard Price equation is influenced by fitness differences whenever $\text{Cov}(w_i, \Delta p_i) \neq 0$. This is often thought to be a merely technical point, since it is usually hard to think of a reason why fitness would co-vary with transmission bias, and in any case many models in the social evolution literature assume transmission to occur with perfect fidelity (Chapter 2).

However, in models that incorporate horizontal transmission, this is not a merely technical point. If a gene of interest is subject to horizontal transmission, there are various reasons why it may be that $\text{Cov}(w_i, \Delta p_i) \neq 0$. For example, plasmid carriage may impose a fitness cost, with the result that organisms which receive a plasmid horizontally during their life cycle may be systematically less fit than organisms which avoid doing so. Alternatively, Δp_i and w_i may be positively correlated in cases where receiving a plasmid confers a direct fitness benefit. More subtly, but relevantly for our purposes here, Δp_i and w_i may be positively correlated even when the plasmid encodes a costly public good, by virtue of being joint effects of a common cause: the number of plasmid bearers in one's vicinity. In other words, an organism surrounded by a high density of public-good-producing plasmid bearers may be both fitter than average *and* more likely than average to receive the plasmid through conjugation.

When, for whatever reason, receiving a gene horizontally co-varies with fitness, the technical problem noted by Frank, Okasha, and Godfrey-Smith becomes significant. Fortunately, Frank provided a solution to the problem, in the form of a modified version of the Price equation (see the Appendix, and also Frank, 1998):

$$\overline{w}\Delta\overline{p} = \text{Cov}(w_i, p_i') + \overline{w}\text{E}(p_i' - p_i) \tag{6.2}$$

The crucial difference here with equation (6.1) is that the transmission bias term is now unaffected by variation in fitness, and p_i (i.e. the ith

individual's initial genic value) has been replaced by p_i' (i.e. the initial genic value of its descendants in the next iteration of the life cycle) in the selection term. Both formulations are mathematically valid—they are algebraic rearrangements of each other—but only the second fully captures the effects of selection in the covariance term when $\text{Cov}(w_i, \Delta p_i) \neq 0$. This makes equation (6.2) a particularly useful formulation of the Price equation in the presence of horizontal transmission.

On the assumption that infidelities of *vertical* transmission between i and its descendants in the next generation do not co-vary with its fitness, we can re-write this equation as follows, where τ is fidelity of vertical transmission:[7]

$$\overline{w}\Delta\overline{p} = \tau\,\text{Cov}(w_i, p_i^{**}) + \overline{w}\text{E}(\tau p_i^{**} - p_i) \qquad (6.3)$$

Let us now assume that $\text{E}(\tau p_i^{**} - p_i) = 0$. This parallels Queller's assumption that $\text{E}(w_i \Delta p_i) = 0$ in the context of deriving HRG. This move, like Queller's, may be interpreted either as an idealization or as an abstraction (in the sense of Thomson-Jones, 2005). On the 'idealization' reading, we are assuming that the net change in the frequency of the plasmid due to its infectivity alone is zero—in other words, we are assuming that every horizontal transfer event is cancelled out, on average, by another event in which the plasmid is expelled by a host—so that natural selection on organismal fitness differences is the sole driver of change. This is not an empirically plausible assumption. On the 'abstraction' reading, we are not assuming anything about the net infectivity of the plasmid; we are simply *omitting* the part of the change attributable to its infectivity alone from our analysis, without assuming anything about its value. I prefer to think of this move as an abstraction; but we should remember that, on this interpretation, the left-hand side of the Price equation only captures part of the total change in gene frequency, to wit, the part attributable to fitness differences between organisms.

This assumption yields a simplified Price equation:

$$\overline{w}\Delta\overline{p} = \tau\,\text{Cov}(w_i, p_i^{**}) \qquad (6.4)$$

---

[7] Formally, τ is defined by the regression equation $p_i' = \tau p_i^{**} + \epsilon_{p_i}$, and the assumption of uncorrelated residuals invoked here is that $\text{Cov}(w_i, \epsilon_{p_i}) = 0$.

6.3.3 Separating Direct and Indirect Fitness Effects

By partitioning this modified and simplified Price equation in the way outlined in Chapter 2, Section 2.1, we arrive at a 'mobile Hamilton's rule'— a variant of HRG that accommodates the effects of horizontal transmission. We begin with a regression model of fitness almost identical to that of Queller's general model (see equation 2.3 in Chapter 2), with $-c$ and b again defined as the partial regression coefficients in this model. The difference is that now the regressors are the genic values of the focal individual (p_i^*) and the average genic value of its social partners $(\hat{p}_i^*)$ at the public goods production stage in the life cycle, i.e. after the first horizontal transmission stage but before the second:

$$w_i = \alpha - cp_i^* + b\hat{p}_i^* + \epsilon_{w_i} \tag{6.5}$$

Substituting this regression model into equation (6.2), and assuming that $\mathrm{Cov}(\epsilon_{w_i}, p_i^{**}) = 0$, we obtain the following partition of the selective change:

$$\overline{w}\Delta\overline{p} = -c\tau\mathrm{Cov}(p_i^*, p_i^{**}) + b\tau\mathrm{Cov}(\hat{p}_i^*, p_i^{**}) \tag{6.6}$$

On the further assumptions that $\tau > 0$ (i.e. the fidelity of vertical transmission is positive) and $\mathrm{Cov}(p_i^*, p_i^{**}) > 0$ (i.e. an organism's genic value in the public goods stage is positively correlated with its genic value after the second horizontal transmission stage), this partition implies the following rule for positive selection:

$$\Delta\overline{p} > 0 \iff -c + b \cdot \frac{\mathrm{Cov}(\hat{p}_i^*, p_i^{**})}{\mathrm{Cov}(p_i^*, p_i^{**})} > 0 \tag{HRM}$$

Because this is a variant of HRG that accommodates gene mobility, I have called it HRM ('M' for 'mobile'). It has the characteristic form of Hamilton's rule, but the covariance ratio that plays the role of r differs in interesting ways from the standard concept of relatedness that we discussed in Chapter 2, and that we defined formally as $\mathrm{Cov}(\hat{p}_i, p_i)/\mathrm{Var}(p_i)$. I will refer to this non-standard relatedness concept as r_M (again, 'M' is for 'mobile'):

$$r_M = \frac{\mathrm{Cov}(\hat{p}_i^*, p_i^{**})}{\mathrm{Cov}(p_i^*, p_i^{**})} \tag{6.7}$$

In contrast to the standard concept of relatedness, r_M takes account of genetic correlations between actors and recipients created by horizontal transmission events. These events matter even if they occur in the second horizontal transmission stage, which is to say *after* the time at which public goods were produced. This feature of r_M leads to a more subtle difference from the standard concept: it is *diachronic*. It captures the statistical association between genic values at two different time points: the genic value of the actor at the time of public goods production and the genic value of the recipient at the end of the life cycle, after all horizontal transmission has taken place.

This may sound strange on first hearing, but, on further reflection, it is not so counterintuitive, especially if one adopt's a gene's eye view on the process (Williams, 1966; Dawkins, 1976).[8] From a gene's eye perspective, the role of a coefficient of relatedness in social evolution theory is to quantify the value of a recipient to a gene (located in an actor) as a means of indirectly gaining representation in future populations.[9] When genes are mobile, the recipient's value to a focal gene depends not on what genes the recipient has at the time the actor interacts with it, but on what genes the recipient is likely to have further down the line, when it comes to transmitting its genes to the next generation. If there is no tendency for recipients to share the genes of actors early in the life cycle, but a systematic tendency for recipients to come to resemble actors *later on* in the life cycle due to horizontal transmission events, then this confers evolutionary value on those recipients from the perspective of the focal gene. In other words, what matters to the success of a mobile gene under natural selection is that it confers fitness benefits on *future* bearers of that gene, whether or not they are current bearers at the time the gene is expressed. This idea is captured formally in HRM.

In sum, relatedness in the presence of horizontal transmission should be defined as r_M, and hence should be defined as a measure of diachronic genetic similarity between actor genotypes at the time of public goods production and recipient genotypes at the end of the life cycle. The formal

---

[8] The relationship between Hamilton's rule and the gene's eye view of evolution is discussed in the book's conclusion. As I see it, HRG already embodies a subtle form of gene's eye thinking, but this is particularly clear in the case of HRM.

[9] See Frank (1998) and Birch (2014b) for further discussion of relatedness as measuring value of a recipient to the genes of an actor.

argument for taking r_M to be the appropriate measure of relatedness in the presence of gene mobility is simple: if one accepts that equation (6.2) is the appropriate version of the Price equation to use in this context, and if one accepts that equation (6.5), which regresses fitness on genotypes at the time they are expressed, is the appropriate regression model of fitness, then it follows that r_M is the appropriate concept of relatedness. The informal 'gene's eye view' argument is even simpler: the role of relatedness, with respect to a specified locus, is to capture the value of a recipient, to the actor's genes at that locus, as a means of securing genetic representation in future populations. For genes carried on plasmids, the value of a recipient to such a gene depends not just on how likely it is that the recipient currently possesses the plasmid, but also on how likely it is that the recipient will come to possess the plasmid by the end of its life cycle.

6.4 Implications for Empirical Research

The previous section focussed on a conceptual question—how should relatedness be conceptualized in the presence of gene mobility?—and argued for an unorthodox definition of r as a measure of the association, at a specific locus, between genotypes of actors at the time the gene in question is expressed and the genotypes of recipients at the end of their life cycle. But does this proposed revision have practical consequences for social evolution research in microbiology? If not, one may question whether the payoff justifies the effort involved in changing the way we think about a central theoretical concept. But I contend that it does have practical consequences.

In the theoretical models of Nogueira et al. (2009) and Mc Ginty et al. (2013), and in the experimental framework of Dimitriu et al. (2014), the opportunity for horizontal plasmid transfer through conjugation precedes the production of the 'public good'. This is a natural choice for investigating the hypothesis that producers are able to convert free riders into producers before the public good is produced, thereby increasing the number of producers in their neighbourhood. It is also a choice constrained by the practical details of the Dimitriu et al. (2014) setup. However, this naturally leads to the question: what happens if the opportunity for horizontal plasmid transfer occurs partially or wholly *after* the expression of the plasmid?

One possibility is that transfer events after social interaction make no difference to relatedness or to the direction of organism-level selection, and can only effect the 'pure infectivity' component of the total change. This is the view taken by Mc Ginty et al. (2013), who write that 'our results clearly depend on our life cycle and, if transmission were to occur after the public goods interaction . . . then we would no longer see the kin selection effect but the infectivity effect would remain' (2013, p. 6). However, they are led to this view because they are working with a synchronic conception of relatedness, evaluated at the time of public goods production. A diachronic conception of relatedness leads to a different answer: opportunities for gene transfer still matter to the direction of selection even if they occur after social interaction, because they increase the value of a recipient to a plasmid as a means of securing genetic representation in future populations.

We can, in fact, formally decompose the numerator of r_M into a component reflecting the synchronic assortment present at the time of public goods production and a component reflecting the effects of transfer events after public goods production. For note that (trivially) $p_i^{**} = p_i^* + (p_i^{**} - p_i^*)$. Substituting this identity into (6.7), we obtain:

$$\text{Cov}(p_i^*, p_i^{**}) \cdot r_M = \overbrace{\text{Cov}(\hat{p}_i^*, p_i^*)}^{\text{Assortment present in public goods stage}}$$

$$+ \overbrace{\text{Cov}(\hat{p}_i^*, [p_i^{**} - p_i^*])}^{\text{Effect of subsequent plasmid transfer}} \tag{6.8}$$

The first component captures the synchronic assortment at the moment the social behaviour encoded on the plasmid is expressed, whereas the second component captures the tendency for organisms who interacted with a plasmid bearer to obtain the plasmid later on, by virtue of a plasmid transfer event in the second horizontal transmission stage. This allows us to see that, in principle, it is possible that a plasmid encoding a costly social trait could spread even if there is zero synchronic assortment at the time the trait is expressed, provided an organism that expresses the trait is sufficiently likely to conjugate later in the life cycle with neighbours who free-rode on its actions in the public goods stage. In short, plasmids encoding costly social traits may be favoured by selection if they are able to help potential future hosts, even when those potential future hosts are not current bearers of the plasmid.

To my knowledge, this possibility has not been investigated empirically, and nor have detailed, realistic models of this hypothetical 'helping potential hosts' process yet been constructed.[10] This is perhaps because it is a possibility that only comes into view once we switch from thinking about relatedness as a synchronic population statistic, evaluated at the time of social interaction, to a diachronic statistic that can be affected by gene transfer events that occur some time *after* the expression of a social trait. It is still a mere possibility, but it is one that merits further investigation.

6.5 'But is it Still Kin Selection?'

Giraud and Shykoff (2011), responding to Rankin et al. (2011b), question whether a selection process in which a social trait is favoured because of gene mobility can be described as one of 'kin selection'. They argue that, fundamentally, the trait's infectivity is the causal explanation for its evolutionary success. They have in mind a picture in which gene transfer precedes social interaction, converting potential free riders into cooperators by the time the trait is expressed, but one might argue that this objection applies even more acutely if horizontal transmission occurs after public goods production, so that the trait spreads by virtue of infecting organisms who had been free riders during the social phase of the life cycle.

I have some sympathy with this criticism. In Chapter 4, I put forward a view on which a paradigm case of kin selection involves kinship-dependent sources of relatedness. Processes in which relatedness at the relevant locus arises largely or entirely from kinship-independent sources such as greenbeard mechanisms or gene mobility are best regarded as, at most, marginal cases of kin selection, owing to the potential for intragenomic conflict (discussed below, in Section 6.6). However, what should not be in doubt is that the process being envisaged here genuinely involves natural selection on indirect fitness differences and not simply infectivity, because the positive selective change in plasmid frequency, though reliant on the plasmid's ability to transfer horizontally, is driven by the fitness consequences for the host organism of the public good it produces. Horizontal transmission will probably also have an effect on the 'pure

---

[10] What I have aimed to provide here is an organizing framework, not a detailed dynamical model. See Chapters 2 and 3 for discussion of the difference.

infectivity' component of the total change, but it will also influence the response to selection via its effects on relatedness, as Rankin et al. (2011a) correctly point out.

When populations are group-structured, as we are assuming here, an interpretation in terms of group selection (in the sense of Chapter 4) is often attractive. As I see it, the models of Mc Ginty et al. (2013) and the experimental studies of Dimitriu et al. (2014), in which plasmid transfer occurs wholly *before* social interaction, more closely resemble paradigm cases of group selection than paradigm cases of kin selection. The basic idea is that groups with a higher density of public goods producers outcompete groups with a lower density, and plasmid transfer generates (at least some of) the clustering of producers that is necessary for group selection for public goods production to outweigh selection within groups for free riding. The only difference here from standard examples of group selection is that within-group genetic variance is suppressed by an unusual mechanism.

However, if plasmid transfer occurs wholly *after* social interaction, then the intuitive idea is different. The idea is roughly that plasmids, by producing a public good, surround themselves with fitter than average potential hosts, and spread for that reason. Another way of putting this is to say that a free rider surrounded by a high density of public goods producers is likely to be both fitter than average and more likely than average to be infected by the plasmid before it divides. This may lead to positive covariance between fitness and change in genic value during the life cycle,[11] which, if the effect is large enough, may lead to positive selection of the gene.[12] This is still a form of selection for social behaviour: change is driven by covariance between organismal fitness and genic value, and not (or not only) by infectivity. But, if such a process does occur, it is a very interesting and unusual form of selection. It resembles neither a paradigm case of kin selection nor a paradigm case of group selection, and it simply could not occur in a species in which genic values cannot change during the life cycle.[13]

I should add that, although these processes are forms of natural selection, they also involve an element of niche construction, in the sense of Odling-Smee et al. (2003). Plasmids, by transferring horizontally, create

---

[11] That is, $\mathrm{Cov}(w_i, \Delta p_i) > 0$. [12] That is, $\mathrm{Cov}(w_i, p_i^{**}) > 0$.
[13] See Birch (2014a) for further discussion of this idea.

through their own activities the genetic assortment that sustains the production of public goods. Moreover, by causing their hosts to produce a public good, they create an environment for themselves that contains fitter than average targets for infection, and this is an environment in which they are potentially able to spread faster than they otherwise would have done. This can be interpreted as an instance of what Powers et al. (2011) have called 'social niche construction': the adaptive manipulation by evolutionary agents, in this case plasmids, of their own social environment.

6.6 Gene Mobility as a Source of Intragenomic Conflict

There is much we do not yet understand about the role of mobile genetic elements in microbial cooperation. One significant open question jumps out: if a plasmid encodes a social trait that, when expressed, is costly for the fitness of its host, why is that plasmid not suppressed or expelled by the rest of the genome? After all, there is a sense in which gene mobility is akin to a greenbeard mechanism: just as in a classic greenbeard scenario, a gene for altruism is able to spread by virtue of generating genetic correlation between social partners *at its own locus*, without thereby generating correlation at other genomic loci, or indeed any of the chromosomal loci. We thereby intuitively expect that genes at chromosomal loci will be selected to inhibit the uptake of the plasmid or the expression of the genes it carries. More precisely, we should expect intragenomic conflict when $r_M b > c > r_H b$, where r_M is the coefficient of relatedness at the mobile locus (defined as earlier) and r_H denotes the coefficient of relatedness at a locus in the host's chromosome (Mc Ginty and Rankin, 2012).

Which should we expect to find: resistance to uptake or suppression of gene expression? A formal analysis by Mc Ginty and Rankin (2012) compares full resistance (of the sort that might be accomplished by the CRISPR-Cas system, a simple form of immune system) with the suppression of plasmid gene expression by the chromosome once the plasmid is acquired. One might intuitively expect full resistance to be favoured by organism-level selection, since plasmid carriage imposes physiological costs, even if the plasmid is not expressed. However, Mc Ginty and Rankin (2012) argue that full resistance leads to cyclical 'rock-paper-scissors' dynamics, essentially because full resistance itself imposes a cost on the organism that is worth paying when the plasmid is common but not worth paying when the plasmid is rare. The spread of full resistance causes a collapse in the plasmid population that leads to the loss of resistance, creating a new opportunity for the plasmid to spread. This leads Mc Ginty and Rankin (2012) to propose that mechanisms for suppressing the expression of mobile genes are more stable than mechanisms that suppress their uptake. To this argument we can add the further consideration that a host which merely suppresses the expression of a plasmid rather than preventing its uptake may have the opportunity to transfer that plasmid onward to its own neighbours, through further conjugation events. If those neighbours fail to suppress its expression, they may end up conferring fitness benefits back on the organism from which they received it. This too may favour the suppression of gene expression over full resistance. Moreover, since plasmids often contain multiple genes, it may be advantageous to suppress the expression of a plasmid partially, rather than expelling it totally.

In sum, there are plausible, albeit hardly conclusive, reasons to think that genes which suppress the expression of costly plasmids—without preventing their uptake—would spread under organism-level natural selection. This leaves us with a puzzle when we find apparently costly plasmids that are being expressed. Two broad possibilities come to mind, both of which merit further exploration. One is that r_H, the *chromosomal* relatedness between actors and recipients, is typically high enough for the suppression of public goods production to detract from the inclusive fitness of the chromosome, in which case there is no intragenomic conflict in the first place. In patch-structured populations, chromosomal relatedness can be extremely high, lending some credence to this suggestion. The other is that, although there is genuinely intragenomic conflict here, costly plasmids and their hosts are locked in an arms race that neither side has yet decisively won. In some cases it may be that a point has been reached at which the cost of detecting a cost-imposing plasmid has become too high, either due to the physiological cost of the suppression mechanism or because the mechanism leads to too many false positives (i.e. the suppression of beneficial plasmids), so that hosts have evolved to tolerate certain kinds of cost-imposing plasmid in order to retain a horizontal transmission system that is on the whole beneficial.

Gintis (2003) argues that the same may be true of another form of horizontal transmission, namely cultural transmission in humans.

Here there is a similar problem: we often seem to find cultural variants (beliefs, desires, etc.) that detract from the biological fitness of their hosts. The general line of thought Gintis develops is that, although opening oneself up to cultural transmission inevitably leaves one vulnerable to 'infection' by cultural variants that detract from one's biological fitness, this is a price worth paying for a transmission system that is on the whole beneficial. The parallels between horizontal transmission in humans and microbes are suggestive, and we will revisit them in Chapter 8.

6.7 Summary of Chapter 6

Sociality is rife in the microbial world, yet our best current theories of social evolution were developed with multicellular animals in mind. In importing these traditional approaches to a microbial context, we must take account of the significant differences between microbes and multi-cellular animals, and we must be ready to make conceptual revisions to social evolution theory in light of these differences.

One crucial difference between multicellular organisms and microbes is the prevalence of mobile genetic elements, such as plasmids, in microbial populations. There is evidence that plasmids are frequently implicated in the production of so-called public goods (Nogueira et al., 2009). There is also evidence that enabling the horizontal transfer of a public-goods-producing plasmid can cause it to be favoured by selection (Dimitriu et al., 2014).

As researchers in this area have noted, relatedness may be at the heart of this curious phenomenon. Because the transmission of plasmids through bacterial conjugation is a replicative process, it is a potential source of relevant genetic similarity between interacting organisms. As a result, it makes a difference to relatedness at mobile loci, which may help explain the evolutionary success of costly cooperative traits carried on mobile genetic elements.

What follows from this for the concept of relatedness? Gene mobility introduces a novel, temporal aspect to relatedness: because genotypes can change over the life cycle, two organisms may share a gene at one point in the life cycle, but not at some earlier or later time point. This means we must specify the point in the life cycle at which genotypes should be evaluated for the purposes of calculating relatedness.

I have argued that the best concept of relatedness in this context—assuming the aim is to capture fully the effects of horizontal transmission on the response to selection—is a diachronic measure that quantifies the association between actor genotypes at the moment of gene expression and recipient genotypes at the end of the life cycle.

This measure takes into account not only genetic correlations between actor and recipient that exist at the moment of social interaction, but also genetic correlations created by subsequent horizontal transfer events. These subsequent transfer events matter because the evolutionary success of a gene for a costly trait relies on the benefits falling differentially on future bearers—not necessarily current bearers—of the gene.

This conceptual point leads to an empirical conjecture: public-goods-producing plasmids may be able to spread by natural selection even if there is no genetic assortment at the moment of social interaction, if they are likely to have an opportunity to transfer horizontally at a later time point into individuals who, by virtue of having been free riders when the public good was produced, are fitter than average. This conjecture merits further exploration.

However, the very idea of costly social traits being sustained by gene mobility leads to a worry about intragenomic conflict. Why are these plasmids, which benefit other copies of themselves at a cost to their host, not expelled or suppressed? This remains an open question. But it is worth noting the suggestive parallels with cultural transmission in humans, where similar questions arise.

7

The Multicellular Organism as a Social Phenomenon

7.1 The Return of the 'Cell State'

The cell theory, arguably the cornerstone of all modern biology, states that organisms are composed of one or more cells, that the cell is the basic functional unit of the organism, and that all cells arise from other living cells. One of the original contributors to the cell theory, the German pathologist Rudolf Virchow, realized that the theory brought with it a new way of seeing the organism. He described the organism as a 'cell state', or *Zellenstaat*, a 'society of cells, a tiny, well-ordered state, with all of the accessories—high officials and underlings, servants and masters, the great and the small' (Virchow, 1859, p. 124).[1]

Virchow's vision of the organism was widely discussed, and widely supported, in late nineteenth-century German biology. Notably the naturalist Ernst Haeckel, best known as an influential early advocate of Darwinism, propounded the 'cell state' metaphor throughout his career, reflecting towards the end of it that:

[t]he conception of cells as 'elementary organisms' led to the further opinion that our own human organism, just like all higher animals and plants, is actually a 'cell state', composed of millions of microscopic citizens, the individual cells, which work more or less independently, and co-operate for the common purpose of the entire state. (Haeckel, 1904, p. 167, quoted in Reynolds, 2008, p. 128)

---

[1] For extensive and illuminating discussion of the history of 'cell state' metaphor, see (Reynolds, 2007a, b, 2008, 2010). The translated quotations in this section are drawn from these articles.

In Britain, meanwhile, the philosopher Herbert Spencer coined the related notion of the 'social organism', a term that encapsulated a complex, two-way analogy between the cells of the body and the members of a society:

> Hence we are warranted in considering the body as a commonwealth of monads, each of which has independent powers of life, growth, and reproduction; each of which unites with a number of others to perform some function needful for supporting itself and all the rest; and each of which absorbs its share of nutriment from the blood. And when thus regarded, the analogy between an individual being and a human society, in which each man, whilst helping to subserve some public want, absorbs a portion of the circulating stock of commodities brought to his door, is palpable enough.   (Spencer, 1851, p. 451)

In the twentieth century, the 'cell state' metaphor fell out of favour among biologists. As Reynolds (2007b, p. 91) notes, 'as many researchers became increasingly preoccupied with the biochemistry of the cell and its nuclear hereditary mechanisms, the idea that higher plants and animals are "states" of amoeba-like elementary organisms ceased to have much relevance or allure'. The rise of biochemistry and, later, molecular biology was accompanied by the emergence of a new metaphor: the notion of a cell as a factory, subordinate to the organism as a whole and dedicated to serving its biochemical needs.

Has the time now come for a revival of the 'cell state' perspective? Three trends in recent social evolution research—trends we have already encountered in earlier chapters—suggest that it has.

Firstly, in microbiology, a growing awareness of the scale of cooperation among unicellular organisms (described in Chapters 1 and 6) has made it impossible to deny that social evolution occurs in microbial populations. Moreover, some social behaviours in microbes, such as the formation of a grex in *D. discoideum*, result in phenomena that clearly resemble simple multicellular organisms (Strassmann and Queller, 2011). More controversially, some authors have suggested that even biofilms should be regarded as multicellular organisms in their own right (Shapiro and Dworkin, 1997; Shapiro, 1998; Ereshefsky and Pedroso, 2013).

Secondly, in entomology, the recent resurgence of group selectionist modes of explanation (discussed in Chapter 4) has led to a revival of interest in the 'superorganism' concept: the suggestion that we should think of a complex insect colony as a single, higher-level organism (Wheeler, 1911; Seeley, 1989; Wilson and Sober, 1989; Hölldobler and

Wilson, 2009; Gardner and Grafen, 2009). While this idea remains controversial, even to take it seriously is to recognize that a high degree of social complexity might in principle give rise to a new, organism-like entity, pointing to a close conceptual and/or metaphysical relationship between sociality and organism-status.

Thirdly, the burgeoning 'major transitions' research program has led to a radical re-evaluation of the importance of sociality in the history of life. Far from being confined to a relatively small number of animal taxa, cooperation is increasingly seen as an utterly central element of the Darwinian worldview. Building on foundations laid by, among others, Leo Buss (1987), John Tyler Bonner (1988), and John Maynard Smith and Eörs Szathmáry (1995), major transitions researchers portray the history of life as a series of 'evolutionary transitions in individuality' in which integrated, higher-level individuals have evolved, through social-evolutionary processes, from social groups of lower-level entities (Queller, 1997; Michod, 1999; Calcott, 2008; Queller and Strassmann, 2009; Strassmann and Queller, 2010; Bourke, 2011; Calcott and Sterelny, 2011; Bouchard and Huneman, 2013). When we look at evolution in this new light, we start to see social phenomena where we saw none before: we see cooperation among cells within multicellular organisms, among organelles within eukaryotic cells, even among genes within a chromosome. The result has been a dramatic increase in the explanatory domain of social evolution research, and the return of 'cell state' thinking is one strand within this broader trend.

Among major transitions researchers, the loudest and most direct calls for a social perspective on the multicellular organism have come from David Queller and Joan Strassmann, and from Andrew Bourke (Queller and Strassmann, 2009; Strassmann and Queller, 2010; Bourke, 2011). Strassmann and Queller (2010, p. 605), propose that 'what makes an organism is high and near-unanimous cooperation among its constituent parts, with actual conflicts among those parts largely absent or controlled' (see also Queller, 1997, 2000; Queller and Strassmann, 2009). They envision a 2D space of groups of cells, placed according to their degree of internal cooperation and degree of internal conflict. Strassmann and Queller intend this proposal to encompass both unicellular and multicellular organisms, as well as 'superorganisms' such as eusocial insect colonies (like the leafcutter ants described in Chapter 1) and siphonophores (like the Portuguese man o' war, *Physalia physalis*), which they suggest should simply be regarded as higher-level organisms. In all cases, they suggest, 'organismality' at level n in the biological hierarchy can be explained in terms of high cooperation and low conflict within a social group of entities at level $n - 1$.

Bourke (2011), meanwhile, proposes that we can conceptualize any evolutionary transition in individuality as involving three characteristic processes: social group *formation*, in which a population of lower-level entities becomes group-structured (cf. Chapter 4); social group *maintenance*, in which cooperation within groups is stabilized against the threat of free riding; and social group *transformation*, in which social groups that are already well-defined and stably cooperative are transformed into higher-level individuals. He notes that social evolution research has devoted a great deal of attention to social group maintenance, and some attention to social group formation, but comparatively little attention to the process of social group transformation, which remains poorly understood.

Importantly, for Strassmann, Queller, Bourke, and their collaborators, the 'cell state' is more than an attractive metaphor: it is the foundation for a research program that seeks to understand evolutionary transitions in individuality. In other words, taking a 'social perspective' on the multicellular organism does not simply mean describing the activities of cells in social terms. It implies a commitment to draw on the concepts and methods of social evolution theory to explain the evolutionary origins of multicellular individuals.

7.2 Resistance to the Social Perspective

There are at least three reasons why one might initially be sceptical of the suggestion that the multicellular organism is a social phenomenon. Firstly, there is the concern that cells cannot normally survive outside the body of which they are a part. If they have no 'choice' in the matter, is social evolution theory still applicable? The simple answer is that obligate sociality is still sociality. One might further argue that the survival chances of a somatic cell outside the body are not much worse than those of a solitary leafcutter ant or, for that matter, a solitary human in most environments. It has never been part of the theory that a social organism must 'choose' to be social. In any case, it may well be that cells are often viable outside proto-organisms during the early stages of a transition to multicellularity, only to lose that ability gradually during the process of social group transformation.

Secondly, the concern about cell autonomy that originally caused the decline of the 'cell state' metaphor still holds some force. Don't cells follow the 'instructions' of centralized nervous and endocrine systems? If so, can they really be said to be social actors in their own right? In response, we should first observe that this is not true of all multicellular organisms, or even all multicellular animals: in sponges, for example, we find amoeba-like cells (called archaeocytes) with comparable functional autonomy to free-living amoebae. We should also observe that the coordination of cell function via nervous and endocrine systems is something that calls for evolutionary explanation, and that social evolution theory may usefully play a part in this explanation. More fundamentally, however, I do not see the top-down control of the somatic cells by nervous and endocrine systems as incompatible with thinking of the cells as social actors: we can, if we wish, take a social perspective on this phenomenon too, and regard the cells outside the nervous and endocrine systems as receivers in a signalling system, receiving instructions from senders in the brain and reliably carrying out those instructions, just as workers in insect colonies respond to pheromonal signals from the queen (cf. Cao, 2014; Shea, 2014). Recall in this context Virchow's hierarchical image of the cell state, with its 'high officials and underlings, servants and masters, the great and the small'.

Thirdly, and in my view most seriously, there is a concern that somatic cells should not be regarded as evolutionary agents in their own right because they have zero reproductive value. This is not the place for a detailed discussion of the concept of reproductive value, but the basic idea is that the reproductive value of a certain class of entity is the expected relative genetic contribution of that class of entity to future populations in the long run.[2] For example, in a diploid species with sexual reproduction, the two sexes have equal reproductive value, and this is pivotal to Fisher's famous 'sex ratio argument' (Fisher, 1930). In multicellular animals, there is a clear germ-soma division of labour, and the somatic cells, even if they are able to divide mitotically, are normally unable to leave descendants

---

[2] For detailed discussions, see Frank (1998) and Grafen (2006b).

in future populations beyond the life cycle of the organism, implying zero reproductive value. There are interesting exceptions, such as the terrible facial tumours of the Tasmanian devil (*Sarcophilus harrisii*), which are transmissible through direct contact (Bourke, 2011), or the case of the 'HeLa' cell line, taken from a patient called Henrietta Lacks in 1951 and now used in laboratories around the world (Skloot, 2010). But such exceptions merely serve to remind us of the usual situation, which is that somatic cells, barring some genetic mutation, are incapable of creating lineages that persist beyond the lifespan of the animal.

Of course, one could say the same about obligately sterile workers in insect societies. A natural response here is to point out that, while the existence of a class of entities with zero reproductive value may be a characteristic *end-point* of a transition to multicellularity, or of a transition to advanced eusociality, it need not be true during the transitional stages, and seems unlikely to be true at the beginning of the process. It can therefore be useful to think of cells and sterile workers as distinct evolutionary agents in order to understand how it is that they ultimately came to lose that status. Their loss of reproductive value is something that itself calls for explanation, and the explanation should begin from a starting point at which they do have reproductive value.

In sum, although the above concerns are all reasonable, they are not decisive. In all cases, the key is to appreciate that the social perspective is primarily a methodological stance—a way of approaching evolutionary transitions in individuality—rather than an empirical hypothesis. In taking a social perspective on the multicellular organism, we are making a methological bet: we are betting that there are deep and illuminating (rather than superficial and misleading) parallels between multicellular organisms and other complex societies in the natural world, such as eusocial insect colonies, and we are betting that social evolution theory will provide us with the tools we need to explore these parallels.

There is admittedly an empirical aspect to this bet: we are betting that the evolutionary processes that have driven the evolution of social behaviour in well-known cases and the processes that have driven the evolution of multicellularity are similar in relevant respects, so that theories and models devised to help us to understand the former can, if suitably revised and extended, shed light on the latter. But one should not exaggerate the degree of similarity that is needed for the bet to pay off. The fact that there are obvious differences between cells and more familiar social actors, though grounds for caution, does not imply that a social perspective on the organism will not prove fruitful. Is the bet a good bet? My view is that a social perspective on multicellularity has already proved to be, and will continue to be, extremely valuable. It helps us see the distinctive explanatory puzzles that the evolution of multicellularity presents, and it helps us generate novel hypotheses with the potential to solve those puzzles. But there is no way to make a convincing case for this view except by putting the social perspective to work, and this is the task of the rest of the chapter.

In the next section, I explain why, even though the evolution of multicellularity has been described as a 'minor major transition', the evolution of complex multicellularity, and the relationship between complexity and size, remains rather mysterious. In Section 7.4, I hypothesize that this transition can be explained as the product of a feedback loop in which the redundancy of task structures generated by increasing group size plays a pivotal role. In Section 7.5, I suggest that the fragility of this feedback mechanism may help explain why most of the lineages in which simple multicellularity has evolved have not proceeded to more complex forms with larger numbers of cell types. In the final section, I consider some open questions regarding the account's validity and scope.

7.3 Hamilton's Hypothesis

For Buss (1987), the evolution of multicellularity presented the following puzzle: given that natural selection favours cells that promote their own fitness, how did proto-multicellular organisms avoid being destabilized by conflict among cell lineages? His answer was that such organisms have evolved—through selection at the group level—mechanisms for controlling intra-organismal conflict, such as germline segregation, whereby the capacity to generate a new organism is limited to a very small number of cell lineages, known as the germline, that are set aside from the somatic cell lineages early in development. This, however, led to a 'chicken and egg' puzzle: how could group selection be powerful enough, relative to individual selection, to assemble such mechanisms prior to the existence of such mechanisms?

However, when we view the multicellular organism through the lens of social evolution theory, the puzzle seems to dissolve. Multicellular organisms are clonal groups of cells, and there is no reason to think that the cell lineages in a clonal group are in evolutionary conflict with each other. A clonal group is one in which, barring any mutation events during the formation of the group, the genetic variance within the group is 0 and the relatedness among group members is 1 at all loci, and these conditions are highly favourable to the evolution of altruism. As Hamilton (1964, p. 25) himself noted:[3]

our theory predicts for clones a complete absence of any form of competition which is not to the overall advantage and also the highest degree of mutual altruism. This is borne out well enough by the behavior of clones which make up the bodies of multicellular organisms.

Hence there is no deep puzzle about the evolutionary stability of cooperation among the cell lineages of the first multicellular organisms. These organisms were clonal groups of cells, and they cooperated because they were genetically near-identical (Maynard Smith and Szathmáry, 1995; Queller, 2000; Grosberg and Strathmann, 2007; Fisher et al., 2013). No further mechanisms were needed to suppress competition, so no 'chicken and egg' problem of the sort Buss envisaged actually arises. Let us call this 'Hamilton's hypothesis'.

Queller (2000) has taken this hypothesis further, arguing that relatedness can even explain the origins of a germ-soma division of labour. He suggests that 'the germ line might have originated as a consequence of other cell lineages' altruistically removing themselves from the reproductive line, to perform some somatic benefit to the organism' (Queller, 2000, p. 1653). This turns the explanatory relationship posited by Buss on its head. Far from being a group-level adaptation for suppressing conflict among cell lineages, germline segregation, on Queller's picture, arose as a by-product of somatic altruism—altruism that evolved because the inclusive fitness interests of the cell lineages were aligned by high relatedness.

Hamilton's hypothesis is complicated by the fact that few multicellular organisms are truly clonal. Clonality is a feature of organisms that develop from a single-celled propagule, but not all development is like this. For example, many plants can reproduce vegetatively, with the new individual

---

[3] In a passage also quoted by Grosberg and Strathmann (2007).

developing from a multicellular propagule.[4] In plants under cultivation, many generations of vegetative reproduction can lead to the gradual accumulation of mutations in different cell layers, resulting in individuals containing substantial genetic diversity (Godfrey-Smith, 2009b). In the wild, however, plants frequently reproduce sexually, pushing their lineage through a single-cell bottleneck and thereby restoring high relatedness and low mutational load. Provided this happens often enough, high relatedness and low internal conflict will be maintained (Grosberg and Strathmann, 2007).

Even among organisms that pass through a single-cell bottleneck every generation, such as multicellular animals, clonality is not perfect. Within-organism genetic diversity can arise through chimerism, where cell lineages produced from a different sperm and egg mix in the early stages of development. We see this, for example, in marmosets (*Callithrix kuhlii*; Ross et al., 2007). Genetic diversity can also arise through mutation during mitotic cell division. Occasionally, these mutation events create cancerous cell lineages, and the stability of multicellularity in the long term depends crucially on these 'cheater' lineages being unable to spread between organisms. We see a grim illustration of this point in the Tasmanian devil, which is now threatened with extinction due to an epidemic of the facial tumours mentioned earlier (Bourke, 2011). Given this, we should not be surprised to find that an ability to discriminate 'self' from 'non-self', and to attack intruding cell lineages, is present even in sponges, usually thought to be the most basal of the multicellular animals (Bayne, 1990).

Despite all these caveats, it remains plausible that, for any multicellular organism spawned from a unitary propagule and of a size within certain limits, relatedness is typically high enough to stabilize cooperation among the cells. It is also plausible that organisms that can reproduce vegetatively nevertheless pass through a single-cell bottleneck often enough to generate sufficient relatedness to stabilize cooperation among their cells, given their ecological and physiological circumstances (Grosberg and Strathmann, 2007). If this is correct, then we can endorse

---

[4] There is a long-running debate about whether this process is truly one of reproduction rather than growth, and about whether it produces a new biological individual, but I do not need to take sides on this issue here (Harper, 1977; Janzen, 1977; Fagerström et al., 1998; Pan and Price, 2001; Godfrey-Smith, 2009b; Clarke, 2011, 2012)

Hamilton's claim: the ultimate explanation for the stability of cooperation within multicellular organisms, at least up to a certain size, is genetic relatedness.

This observation has led Grosberg and Strathmann (2007) to suggest that the evolution of multicellularity is no great puzzle at all—that it is a 'minor major transition'. They point out that simple multicellularity has, to our knowledge, arisen around twenty-five times in the history of life on Earth: not very often, but often enough to suggest that we are not dealing with a phenomenon as singular as some of the other 'major transitions', such as the origin of the eukaryotic cell, the origin of sex, or the origin of life itself. Moreover, simple cell aggregates have recently been evolved in the laboratory, often in surprisingly few generations, in various species including the bacteria *M. xanthus* and *Pseudomonas fluorescens*, the green alga *Chlorella vulgaris*, and the budding yeast *Saccharomyces cerevisiae* (Bourke, 2011; Ratcliffe et al., 2012).

So what still needs explaining about the evolution of multicellularity, from the point of view of social evolution theory? As Bourke (2011) has suggested, many of the most tantalizing questions concern the process of social group transformation, by means of which a social group of cells, once formed and stabilized, is transformed over evolutionary time into a multicellular organism with a clear division of labour among distinct cell types. In this context, one particularly interesting question concerns the relationship between the size of a multicellular organism and its complexity. Across all phyla of multicellular organisms, we find a clear positive correlation between the total number of cells an organism contains and the number of distinct, specialized cell types it contains (Bell and Mooers, 1997). What explains this relationship?

A related open question concerns the factors that limit the number of cell types. Grosberg and Strathmann (2007) count twenty-five separate instances of the evolution of simple multicellularity, but in only three of these cases—the plants, animals, and fungi—has the lineage in question proceeded to evolve large numbers of distinct cell types. As Szathmáry and Wolpert (2003, p. 301) note, 'three hits in 3.5 billion years is not that many'. This suggests that evolving high numbers of specialized cell types remains improbable even once a lineage has attained simple multicellularity. Indeed, it suggests that quite restrictive further physiological or ecological conditions are required (Maynard Smith and Szathmáry, 1995). What are these conditions?

Bourke (2011) maintains that a social perspective on the organism can help not only with questions about the evolutionary stability of cooperation among cells, but also with questions such as these—questions that concern the transformation of a social group of cells into a recognizable proto-multicellular organism, replete with division of labour and morphologically differentiated individuals specialized in particular tasks.[5] Here too, he argues, analogies between multicellular organisms and eusocial insect colonies can prove illuminating. I agree, and indeed I think we can develop these analogies even further than Bourke does. That is my aim in the rest of this chapter.

7.4 The Economy of the Cell State: Redundancy, Market Size, and Specialization

Bourke (1999, 2011) argues that the size of a social group and the amount of specialization it contains are connected in a positive feedback loop, whereby greater size enables greater specialization, and greater specialization enables yet greater size. He calls this the 'size-complexity hypothesis' and proposes that it applies to both multicellular organisms and social insect species.[6] In both social insects and multicellular organisms, we see a clear size-complexity trend, with the number of morphological worker-types or cell-types increasing, on average, with group size, and the attraction of the size-complexity hypothesis is that it provides a common explanation for both trends (Bell and Mooers, 1997; Bourke, 2011; Ferguson-Gow et al., 2014). But the nature of the feedback loop is not well understood, and until we understand it better we will not be able to explain why certain phyla of multicellular organisms have attained extremely large sizes and extremely high levels of cell specialization, while others have remained small and with comparatively little differentiation.

---

[5] Michod (1999, 2005, 2006, 2011) has also made a powerful case for this idea, but I focus in this chapter on Bourke's work, which has so far received less attention from philosophers of biology. See Okasha (2006, Ch. 8) and Godfrey-Smith (2011) for discussion of Michod's program.

[6] Sterelny (2012a) argues that a somewhat similar feedback loop was the driving force in human evolution, but there are important differences in the human case (see Section 7.6 of this chapter, as well as Birch, 2013a, for discussion).

In an earlier paper (Birch, 2012), I made an initial attempt at elucidating how Bourke's feedback loop might work, and I now want to revisit and expand that account. The core proposal of my earlier paper was that, as the size of any social group increases, there is typically a transition in the source of robustness with respect to the collaborative tasks the group undertakes. This is inspired by an observation made by George F. Oster and Edward O. Wilson (1978) and Joan M. Herbers (1981) in the context of insect societies.

At a coarse grain of analysis, we can distinguish between two ways in which a group might maintain the robustness of the completion of a collaborative task (e.g. obtaining enough food to feed everyone) in the face of individual failures. One is *functional versatility* at the level of individuals: if an individual fails to perform their part in the task, other individuals modify their behaviour to compensate, and switch tasks if necessary. For example, they might increase their work rate, or abandon other, less important tasks in order to focus on tasks essential to the survival of the group. This source of robustness is especially important in small groups that do not have workers to spare. However, the efficiency of this source of robustness is limited by the costs of switching: a group member who switches between tasks will be restricted in the extent to which they can morphologically specialize in performing one task, and, if the process of switching takes time, they will also spend some of their time not contributing to the productivity of the group.

The second source of robustness, which is especially important in large groups, is *redundancy* in the organizational structure of the workforce. In general, a workforce contains redundancy with respect to a task T when there are more workers available to undertake T than are strictly needed for the completion of T. We see two kinds of redundancy in insect societies. The first sort, *passive* redundancy, occurs when there is a large reserve workforce, idle but ready to step in should any labour shortages arise. This phenomenon is widespread in eusocial societies (Hölldobler and Wilson, 1990, pp. 342–3). The second sort, *active* redundancy, occurs when large numbers of workers actively undertake the same task in parallel, such that the group can tolerate many individuals failing the task, provided enough of them succeed. We see this in the foraging strategies of large ant societies: huge numbers of ants search for food in parallel, then work in parallel to retrieve the food that one individual has found (Oster and Wilson, 1978; Herbers, 1981).

The upshot of organizational redundancy, whether passive or active, is that 'if one worker doesn't complete the task someone else will' (Oster and Wilson, 1978). In other words, task completion becomes more robust, protecting the group against the risk of task failure. Relying on redundancy rather than functional versatility as a source of robustness has distinctive advantages, because it eliminates switching costs and allows for greater morphological specialization. However, it can be inefficient in its use of workers, who spend some of their time idle (in cases of passive redundancy) or performing tasks that a sufficient number of workers are already performing (in cases of active redundancy). These are likely to be serious disadvantages in smaller groups. But as group size increases, it becomes more likely that a group has workers to spare, which makes a transition to this source of robustness possible. It is therefore no surprise that redundancy is more commonly observed in larger insect societies than in smaller ones (Herbers, 1981; Anderson et al., 2001).[7]

Multicellular organisms also rely on organizational redundancy as a source of robustness. We find forms of passive redundancy in simple multicellular organisms: for example, in sponges, in addition to several permanently differentiated cell types, there is (as briefly noted earlier) a cell type called an archaeocyte that can specialize to perform any of the other functions as needed. The role of pluripotent stem cells, such as haematopoietic stem cells, in larger multicellular organisms might be interpreted in a similar way. The role of active redundancy in generating robustness in larger multicellular organisms is plain to see: the number of cells that specialize in a given task often dramatically exceeds the minimum strictly required for its completion. To take a particularly extreme example, the human circulatory system can stand to lose one-eighth of its total stock of red blood cells during a routine blood donation without any adverse effects. In the wild, this excess stock of red blood cells protects multicellular animals against the risk of blood loss through injury. 'Redundancy' might be considered a misnomer for a phenomenon that, as a source of robustness, has an obvious adaptive

---

[7] There is an interesting parallel here with the work of Wagner (1999, 2005a, b), who suggests that the redundancy of genes in genetic networks may to some extent be explicable as an adaptation for promoting the robustness of development in the face of mutation. Here, however, I am considering the redundancy of cells in a multicellular organism, and more generally the redundancy of actors in a social group, rather than the redundancy of genes.

function. To be clear, however, in calling the surplus cells 'redundant', I am not claiming they are functionless; rather, my claim is that their function is to generate redundancy in the organizational structure of a task, in this case oxygen transport, so that it can still be completed when many of its workers are lost.

My hypothesis is that in proto-multicellular organisms, as in social insects, the evolutionary relationship between size and specialization is mediated by redundancy: larger groups can sustain greater levels of redundancy; this makes them less reliant on functional versatility as a source of robustness; and this enables them to evolve more extreme forms of specialization that sacrifice functional versatility for the sake of improved efficiency at task completion. This improved efficiency allows the group to meet its needs more easily, enabling a further increase in the size of the group, which in turn leads to a greater number of spare workers and the possibility of sustaining yet greater levels of redundancy.[8]

However, there is more to be said here. As Anderson et al. (2001) and McShea (2002) have noted, a specialized workforce may exhibit *less* complexity at the individual level, as measured by the number of recognizably distinct parts an individual contains or by the number of recognizably distinct behaviours it can perform: a phenomenon McShea calls a 'complexity drain'. We see evidence of this in multicellular organisms, since their cells tend to have fewer parts on average than unicellular eukaryotes (McShea, 2002). Red blood cells are an extreme example: they are, individually, far less complex than any free-living unicellular organism, lacking nuclei, mitochondria, ribosomes, lysosomes, and Golgi complexes. Many other animal cell types, while retaining these parts, have dispensed with parts such as flagellae. As McShea (2002) suggests, this may be a common by-product of specialization: as a cell-type

---

[8] The 'proximate' literature on division of labour in social insects contains ingenious attempts to model the process of self-organization whereby division of labour emerges from simple individual-level behavioural rules, or 'response thresholds'. A model of this sort by Jeanson et al. (2007) gives a role to group size: the idea is that, as group size increases, there are more tasks to be performed but reduced demand for work relative to the size of the workforce (i.e. greater redundancy), with the result that tasks tend to be undertaken by workers with a preference for that particular task. However, this model does not incorporate evolutionary processes. My hypothesis here is that, over evolutionary timescales, greater redundancy would lead to the evolution of morphologically differentiated task specialists. Recent work by Duarte et al. (2011, 2012) attempts to integrate proximate models of self-organization with evolutionary models, although without (yet) incorporating group size effects. This may provide an attractive framework in which to investigate more formally the feedback hypothesis set out qualitatively here.

becomes more specialized for a particular task, those parts it contains that are dispensable with respect to that task become maladaptive (they still require energy to maintain, but they no longer contribute to its functioning), and selection favours processes of cell differentiation in which functionally dispensable parts are lost.

There are limits to this complexity drain, since most cells need to retain a core set of parts to perform basic 'housekeeping functions' such as respiration, but McShea argues persuasively that there is a trend here, and that it applies to plants as well as to animals (he does not discuss its applicability to fungi). This loss of physical parts as group size increases seems likely to feed back into group size, by reducing the cost of producing new cells. It may also have positive effects on their reliability, since fewer parts implies less that can go wrong. If so, this would further promote the efficiency of task completion, further promoting an increase in the size of the group.

These considerations help explain why increasing size may promote greater specialization in specific tasks, and why this may feed back into further group size increases. They do not, however, shed much light on the *number* of distinct specialisms we should expect to find. Why do larger groups tend to contain more specialisms? The crucial factor here, I suggest, is market size. New specialisms can evolve only if there is a sufficiently large 'market' in the economy of the cell state for their services, and this becomes more likely as group size increases. For example, it is adaptive to have a population of specialist cells dedicated to the storage and release of insulin only if there is adequate demand for insulin to make use of the supply provided by those cells, and this implies a lower bound on group size before such a cell type can evolve. This may help explain why, although insulin-like molecules exist in the endocrine systems of invertebrates such as molluscs and insects, we do not find cells specializing in the secretion of this hormone, as we do in vertebrates, which tend to be larger (Ebberink et al., 1989; Reinecke and Collet, 1998).

The feedback loop in Figure 7.1 combines all of these considerations into a single hypothesis. The figure should be understood as an elaboration of Bourke's size-complexity hypothesis. Like Bourke's version, it is intended to be sufficiently abstract to apply to both eusocial insect colonies and multicellular organisms, and to shed light on the size-complexity trend we see in both contexts. It is important to note that the arrows in the figure represent hypothesized *enabling* relationships (e.g. the reduced need for functional versatility enables the evolution of a larger number

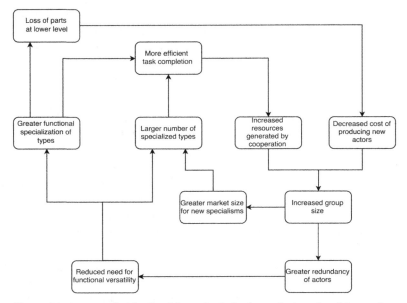

Figure 7.1 An expanded feedback hypothesis for the evolution of social complexity. The arrows represent hypothesized enabling relationships, e.g. greater market size for new specialisms enables the evolution of a larger number of specialized types.

of specialized cell types), not relationships of necessitation. An enabling relationship makes it possible for a new trait to evolve if the ecological conditions are right, but it does not guarantee the presence of those conditions. As I will argue in the next section, this is crucial in explaining why very high levels of specialization have rarely been achieved in phyla that have evolved multicellularity. The size-complexity feedback loop is not a recipe for a 'runaway selection' process; it is a fragile mechanism that can easily stall.

7.5 Limits to the Number of Cell Types

Let us now return to the puzzle introduced earlier in the chapter. This hypothesis, if it is on the right lines, may shed light on why the evolution of complex multicellularity (and indeed complex eusociality) has been so rare in the history of life.

The key here is to understand the arrows in the model represent enabling relationships, not relationships of causal sufficiency or necessitation. For example, increasing the market size for new specialisms merely enables the evolution of a larger number of cell types—it does not necessitate it. It is still crucial that the ecological circumstances confer an advantage on groups with a larger number of cell types, and this will not always be the case.

As Grosberg and Strathmann (2007, p. 643) argue, part of the explanation for the rarity of complex multicellularity may be:

a lack of selective pressure or trade-offs. For example, the vertebrate immune system generates different cells in indefinite variety because variety is favored by selection. We expect that functional requirements limit the number of cell types in organisms that develop from a single cell. . . . Once the major functional specializations are satisfied, there is presumably a diminishing return in added capabilities from each additional cell type.

Grosberg and Strathmann's point here is simply that we should not expect more specialized types to evolve, even when the need for versatility is removed, if the evolution of new specialized types would not increase the efficiency with which tasks are completed. Further specialization is not always advantageous.

For a suggestive example, consider the colour photoreceptors, or cone cells, of the mammalian eye. Most placental mammals are dichromats: they have two types of cone cell. Why not more? After all, further specialization is quite possible here: there are plenty more regions of the electromagnetic spectrum to specialize in, and room for more fine-grained specialization at visible wavelengths. Primates, including humans, have an extra type of cone cell (allowing most of us to discriminate red from green), and various species of bird, fish, and reptile have been found to have four. The explanation for dichromacy in placental mammals may simply be that having two-types of cone cell efficiently meets their ecological needs: adding another would require devoting more time and energy to the processing of visual information, and the benefits would not outweigh the costs.

While I agree with Grosberg and Strathmann about the limited advantage of specialization beyond a certain level, I think there is more to say here about the factors that make complex multicellularity so rare. In particular, we should consider the factors that limit the loss of parts at the lower level, and we should also pay attention to the role of redundancy in mediating the relationship between increased group size and loss of functional versatility.

In a sense, the limitations on a complexity drain are easy to see. An actor specializing in a particular task cannot afford to lose parts that are indispensable to the performance of that task. So a complexity drain can occur only if the task in which the actor specializes is simple enough to make at least one of its parts functionally dispensable. The red blood cell is (once again) a clear illustration: it is only because its task (the carrying of oxygen and carbon dioxide) is simple enough to require no nucleus that it has lost this part. This is an exceptional case. On the whole, the cells of a multicellular organism retain what McShea (2002) calls a 'standard set' of parts including a nucleus, mitochondria, ribosomes, and Golgi apparatus. This provides one reason why at least part of the feedback loop might stop: there may come a point at which actors no longer have any more parts or capacities to lose, because any further losses would impair their ability to perform the tasks for which they are specialized. This will then limit any further reduction in the cost of producing new actors.

Let us turn now to the idea, central to my feedback loop, that increasing group size enables greater organizational redundancy. This relies on the idea that, as task efficiency and group size increase, the number of 'workers to spare' (i.e. the number of workers the group can afford to hold in reserve, or to put towards the parallel performance of the same tasks) will increase. There is some evidence that this is indeed the case in insect societies (Jeanson et al., 2007). But there is no reason to suppose it is a necessary truth about biological systems. It requires that each new actor, on average, contributes more to the productivity of the group than it takes from the group's resources. If there comes a point at which the burden a new actor imposes on the group tends to exceed its contribution to the group's productivity (e.g. because the group must explore a larger and larger area to feed its members, so that new members become increasingly hard to support), the number of redundant workers may be eroded with group size, and the feedback loop may stop.

We should also revisit in this context the relationship between passive and active redundancy. Reliance on passive redundancy, in the form of a versatile reserve workforce, imposes limits on morphological specialization. Some workers may be highly specialized, but the reserve workers must be versatile enough to step in as needed. This constrains both the extent to which these workers can specialize and the extent to which tasks can require specialist abilities. By contrast, active redundancy, of the sort we see on a dramatic scale in larger multicellular animals, enables more extreme specialization. However, active redundancy has its own disadvantages. Workers actively doing work will tend to require more energy than idle reserve workers. Moreover, more workers are likely to be needed: a full reliance on active redundancy requires that every essential task has an excess of workers participating in it, whereas passive redundancy requires only that there are enough excess workers to maintain a reserve workforce. This provides a tentative reason to hypothesize that active redundancy is only sustainable in very large groups, and that a reliance on passive redundancy is a transitional phase, commonly found in groups of intermediate size, on the road from a total (or near-total) reliance on the functional versatility of unspecialized workers to a near-total reliance on active redundancy in task structures ('near-total' because even large multicellular animals have some passive redundancy, as noted earlier).

This line of argument may help shed light on the presence of a large reserve workforce in eusocial insect species. Even the most complex maintain a large reserve workforce of significant versatility, in addition to active redundancy in foraging strategies (Oster and Wilson, 1978; Anderson and McShea, 2001). This may be because, large as these colonies are, they are not large enough to have achieved a full transition to active redundancy. Similar considerations may also help shed light on the function of the archaeocyte in sponges.

To sum up, there is no reason to think that the size-complexity feedback loop will carry on ratcheting up indefinitely. The links describe enabling relationships, some of which are quite fragile, and not relationships of necessitation. We can understand how the loop works, when it works. But I think we can also see various different kinds of circumstance in which it would not work, or in which it would work for a while but then stop. I see this as a virtue of the hypothesis. A cast-iron engine of complexity is not what we want, because it would fail to explain the rarity with which large numbers of specialized actor-types are achieved in nature. To explain that rarity, we need an engine that can easily stall.

I have focussed in this section on the ecological factors that may cause the number of specialized cell types in a multicellular organism to stop at a relatively small number, but I should note that developmental factors are surely also a very important part of the picture. In the special case of the radiation of the bilaterians (i.e. organisms with bilateral symmetry) in the Cambrian, which led, uniquely in the history of life, to the evolution of organisms containing over 100 distinct cell types, it seems likely that a unique set of developmental changes were involved. Carroll, Davidson, Sterelny, and others have argued that a 'developmental revolution', characterized by delayed cell differentiation in a pattern determined by a cell's region in the embryo, rather than by local signalling patterns, was critical to this transition (Carroll, 2001, 2005; Erwin and Davidson, 2002; Peterson and Davidson, 2000; Sterelny, 2007). I regard my approach, based on the 'economy of the cell state' and its workforce, as complementary to approaches based on developmental considerations. Both provide illuminating perspectives on the evolution of multicellularity.

7.6 Other Major Transitions

Although I have not attempted to make a detailed empirical case for the size-complexity feedback model here, it does seem to me that several important lines of evidence tell in its favour. First, there is the evidence for a link between group size and social complexity (measured in terms of number of actor types), comprehensively surveyed by Bourke (2011). Second, there are the correlations between group size and redundancy in cooperative tasks, and between social complexity and the loss of totipotency on the part of individual social actors, as surveyed by Anderson and McShea (2001). Third, there is the evidence of a complexity drain (measured in terms of loss of parts) in the cells of multicellar organisms, as presented by McShea (2002). So although I have characterized my hypothesis as speculative, this should not be taken to imply that it has no empirical support.

The best sort of evidence for the hypothesis would be experimental. So far, attempts to evolve multicellularity in the lab have resulted in simple cell aggregates. Ratcliff et al. (2012) report evolving a simple form of 'specialization' in budding yeast, in which some cells undergo apoptosis (programmed cell death) more readily in a way that aids the fragmentation, and hence 'reproduction', of the multicellular group. But this is not morphological specialization for complex tasks, of the sort we find in complex multicellular organisms, and to evolve this remains a major challenge for further experimental work. If it turns out to be possible, then we may find ourselves in a position to perform direct tests of hypotheses regarding the origins of multicellularity.

I want to close by considering the potential applicability of the same model to other evolutionary transitions. The focus of this chapter has been on the evolution of multicellularity. That said, in arguing for the utility of a social perspective on the multicellular organism, I have emphasized the parallels that can be drawn with the evolution of eusociality, and I have proposed that the basic feedback loop outlined earlier may have operated in both cases. This naturally leads to the thought that the feedback model may offer a general account of so-called 'fraternal' transitions, in which the social groups that come to constitute new, higher-level organisms are composed of units related by kinship (Queller, 1997, 2000; Birch, 2012).[9]

The evolution of multicellularity and eusociality are two prominent examples of this, but they they are not the only examples. Another is the origin of the first protocells. Maynard Smith and Szathmáry (1995, p. 41) hypothesized that the evolution of division of labour among replicating molecules in compartments may have involved 'processes analogous to kin selection', whereby limited dispersal led to similarity between interacting replicators, helping to stabilize a form of altruism (Maynard Smith and Szathmáry, 1995, p. 41). The basic idea is that some replicators may have sacrificed their own replicative capacity in order to catalyse the replication of other, similar replicators, giving rise to a rudimentary division of replicative labour, and ultimately to recognizable protocells. Could the feedback model apply to this transition?

As much as I would like this to be the case, the evolution of protocells presents its own distinctive problems. For example, Maynard Smith and Szathmáry's kin selection hypothesis regarding the origin of protocells is closely tied up with the 'stochastic corrector model', which aims to explain the persistence of a division of replicative labour across the generations by appealing to the stochastic nature of protocell division (which leads to at least some offspring groups possessing the same number of altruistic replicators as the parent, even when altruists replicate more slowly than non-altruists), together with selection for groups with the optimal composition (Szathmáry, 1986; Szathmáry and Demeter, 1987; Maynard Smith

---

[9] 'Sororal' might be a better term, given that workers in insect societies are female, but the 'fraternal' terminology appears to have stuck.

and Szathmáry, 1995). However, the stochastic corrector model relies on small group size. If the group size is too large, the frequency of altruistic replicators in daughter cells becomes less variable, the 'stochastic corrector' effect becomes weaker, and the division of labour becomes less stable. In short, the need for a stochastic corrector effect limits the size a social group can attain while maintaining reliable inheritance of a division of labour. This marks an important difference with the case of multicellularity. To understand the relationship between size and complexity in protocells, we would need to take account of the way increasing group size might erode the heritability of altruism.

Finally, I want to comment briefly on the case of humans. Might human evolution fit the model? Although some authors, notably including Edward O. Wilson and David Sloan Wilson, have attached great weight to parallels between the evolution of human sociality and the evolution of insect eusociality, I think there is a danger of overstating these parallels (Wilson and Wilson, 2007; Wilson, 2012). True, humans throughout much of their history lived in small, close-knit bands with non-zero (though probably not high; see Chapters 2 and 8) genetic relatedness. And true, they achieved a substantial degree of social complexity, characterized by impressive degrees of division of labour, specialization, and coordination, during that time. But we should not lose sight of the differences. Morphological differentiation in humans is nothing like as extreme as that found in eusocial colonies, let alone multicellular organisms. With the exception of sexual dimorphism, we remain more or less totipotent, in the sense that we are biologically capable of taking on any social role. We have not lost parts; we have not undergone a complexity drain. And although human societies are now very large, this is an aberration in evolutionary terms: for the vast majority of our history our groups were small, numbering in the hundreds or less.

Sterelny (2012a) has argued that there may have been an interesting role for redundancy, enabled by increased group size, in early human social evolution. However, the main role he has in mind differs from the role of redundancy in my feedback model. For Sterelny, the main role of redundancy was to generate robustness in the process of social learning. Crucial specialist skills and knowledge, rather than being stored in a single head, could be stored in multiple heads, preventing information from being lost if skilled practitioners were accidentally killed. Sterelny (2012a) goes so far as to suggest that this effect may even help explain why *Homo sapiens* survived when the Neanderthals went extinct.

Plainly, this is not the same role that redundancy plays in my feedback loop, which is the role of providing robust task completion without the need for functionally versatile actors, thereby enabling the evolution of distinct morphological types. Might redundancy also have played this role in humans? This seems unlikely on the face of it, since, as noted earlier, the evolution of distinct morphological types has not occurred to any substantial degree in humans, perhaps because our social groups were never large enough to enable it. Human agents remain extremely versatile, although some of the foregoing considerations may apply to the non-genetic, cultural specialization of actors in particular skills (such as the manufacture of particular types of stone tool).

In short, despite the suggestive similarities with the evolution of eusociality and multicellularity, the evolution of human societies poses its own distinctive problems, which require their own distinctive solutions. In the former two cases, we are faced with genetically inherited altruism, stabilized by genetic relatedness, in very large, morphologically differentiated groups. In the human case, the groups are much smaller, genetic relatedness is much lower, the agents are intelligent and versatile, and the traits tend to be socially learned. Yet this does not make relatedness irrelevant—or so I will argue in the book's final chapter.

7.7 Summary of Chapter 7

In the nineteenth century, the idea of the multicellular organism as a 'cell state' was widespread. Although it fell out of favour in the twentieth century, three recent trends suggest that a social perspective on the organism is due a revival: our growing understanding of microbial cooperation, the resurgence of the 'superorganism' concept, and the 'major transitions' research program.

From the perspective of social evolution theory, the stability of cooperation within clonal groups of cells is no mystery, since their inclusive fitness interests are aligned. However, the process of social group transformation, by means of which a social group of cells, once formed and stabilized, is transformed over evolutionary time into a multicellular organism with a division of labour among multiple cell types, remains mysterious.

In both multicellular organisms and eusocial insects, the size of a group and the amount of specialization it contains are closely linked. This leads to the puzzle of what explains this relationship, and the further puzzle of why simple forms of multicellularity have only rarely evolved into more complex forms with large numbers of specialized cell types. As Bourke (2011) has argued, positive feedback is likely to be crucial in explaining the relationship between size and complexity, and a social perspective on the organism helps us understand this feedback loop. I have set out an expanded feedback loop on which the relationship between group size and specialization is mediated by the degree of redundancy (which may be either passive or active) in task structures.

In brief, greater morphological specialization enables more efficient task completion, and more efficient task completion enables an increase in group size, which enables greater redundancy in task structures, which reduces the need for functional versatility on the part of individual actors, allowing for yet greater morphological specialization. Meanwhile, group size also increases the market size for new specialisms. At the same time, greater specialization can sometimes cause the loss of functionally redundant parts at the lower level (McShea, 2002), feeding back into group size by making new actors cheaper for the group to produce.

The links in this feedback loop should be understood as enabling relationships rather than relationships of causal sufficiency, and the loop will only operate if the ecological conditions are right. For example, new cell types will not evolve unless there is an ecological need for them, and increased group size will not lead to greater redundancy unless each new actor adds more to the productivity of the group than it consumes. Active redundancy is likely to be particularly difficult to maintain, and requires particularly large groups. Such considerations may help explain why the evolution of simple multicellularity only rarely leads to complex multicellular forms with large numbers of cell types.

While the hypothesis remains speculative, several lines of evidence tell in its favour. Moreover, although it is mainly intended as an hypothesis regarding the origin of complex multicellularity, it may also help shed light on the evolution of complex eusociality. That said, it is not a general theory of major transitions. Other transitions, such as the origin of division of labour among replicators in compartments, and the origin of human sociality, pose their own distinctive problems.

8

Cultural Relatedness and Human Social Evolution

8.1 Broad-Scope Prosocial Preferences

As Haldane (1955) observed, in the passage quoted at the start of this book, humans often set aside their own self-interest in order to help others. This behaviour is not rare or exceptional, and it need not take the form of dramatic acts of altruism, such as jumping into a river to save a drowning child. Over the past thirty years, experimental studies have gradually revealed the extent to which unselfish behaviour is a routine aspect of human social life. We are disposed to cooperate with others, and to punish those who do not cooperate, even if this cooperation or punishment comes at a cost, even if there is no possibility of reputational effects, and even if the people we help or punish are strangers with whom we have never interacted before and with whom we may never interact again (for an overview, see Bowles and Gintis, 2011, Ch. 3).

Consider, for example, a game commonly used in such studies: the ultimatum game. There are two players. Player 1 decides how to divide a sum of money between the two players. Player 2 must then decide whether to accept or refuse the proposed division. If Player 2 refuses, both players receive nothing. If both agents were rational and self-interested, and if their rational self-interest were a matter of common knowledge, Player 1 would make the lowest possible offer to Player 2, and Player 2 would always accept that offer. Numerous experiments have shown that a large fraction of human subjects depart systematically from self-interest in ultimatum games.[1] The mean offer from Player 1 is around 40% of the sum

---

[1] Landmarks in the experimental literature on ultimatum games include Güth et al. (1982); Binmore et al. (1985); Kahneman et al. (1986); Ochs and Roth (1989); Henrich (2000), and Sanfey et al. (2003). For an overview of the key findings, see Camerer (2003); Oosterbeek et al. (2004).

of money, and players in the Player 2 role tend to reject offers that they perceive as unfair, which happens in about 16% of cases (Camerer, 2003; Oosterbeek et al., 2004). In the ultimatum game, then, we see two kinds of deviation from self-interest: a tendency to cooperate even when one stands to gain by not doing so, and a tendency to punish non-cooperators (through the rejection of an unfair offer) even at a cost to oneself.[2] Experiments with public goods games have elicited similar tendencies. Here too, people cooperate to a much greater extent than one would expect from purely self-interested rational agents, although agents vary substantially in their willingness to cooperate, and the level of cooperation declines over time in repeated public goods games, suggesting that the tendency to cooperate is conditional on how others behave (Fischbacher et al., 2001). Moreover, here too there is a strong tendency to punish free riders who contribute nothing to the public good (Fehr and Gächter, 2000).

I will refer to the combination of these two tendencies as the phenomenon of *broad-scope prosocial preferences*. 'Prosocial' because, in promoting cooperation and punishing failures to cooperate, the preferences agents express in these experiments display a systematic bias in favour of cooperation. 'Broad-scope' because these prosocial preferences not only encompass interactions with close kin, repeated interactions, and interactions with reputational effects, but also appear to encompass one-off interactions with strangers.[3]

Evidence from experimental games is not enough to show that these preferences are *altruistic*, or even *cooperative*, in the technical sense of these terms introduced in Chapter 1.[4] To show that they are cooperative, one would need to show that they belong to a strategy that has, in recent evolutionary history, been maintained by selection in virtue of its positive effect on the reproductive success of other agents. To show that they are

---

[2] These tendencies, which are entangled in the ultimatum game, can be disentangled using different games. Dictator games isolate the first tendency, while third-party punishment games isolate the second (see Camerer, 2003). On public goods games, which are more directly relevant to the discussion of Section 8.4, see Ledyard (1995); Fehr and Gächter (2000); Fischbacher et al. (2001); Fehr and Fischbacher (2003).

[3] Gintis (2000); Fehr et al. (2002); Bowles and Gintis (2011), and collaborators refer to these preferences as 'strong reciprocity', but I find this term misleading: talk of 'reciprocity' suggests behaviour that is conditional on repeated interactions or reputational effects, and the point is precisely that this behaviour does not have this pattern.

[4] West et al. (2011) also make this point.

altruistic, one would have to additionally show that they were maintained by selection despite causally detracting from the reproductive success of the actor. I suspect that these things may well be the case—with the qualification that the form of 'selection' in question is a form of cultural selection (see Section 8.3)—and I therefore suspect that these preferences are indeed altruistic. Even so, it is important to note that experimental games alone do not establish this.

The existence of such preferences, in one form or another, appears to be a cross-culturally robust phenomenon. Experiments testing for prosocial preferences were originally carried out, like most psychology experiments, on samples from predominantly 'WEIRD' (white, educated, industrialized, rich, and democratic) populations (Henrich et al., 2010b). However, in two separate comparative studies, Henrich et al. (2004, 2010a) investigated behaviour in experimental games, including the ultimatum game, in fifteen small-scale societies from around the world. In all societies, agents tended to make offers above the minimum in the ultimatum game, deviating from self-interest in a way that indicates prosocial preferences. There is substantial variation across (and indeed within) cultures in the nature of these preferences, but their existence seems to be a cultural universal.[5]

In a sense this is unsurprising, since prosocial preferences play a pivotal role in holding any human society together. In modern nation states, state-backed coercion imposes a limit on the extent to which it is rational for a purely self-interested agent to free ride, since such an agent would want to avoid fines, prison sentences, and other sanctions. However, at least outside of totalitarian regimes, coercion never completely eliminates the incentive to free ride. A purely self-interested agent would not buy a ticket to travel on a route they knew to have no ticket inspectors, would not work harder than necessary when unsupervised, would not vote in an election if the probability of swinging the outcome was negligible, and would never donate blood. The fact that we do not all behave like this, all of the time, is crucial to the functioning of society. This 'everyday prosociality' is the glue that, in myriad ways, holds human communities together (Bowles and Gintis, 2011).

---

[5] The question of how the variance 'between cultures' compares to the variance between individuals within a culture remains a source of heated debate; see Lamba and Mace (2011, 2012); Henrich et al. (2012).

It seems likely that broad-scope prosocial preferences would have been even more important in holding together the very earliest human societies, prior to the existence of states. In these societies there was no state-backed coercion to speak of, and the only punishment of free riders would have been carried out by coalitions of individuals, potentially at a cost to themselves, which would itself have been a prosocial act. So it seems reasonable to hypothesize that robust prosocial preferences were already present in Palaeolithic human societies, and that their apparent ubiquity in present-day societies is explained at least in part by common descent from these early ancestors. Yet they appear to be absent in our closest living relatives, suggesting they originated after the divergence of the hominin lineage from the other great apes (Jensen et al., 2007).

Assuming that broad-scope prosocial preferences do indeed have a deep history, we are led to the question of how they originated in early human populations. I take it for granted here that the explanation for prosocial preferences in humans involves cultural, and not simply genetic, processes of inheritance (Richerson and Boyd, 1998, 2005; Boyd et al., 2003; Gintis, 2003; Henrich, 2004; Bowles and Gintis, 2011). Culture may not be the whole story, but it is at least part of the story.[6] We have the beliefs, desires, preferences, and normative attitudes we have at least in part because of our interactions with other members of society. We observe others, we learn from others, and we internalize the norms of our community. This is reinforced by the aforementioned evidence that, despite the cross-cultural robustness of prosocial preferences of one form or another, the precise form these preferences take (e.g. as manifested by behaviour in the ultimatum game) varies substantially across cultures (Henrich, 2000; Bowles and Gintis, 2011).

Acknowledging the importance of cultural inheritance in explaining broad-scope prosocial behaviour leaves two possibilities regarding the proper role of evolutionary theory. One is that its role should be restricted to that of explaining the origin of the basic cognitive capacities that make culture of any kind possible: mechanisms of learning, language, and so on. On this view, once these core capacities are in place, evolutionary theory

---

[6] I am sympathetic to the notion of 'gene-culture co-evolution' (Richerson and Boyd, 2005; Bowles and Gintis, 2011), but it is not my focus here. I focus in this chapter on cultural evolution, before briefly considering (in Section 8.6) how genetic evolution might react to the cultural evolutionary processes I have considered.

should take a back seat, so that explanatory frameworks better suited to explaining cultural change can take over. The other possibility is that evolutionary theory has a more substantial role to play: that, in addition to explaining the origins of culture, it can also shed light on the population-level dynamics of cultural change, and thus on the circumstances in which cultural processes might help stabilize prosocial preferences.

Over the last few decades, a great deal of work has explored the second possibility (landmarks include Cavalli-Sforza and Feldman, 1981; Boyd and Richerson, 1985, 2005; Bowles and Gintis, 2011). This work is not uncontroversial: indeed, the very idea of 'cultural evolution' remains controversial in some quarters (see Lewens, 2013 for an overview). This is partly due to its association with Dawkins's (1976) meme concept, which many cultural evolution theorists now reject. My aim in this chapter is not to dissect these criticisms or to defend cultural evolution theory against its critics: I leave that to others (Richerson and Boyd, 2005; Mesoudi, 2011; Laland and Brown, 2011; Lewens, 2015). I will instead assume the basic legitimacy of drawing on evolutionary theory to help explain cultural change, in order to consider a much more specific question: to what extent can the ideas that have been the focus of this book—in particular, relatedness and Hamilton's rule—be usefully applied to the cultural evolution of broad-scope prosocial behaviour?

In the context of early human populations, the problem of explaining broad-scope prosocial preferences can be usefully recast as the problem of explaining prosocial preferences that extend beyond the limits of one's residential camp, or 'band'. The ethnographic record of present-day hunter-gatherer societies indicates typical camp sizes of 20–30, with a maximum of about 100 (Binford, 2001; Marlowe, 2005; Bowles and Gintis, 2011; Boehm, 2012). Camps are typically composed of multiple families, and migration from one camp to another is frequent. We should be cautious about inferring anything about population structure in ancestral populations from modern-day hunter-gatherer societies, which tend to have a history of interaction with settled agragrian societies and tend to exist on the margins of such societies, in environments that would not have been typical in the Palaeolithic. That said, it seems reasonable to take the available ethnographic evidence as a starting point for our purposes.

Sterelny (2012a, 2016) has argued that cooperation *within bands* can be explained largely by immediate returns, and I am inclined to agree.

Members of the same would have collaborated in tasks such as the hunting of big game, and the profits of collaboration would have been immediately shared among the participants. Unreliable cooperators would have found themselves excluded from these collaborative projects and unable to share directly in their profits. Reciprocity, both direct and indirect, may also have been important: these mechanisms are known to be effective in small, close-knit groups in which individuals interact repeatedly and information about past behaviour is readily available (Bowles and Gintis, 2011). It is, however, in the context of interactions between bands that 'one-shot interactions with strangers' would have been more likely to arise.

Drawing on studies of social networks in industrialized societies, foraging societies, and non-human primates, Clive Gamble and colleagues (2014) argue that humans have cognitive adaptations for maintaining communities (or 'effective' social networks) of approximately 150 individuals and super-communities (or 'extended' social networks) of approximately 450–500 individuals (see also Dunbar, 1992, 1998; Gamble, 1998, 1999). I will take this as a second starting point. For if we compare these estimates with typical estimates of the size of residential bands, we see straight away that, if they are even approximately correct, the social networks of Palaeolithic foragers must have extended well beyond their local residential group. The effective network of 150 might have consisted primarily of members of one's band, plus other individuals with whom one had been co-resident in the past. But the extended network of 450–500 must have included more remote connections: friends of friends, cousins of cousins, virtual strangers with whom one would very rarely interact. We can therefore put our question regarding the origin of broad-scope prosocial preferences like this: what might have promoted and stabilized prosocial preferences that encompassed interactions with individuals outside one's effective social network?

Could genetic relatedness have played a role? The idea that genes for altruism can be selected by virtue of genetic relatedness between actors and recipients has been central to all the preceding chapters of this book. Yet important as this is in explaining altruistic behaviour throughout the natural world, it seems to be of limited relevance in the context of human sociality, because there is evidence that genetic relatedness would already have been very low within bands, let alone between members of neighbouring bands. In a cross-cultural study of thirty-two present-day hunter-gatherer societies, Kim R. Hill and colleagues (2011) document that 'primary kin generally make up less than 10% of a residential band' (p. 1288) and estimate that in the Ache, a hunter-gatherer population in the Amazon, genetic relatedness between interacting agents within bands is only around 0.05. The fundamental reason for this low relatedness is intermarriage between bands, which typically leads to either the male or female moving. Bearing in mind the standard caveats about inferring ancestral social structure from present-day hunter-gatherers, the proper message to take from this study is not that genetic relatedness in early human bands was certainly low, but rather that we cannot safely assume that it was even moderately high (e.g. $r > 0.1$), given the ethnographic reality of stable hunter-gatherer societies with low within-band genetic relatedness.

Here, however, an attractive thought arises. If broad-scope prosocial preferences are culturally transmitted, then perhaps it was always mis-guided to look to *genetic* relatedness for an explanation of their evolutionary stability. Perhaps a form of *cultural* relatedness is what really matters in the cultural case. Perhaps cultural relatedness can be high where genetic relatedness is low, and perhaps it can help to stabilize costly prosocial preferences in much the same way genetic relatedness helps to stabilize altruism-promoting genes. I will call this the *cultural relatedness hypothesis* for the evolution of broad-scope social preferences.

This idea has a history in cultural evolution theory: Luigi Luca Cavalli-Sforza and Marcus W. Feldman (1981) discussed cultural relatedness under the heading of 'cultural inbreeding'; Paul D. Allison (1992a, b) developed a formal treatment of cultural relatedness and linked it to the evolution of altruism in much the same way I do here; and, more recently, concepts of cultural relatedness have featured in papers by Lehmann and Feldman (2008), and Claire El Mouden and colleagues (2014), as well as in an unpublished paper by Tom Wenseleers, Siegfried Dewitte, and Andreas De Block. For all that, the cultural relatedness hypothesis remains a comparatively neglected idea. My aim in this chapter is to articulate a version of it—and then to defend it.

8.2 Cultural Variants

Before we can consider the relationship between cultural relatedness and cultural selection, we must get a grip on what we mean by 'cultural selection'. In very broad terms, I take cultural selection to mean selection on differences between individuals with respect to their *cultural variants*. There is an ambiguity here between two possible meanings of 'selection', which I will revisit in due course, but first I must address a prior question: *what is a cultural variant?*

I propose the following, four-part definition: a cultural variant is (i) a property of an individual that (ii) varies between individuals, (iii) originates, at least in part, in a process of social learning, and that (iv) admits of a quantitative characterization. This definition is deliberately minimal. The requirement that a cultural variant 'admits of a quantitative characterization' is necessary if we want to make models of how variant frequencies change over time, but it is not a very onerous requirement. In the case of an 'all-or-nothing' property, we can simply define a dummy variable that takes the value 1 if an individual has the property and 0 otherwise; this is a common technique in the cultural evolution literature.

Paradigm cases of cultural variants are mental representations, such as beliefs, desires, plans, values, or pieces of know-how.[7] Mental representations that come naturally in degrees, such as degrees of belief, are cultural variants par excellence. On this point I am broadly aligned with Peter J. Richerson and Robert Boyd (2005, p. 61), who write that 'culture is (mostly) information stored in human brains, and gets transmitted from brain to brain by a variety of social learning processes'. That said, I see no reason why cultural variants *must* be mental states: to the extent that they are mental states in paradigm cases, this represents a contingent fact about the form socially learned properties tend to take in humans.

We should, I think, leave room for cultural variants that are external and non-mental: for example, the shape of a pandanus leaf tool constructed by a New Caledonian crow might be a well-defined cultural variant, if it turns out to originate at least partly in social learning, and if it can be given a quantitative characterization (Holzhaider et al., 2010). If one prefers human examples, the same might be said of the shape of an Acheulean handaxe (Lycett, 2008). In general, I contend that cultural evolution theorists are under no obligation to delimit sharply the variables that may be modelled as cultural variants. On the contrary, it is right

---

[7] The idea that know-how consists of mental representations is controversial, but that is not a debate I intend to weigh into here (see e.g. Stanley, 2011; Levy, 2017).

to remain open-minded as regards the kinds of properties that originate in social learning and that admit of a quantitative characterization. The notion of a cultural variant, or a cultural trait, has attracted criticism from anthropologists (e.g. Ingold, 2007) who see it as little more than a re-labelling of Dawkins's (1976) meme concept, and as a way of diminishing the role of human agency—a way of reducing agents to the status of mere vehicles built for the transmission of selfish replicators. The minimal conception of a cultural variant outlined earlier should make it clear why this worry is misplaced. Suppose, for example, that the cultural variant we are interested in modelling is an individual's degree of belief in a proposition k—for example, the proposition that one ought to help unknown individuals when they are in need.[8] This is a good, well-defined cultural variant, provided every individual in the population has a determinate degree of belief in k. Yet it would be a mistake to conclude from this that degrees of belief are 'selfish replicators', or that individuals are somehow mere vehicles of their degrees of belief. The fact that a degree of belief is a well-defined cultural variant is compatible with every individual arriving at its degree of belief by a complex process of learning and rational reflection, and not by a process that is in any sense one of mere copying. It is true that cultural evolution theory does not aim to provide a mechanistic account of this process, but this is a deliberate choice rather than a failure of the theory. Cultural evolution theory, like population genetics, intentionally abstracts away from individual-level processes in order to study the population-level processes by means of which the distributions of properties change over time (Richerson and Boyd, 2005; Lewens, 2015).

8.3 Two Types of Cultural Selection

With this notion of a cultural variant in hand, it is helpful to distinguish between two types of Darwinian process that may act on differences in cultural variants, and that are deserving of the name 'cultural selection'. The first—which I will call type-1 cultural selection, or CS_1—occurs when phenotypic differences that are *culturally transmitted from parents to offspring* cause differences in *reproductive success*. The idea here is that, just

---

[8] Conventionally, philosophers use 'p' to denote an arbitrary proposition, but 'p' is chronically overworked in this book and needs a rest.

as in a traditional process of natural selection, phenotypic differences cause differences in the number of offspring an organism produces. However, unlike in a traditional process of natural selection, the phenotypic differences are explained by underlying differences in cultural variants, not genes, and they are transmitted from parents to offspring through social learning rather than genetic inheritance. It is easy to imagine how such a process might occur in any species in which offspring learn from their parents. The organisms need not be humans. A particularly lovely example of parent-offspring learning is provided by bottlenose dolphins (*Tursiops* genus): in a field study of wild dolphins in Shark Bay, Western Australia, Michael Krützen and colleagues (2005) documented a foraging technique whereby 'a dolphin breaks a marine sponge off the seafloor and wears it over its closed rostrum [beak] to apparently probe into the substrate for fish' (Krützen et al., 2005, p. 8939). This technique was transmitted vertically through social learning from mothers to their female offspring. Assuming this trait confers a fitness advantage, mothers who possess the technique will tend to have more offspring than mothers who do not, potentially causing the trait to spread through the population. This selection process, which has not been documented but seems empirically plausible, would be a paradigm case of CS_1. It is quite possible that CS_1 is a very significant driver of behavioural evolution in apes and cetaceans, and indeed in any species in which cultural variants are transmitted from parents to offspring.[9]

Importantly, although CS_1 relies on vertical (i.e. parent to offspring) cultural transmission, it does not assume that transmission is *exclusively* vertical. On the contrary, CS_1 can occur in the presence of horizontal transmission and be influenced by it—an idea that, as I will argue in due course, has implications for the evolution of prosocial behaviour. There is an analogy here with microbes. The idea that a plasmid might spread in virtue of its effects on the fitness of its host relies on the fact that plasmids tend to be vertically transmitted through lineages of hosts; if they were not, the effects of a plasmid on the fitness of its host would be irrelevant to its own evolutionary prospects. But to understand the factors

---

[9] A number of authors have argued for the importance of this kind of selection in humans and other species, notably Avital and Jablonka (2000); Mameli (2004); Jablonka and Lamb (2005). For a review of culture in whales and dolphins, see Rendell and Whitehead (2001). On culture in chimpanzees, see Whiten et al. (1999).

influencing the direction of selection on a plasmid-borne trait—and, in particular, to see why a plasmid might gain from causing its bearer to produce a costly public good—it is crucial to take account of the fact that plasmids are *also* transmitted horizontally, since this affects the coefficient of relatedness. The same goes for cultural variants in the context of CS_1. Horizontal transmission can be interpreted in the context of CS_1 as a source of cultural relatedness.

The second type of cultural selection—which I will call type-2 cultural selection, or CS_2—occurs when culturally transmissible phenotypic differences between individuals cause variation in their *cultural fitness*, where cultural fitness is defined differently from biological fitness. In CS_2, the role of culture is not simply that of an alternative, non-genetic inheritance system through which fitness-relevant properties are transmitted; culture also gives rise to a distinctive form of individual fitness that is decoupled from biological fitness.[10]

The key to making CS_2 intelligible and coherent is to define a workable concept of an individual's cultural fitness. This has proven to be a non-trivial challenge for cultural evolution theorists. In spite of this, I agree with Grant Ramsey and Andreas de Block (2017) that the concept of the cultural fitness of an individual is not 'hopelessly confused', and that there are at least some circumstances in which such a notion may be well-defined and useful.

For example, Sterelny (2012a) has argued that one of the central strands in the story of human evolution was the evolution of a distinctive form of teacher–apprentice learning, in which teachers would construct scaffolded learning environments to enable their apprentices to acquire important skills more rapidly. Where we have well-defined teacher–apprentice relationships, we have well-defined lineages, and it is possible to define an individual's cultural fitness as, roughly, the number of apprentices to whom that individual successfully teaches the cultural variant of interest (El Mouden et al., 2014).[11] We could imagine, in principle at

---

[10] Cavalli-Sforza and Feldman (1981, pp. 15–16) foreshadow the 'CS_1/CS_2' distinction, writing that '*cultural selection* must be clearly differentiated from the *Darwinian* or *natural selection* due to the cultural trait'. Their 'natural selection due to the cultural trait' is equivalent to my CS_1. However, as I explain later, their definition of 'cultural selection' differs from my definition of CS_2.

[11] Note that cultural fitness, thus construed, is a *trait-relative* property of an individual, in contrast to classical Darwinian fitness, which can be defined without specifying a focal

least, a process in which the spread of a cultural variant is driven by the differential ability of bearers of that variant to recruit apprentices to whom they can teach it successfully. This would be a paradigm case of CS_2. I want to resist the use of the term 'cultural selection' to describe any other type of cultural-evolutionary process. Some authors, such as Cavalli-Sforza and Feldman (1981, pp. 15–16), define the term more broadly, apparently taking it to encompass all cases of the differential adoption and retention of cultural variants by individuals, regardless of whether there are well-defined teacher–apprentice lineages.[12] Richerson and Boyd (2005, pp. 79–80) protest against this broad usage, arguing that one must distinguish changes driven by cultural selection from changes driven purely by transmission biases. I have already drawn a similar distinction in relation to microbial evolution (see Chapter 6), where I used a modified Price equation to separate the effects of 'pure infectivity' from the effects of fitness differences between organisms, and I think a partition between the effects of selection and the effects of transmission alone is also helpful in the case of cultural change. As in the microbial case, however, we should add an important (and by now familiar) caveat: transmission biases, as well as causing change independently of selection, can also influence the direction of selection via their effects on relatedness (see Section 8.4).

The CS_1/CS_2 distinction may appear sharp, but it is possible to imagine intermediate cases: cases in which change is driven by differences in cultural fitness, but where cultural fitness is a function of biological fitness, and is therefore not wholly decoupled from it.[13] For example, suppose offspring are very commonly taught only by their biological parents, but there are some exceptions: some offspring are disavowed by their biological parents and adopted by genetically unrelated teachers. In such a scenario, an individual who adopted many offspring from other

---

trait. If teacher–apprentice relationships were such that all the cultural variants of the teacher were transmitted together as a package to the apprentice, we could have a trait-independent measure, but this is not a plausible picture of how such relationships work.

[12] Cavalli-Sforza and Feldman (1981, p. 64) later add the condition that cultural selection only occurs when individuals adopt or retain a variant due to 'a true persuasion that [it] is good or adaptive', and not simply due to an instruction from a leader. This extra criterion makes their definition significantly narrower than it initially appears.

[13] Okasha (2006, Ch. 8) makes a similar point regarding Heisler and Damuth's (1987) MLS1/MLS2 distinction.

individuals could attain much higher cultural fitness than biological fitness, but cultural fitness would still be closely linked to biological fitness in the population as a whole.

I conjecture—and it is really only a conjecture—that the course of human social evolution in the Palaeolithic involved a gradual decoupling of cultural fitness from biological fitness, and that there was a gradual transition in the most important form of cultural selection from CS_1 to CS_2. As we noted earlier, CS_1 is not uniquely human, and I suspect that it plays at least some role in explaining the spread of cultural variants in other mammals and birds that are capable of social learning. But since the fidelity and scope of social learning in other species is very limited in comparison with humans, the scope for CS_1 is similarly limited, and it seems likely that natural selection acting on genetic variation remains the most important driver of adaptive evolution in these species. In early hominins, biological fitness differences would still have been the primary driver of adaptive change; but, as our ancestors evolved ever more sophisticated capacities for social learning, the relative significance of cultural as opposed to genetic variation in producing heritable fitness differences would have gradually increased, until CS_1 was a central rather than peripheral cause of adaptation. At this time, cultural inheritance would still have been primarily—but not exclusively—vertical (Mameli, 2008).

As social learning continued to increase in bandwidth and fidelity, well-defined cultural lineages, formed of teacher–apprentice relationships that did not necessarily align with parent–offspring relationships, would have started to appear, bringing with them the possibility of a new kind of selection. Cultural fitness—the number of apprentices one recruits and successfully teaches—would initially have been closely tied to biological fitness, but with the onset of kinship norms that allowed for the adoption of biological non-relatives as socially recognized offspring, a partial decoupling became possible. I suspect that it is only in the Holocene (i.e. approximately the last 12,000 years) that institutions such as religions and professions have allowed cultural fitness to become almost entirely decoupled from biological fitness, so that (for example) a religious leader can enjoy high cultural fitness with respect to the transmission of their religious beliefs by recruiting large numbers of followers, independently of whether or not they produce any biological offspring.

This speculative history of cultural selection leads to a methodological proposal. When our aim is to explain a pattern of behaviour that has a deep history in the hominin lineage but that cannot be explained 'by genes alone', we should look in the first instance to CS_1 as a possible explanation. If CS_1 still seems incapable of explaining the target phenomenon, we should then consider CS_2, and start grappling with the complexities of defining a concept of cultural fitness. I suspect that CS_1 alone can explain a great deal about the early stages of human social evolution and that approaches based on CS_2, although intrinsically interesting, are often unnecessary.[14] In particular, I suggest that, when it comes to explaining the origin of broad-scope prosocial preferences, CS_1 is an attractive option. Moreover, I suggest that a cultural analogue of Hamilton's rule can give a better understanding of the conditions under which a prosocial cultural variant can spread by CS_1.

8.4   A Cultural Analogue of Hamilton's Rule

In Chapter 2 and again in Chapter 6, we saw the close relationship between Hamilton's rule and the Price equation. In short, Queller's (1992a) 'general' version of Hamilton's rule is derived by means of a very coarse-grained statistical partitioning of the term in the Price equation that represents the response to selection. So, once we have a Price equation for cultural change, it is straightforward to derive a cultural analogue of Hamilton's rule.[15,16]

A number of authors have noted that a cultural version of the Price equation can be used to represent the response to selection in a cultural variant (Henrich, 2004; Lehmann and Feldman, 2008; Lehmann et al., 2008; Helanterä and Uller, 2010; El Mouden et al., 2014).[17] Indeed, any selection process can be represented using a Price equation provided three basic ingredients are in place. First, we need an ancestral

---

[14] Mameli (2008) makes a similar suggestion.

[15] Readers wishing to avoid mathematical details can skip to the last subsection of this section—but note the key result labelled HRC.

[16] El Mouden et al. (2014) also make this point, and they go on to derive a cultural analogue of Hamilton's rule for what I have termed type-2 cultural selection. My framework differs from theirs in so far as it analyses type-1 cultural selection. On a technical level, my framework also differs in that it employs a modified Price equation and a diachronic definition of relatedness, for reasons explained later.

[17] Price (1995) himself arguably anticipated this, in so far as he always intended the Price equation to be a representation of selection in general, and not merely of natural selection on genetic variation.

and a descendant population, which may be discrete generations in a discrete generations model or earlier and later census points in an overlapping generations model. Second, we need a well-defined property of individuals for which every individual can be given a determinate value. Third, we need a mapping relation from ancestors to descendants such that all descendants have the same number of ancestors; we then define the 'fitness' of an ancestor as the number of descendants to which it maps.

When the aim is to represent natural selection on genetic variation, the property of interest is usually an individual gene frequency or breeding value, and the most appropriate mapping relation is biological reproduction: ancestors map to their direct biological descendants. But we can equally well use a Price equation to represent cultural selection on cultural variation, by taking a well-defined cultural variant as the property of interest and by choosing a mapping relation appropriate to the type of cultural selection we wish to analyse. For CS_1, in which change is driven by culturally heritable differences in biological fitness, biological reproduction is still the appropriate mapping relation, and fitness retains its usual meaning. For CS_2, in which change is driven by variation in cultural fitness, the appropriate mapping relation maps teachers to their apprentices, and an individual's fitness is redefined as the number of apprentices it teaches.

Here, in keeping with my earlier methodological proposal, I will focus on CS_1 (see El Mouden et al., 2014 for discussion of CS_2). Because fitness retains its usual meaning in a case of CS_1, we can sidestep the complexities involved in defining a notion of cultural fitness in the context of the Price equation;[18] but there is one complexity we must still consider. In the presence of horizontal transmission, an individual's cultural variants—like the mobile genetic elements of a bacterium—can vary over time during its life cycle. We therefore cannot talk of an individual's cultural variant *simpliciter*—only of its cultural variant at a particular time.

---

[18] As noted in Chapter 2, Price (1970) assumed that all offspring have the same number of parents. This is normally a reasonable assumption when lineages are defined by biological reproduction, but it becomes a problem when we switch to cultural lineages, because two apprentices might differ in their number of teachers. This obstacle can be overcome either by adding an extra term to the Price equation (as in Kerr and Godfrey-Smith, 2009) or by weighting teacher–apprentice relations by relative influence, so that an apprentice with more teachers counts less towards the fitness of each teacher than an apprentice with fewer (as in El Mouden et al., 2014).

To accommodate this, we can—as we did in Chapter 6—introduce an idealized life cycle in which horizontal transmission, social interaction, and reproduction all take place in separate stages. This is a fairly common idealization in cultural evolution theory (e.g. Lehmann and Feldman, 2008; Lehmann et al., 2008), and one that strikes me as reasonable when the aim is to fix ideas about the population-level causes of cultural change, rather than to produce accurate and detailed models of particular historical episodes.

8.4.1 An idealized life cycle

We can, in fact, use a broadly similar basic life cycle to that we used in Chapter 6, but with the individuals now interpreted as human agents rather than microbes, with the focal property now interpreted as a cultural variant—specifically, a culturally inherited propensity to contribute to a public good—rather than a mobile genetic element, and with horizontal transmission now interpreted as social learning rather than plasmid transfer (and a few other differences, which I will explain later). Here are the stages:

- *Social network formation*: Agents form a social network. For example, the network might be a square lattice in which each agent interacts with its four von Neumann neighbours or its eight Moore neighbours, or the network may be group-structured with discrete groups (see Chapter 4 for discussion of the varieties of population structure). Network formation may be assortative or random; this is also left open.

- *Horizontal transmission 1*: Agents have an opportunity to learn socially from their neighbours. The cultural variant of individual i prior to this stage is denoted by v_i, and must take a value between 0 and 1. The potentially modified cultural variant of i after this stage is denoted by v_i^*. The average initial and modified cultural variants of i's social partners are denoted, respectively, by $\hat{v}_i$ and $\hat{v}_i^*$.

- *Public goods production*: Agent i contributes to a public good with probability v_i^*, incurring a net cost to its own viability but conferring a net benefit on its neighbours.

- *Horizontal transmission 2*: Agents have a second opportunity to learn socially from their neighbours. The cultural variant of i after this stage is denoted by v_i^{**}.

- *Global competition*: Agents are killed off with a probability proportional to the total payoff they received in the public goods production stage.
- *Reproduction* All surviving agents reproduce. The network dissolves, and a new network is formed from the new population. The average cultural variant of the descendants of i in the new population is denoted by v_i'.

In contrast to the idealized microbial life cycle described in Chapter 6, we are not here assuming a 'patch-structured' population, but rather a structured social network that may or may not be group-structured. The idea is to derive a very abstract partition of selective change under CS_1 that will hold for any population with this life cycle, regardless of the structure of the network.[19] We are also allowing the cultural variant v_i to take any value between 0 and 1, to allow for the fact that individuals can vary continuously in their culturally inherited propensity to contribute to a public good. Finally, we have omitted the cell division phase in which each agent populates its local patch by dividing many times over. Despite these differences, this idealized life cycle is still broadly similar to the one we employed in Chapter 6.

8.4.2 A cultural Price equation

We noted in Chapter 6 that, in the presence of horizontal transmission, Frank's modified Price equation should be preferred to the standard Price equation, since it captures all the effects of differential fitness in a single term. In the context of our idealized life cycle, earlier, we can write a Frank-style modified Price equation as follows:

$$\overline{w}\Delta\overline{v} = \text{Cov}(w_i, v_i') + \overline{w_i}\text{E}(v_i' - v_i) \qquad (8.1)$$

We can now follow the series of moves we made in Chapter 6 to derive, from this cultural Price equation, a cultural analogue of Hamilton's rule. The first step is to separate out the fidelity of vertical transmission, τ. On the assumption that infidelities of vertical transmission between i and its

---

[19] For a rich discussion of various possible network structures, and their consequences for the cultural evolution of cooperation, see Alexander (2007).

descendants in the next generation do not co-vary with its fitness, we can re-write (8.1) as follows, where τ is fidelity of vertical transmission:[20]

$$\overline{w}\Delta\overline{v} = \tau\,\mathrm{Cov}(w_i, v_i^{**}) + \overline{w_i}\mathrm{E}(\tau v_i^{**} - v_i) \tag{8.2}$$

The next move is to assume that $\mathrm{E}(\tau v_i^{**} - v_i) = 0$. This sets the 'pure transmission bias' term of the Price equation to zero, just as we did in deriving HRG (Chapter 2) and HRM (Chapter 6). It is worth once more reiterating the point that this may be interpreted as an idealization or as an abstraction. On the 'idealization' reading, we are assuming that the net change in the frequency of the cultural variant due to social learning *alone* is zero—in other words, we are assuming that there is no systematic tendency for the variant to increase or decrease in frequency independently of its effects on reproductive fitness. On the 'abstraction' reading, by contrast, we are not assuming anything about the net change due to social learning alone; we are simply *omitting* the part of the change independent of fitness differences from our analysis in order to home in on the part of the total change that does depend on fitness differences.

I favour the 'abstraction' reading. It is a central feature of cultural evolution that traits do change in frequency due to social learning alone, independently of Darwinian selection processes. Consequently, it is not clear what is 'ideal' about a representation from which the non-Darwinian component has been stripped away. On the abstraction reading, however, the rationale for setting aside the non-Darwinian component is easier to see. For even if the non-Darwinian part of the change is substantial, it is still interesting and worthwhile to *abstract away* from the non-Darwinian 'background noise' in order to study the part of the total change that is Darwinian in character. As I interpret it, that is what we are doing here.

Introducing this assumption yields a simplified Price equation:

$$\overline{w}\Delta\overline{v} = \tau\,\mathrm{Cov}(w_i, v_i^{**}) \tag{8.3}$$

8.4.3 Separating direct and indirect fitness effects

We now partition change using a regression model nearly identical to that employed in Chapter 6, except now the regressors are the cultural variant of the focal individual and the average cultural variant of its social

---

[20] Formally, τ is defined by the regression equation $v_i' = \tau v_i^{**} + \epsilon_{v_i}$, and the assumption of uncorrelated residuals invoked is that $\mathrm{Cov}(w_i, \epsilon_{v_i}) = 0$.

partners at the public goods production stage in the life cycle (i.e. after the first horizontal transmission stage but before the second):

$$w_i = \alpha - c_v v_i^* + b_v \hat{v}_i^* + \epsilon_{w_i} \qquad (8.4)$$

The subscripts on c_v and b_v are intended to indicate that we are regressing on cultural rather than genetic predictors; but, this aside, the cost and benefit coefficients retain their standard meanings. Substituting this regression model into equation (8.2), and assuming that $\text{Cov}(\epsilon_{w_i}, v_i^{**}) = 0$, we obtain the following partition of the selective change:

$$\overline{w}\Delta\overline{v} = -c_v \tau \text{Cov}(v_i^*, v_i^{**}) + b_v \tau \text{Cov}(\hat{v}_i^*, v_i^{**}) \qquad (8.5)$$

On the further assumptions that $\tau > 0$ (i.e. the fidelity of vertical transmission is positive) and $\text{Cov}(v_i^*, v_i^{**}) > 0$ (i.e. an agent's cultural variant in the public goods stage is positively correlated with its cultural variant after the second horizontal transmission stage), this partition implies the following rule for positive cultural selection:

$$\Delta\overline{v} > 0 \iff -c_v + b_v \cdot \frac{\text{Cov}(\hat{v}_i^*, v_i^{**})}{\text{Cov}(v_i^*, v_i^{**})} > 0 \qquad \text{(HRC)}$$

I have called this result HRC ('C' for cultural). The role of relatedness in this rule is played by a non-standard relatedness concept that captures the statistical association between the focal individual's *final* cultural variant and the average *expressed* cultural variant of its social partners in the public goods stage. I will refer to this quantity as 'cultural relatedness', or r_v:

$$r_v = \frac{\text{Cov}(\hat{v}_i^*, v_i^{**})}{\text{Cov}(v_i^*, v_i^{**})} \qquad (8.6)$$

There are two main sources of cultural relatedness in our idealized life cycle. One is social network formation: if the network is formed assortatively, such that prosocial individuals differentially form ties with other prosocial individuals, this will contribute to r_v. The second is horizontal transmission, whether it occurs before or after public goods production. This provides an opportunity for agents to influence the cultural variants of their social partners, with the result that they become more similar to each other than they were initially.

Clearly, HRM is a very similar result to HRC, and embodies a very similar idea; the differences in the idealized life cycles do not make any difference to the form of the rule describing the direction of selection.

This may lead to a concern: can it really be the case that such similar basic organizing frameworks can be used to describe the effects of horizontal transmission in both microbes and humans? Although this may initially seem surprising, it is simply a consequence of the high level of abstraction at which organizing frameworks operate. In both cases, the framework deliberately avoids making detailed assumptions about the form horizontal transmission takes, or about the nature of the social phenotype of interest. It simply offers a deliberately coarse-grained partition of change that separates direct and indirect fitness effects in the traditional Hamiltonian way, while making room for the role of horizontal transmission mechanisms in generating the latter.

At this high level of abstraction, social evolution in microbes is indeed relevantly similar to cultural evolution in humans. In both cases, a form of horizontal transmission matters to the direction of selection, and matters for fundamentally the same reason: it generates correlation between actors and recipients with respect to the transmissible basis of social traits. Because of this, similar rules describe the circumstances under which a horizontally transmissible trait will undergo positive selection.

8.4.4 The significance of HRC

HRC embodies several important insights about the cultural evolution of social behaviour by type-1 cultural selection—insights that help us organize our thinking about causes of cultural change, just as HRG helps us organize our thinking about the causes of gene frequency change.

First, HRC enables us to draw a distinction between direct fitness explanations of cultural change (for which $c_v < 0$ and $r_v b_v \leqslant 0$) and indirect fitness explanations (for which $c_v \geqslant 0$ and $r_v b_v > 0$). Second, HRC tells us that, if $r_v b_v \leqslant c_v$ for some cultural variant, positive change in that variant cannot be wholly explained by CS_1, implying that any adequate explanation of positive change must appeal at least partly to other causes (such as CS_2, or non-selective causes). Third, HRC shows us that, in the case of a prosocial variant that confers a positive fitness benefit on others ($b_v > 0$) at a cost to its bearer ($c_v > 0$), the behaviour will be positively selected by CS_1 *only if there is a source of positive cultural relatedness* ($r_v > 0$).

It is worth highlighting the fundamental conceptual point here: when a prosocial trait is transmitted culturally rather than genetically, it is a coefficient of *cultural* relatedness, not a coefficient of genetic relatedness, that provides the appropriate weighting for indirect fitness effects. Relatedness coefficients capture selectively relevant correlations in the transmissible basis of social traits. When the mode of transmission changes, the meaning of relatedness also changes.

In the case of a variant that confers a benefit on others at a cost to its bearer, the intuitive idea (as previewed in Section 8.1) is that such a variant can be favoured by CS_1 when the fitness benefits it produces *fall differentially on other (current or future) bearers of the variant.* These recipients then produce more offspring, and tend to transmit the variant vertically to those offspring, so that, in the absence of countervailing causes of change, the variant increases in frequency. The coefficient of cultural relatedness, r_v, captures the extent to which the benefits of expressing the variant fall differentially on other (current or future) bearers. The condition '$r_v b_v > c_v$' captures the circumstances under which the indirect fitness effects on 'cultural relatives' outweigh the direct cost to the actor, so that the variant is selectively favoured.

8.5 The Cultural Relatedness Hypothesis

We are now in a position to articulate the cultural relatedness hypothesis more precisely and more carefully. I hypothesize that the $r_v b_v > c_v$ condition was, by virtue of positive cultural relatedness ($r_v > 0$) in extended social networks, satisfied by broad-scope prosocial preferences in early human populations, and that these cultural variants were therefore favoured by type-1 cultural selection, causing them to spread to fixation. In other words, cultural variants for broad-scope prosociality imposed a direct cost on their bearers, but they spread because these effects were outweighed by indirect fitness benefits conferred on culturally related recipients. Let me emphasize that it is just a hypothesis. Like all hypotheses concerning early human social evolution, it is speculative. However, I contend that its qualitative empirical assumptions have at least some tentative evidence in their favour.

What are the qualitative empirical assumptions of the cultural relatedness hypothesis? As I see it, here are the most important ones:

1. Differences in reproductive fitness caused by differences in cultural variants (i.e. CS_1) were a significant driver of cultural change in early human populations.

2. Cultural relatedness in *extended* social networks (i.e. between 'friends of friends') was positive in early human populations with respect to broad-scope prosocial cultural variants ($r_v > 0$). In other words, bearers of such variants were differentially likely to have other bearers as members of their extended network.

3. Expressing broad-scope prosocial variants in interactions with members of one's extended network conferred lifetime reproductive fitness benefits on others ($b_v > 0$) at a cost to the bearer ($c_v > 0$).

These are necessary but not sufficient conditions for the cultural relatedness hypothesis: even establishing their truth conclusively would not suffice to show that $r_v b_v > c_v$. But they do represent ways in which the cultural relatedness hypothesis is vulnerable to refutation. Consider, for example, assumption (2). I stressed earlier that present-day hunter-gatherers should not be taken as representative of our Palaeolithic ancestors in all respects; however, it is reasonable to assume that they provide a better model of Palaeolithic societies than modern nation states do, and this makes evidence from hunter-gatherer societies particularly relevant for testing hypotheses about human social evolution. If studies of present-day hunter-gatherers showed that $r_v \approx 0$ in their extended social networks, this would be a mark against the cultural relatedness hypothesis. If they show that $r_v > 0$, that is a mark in its favour.

In a remarkable study of the Hadza, a hunter-gatherer population in Tanzania, Coren Apicella and colleagues (2012) mapped the structure of 'campmate' and 'giftmate' networks, with the links in these networks defined (respectively) by an individual's willingness to share a camp with or donate a gift to another. Typically, an agent had fewer giftmates than campmates. Both notions may be seen as capturing subsets of an agent's effective social network, in Gamble's (1999) sense. Apicella et al. then invited pairs of campmates or giftmates to play a public goods game, and they found that, in both networks, the donations made by directly connected individuals were positively correlated: agents disposed to make larger contributions to public goods tended to form ties with other, similarly prosocial individuals, whereas agents weakly disposed to contribute tended to form ties with other, similarly selfish individuals. This is clear evidence that the campmate and giftmate networks exhibit positive cultural relatedness with respect to prosocial dispositions.

Moreover, in the giftmate network, Apicella et al. also found positive correlation not only between directly connected individuals but also between individuals at *one degree of separation*: in other words, giftmates-of-giftmates were also positively correlated in their tendency to contribute to public goods. This matters for our purposes, because it is this kind of cultural relatedness that might conceivably stabilize *broad-scope* prosocial preferences that extend beyond one's effective social network to encompass an extended social network of 'friends of friends'. This is good news for the cultural relatedness hypothesis: it shows that the sort of correlations the hypothesis requires do in fact exist in modern hunter-gatherer populations.

As Apicella et al. note, there are two possible explanations for these correlations. One is *assortative network formation*: prosocial individuals preferentially form ties with other prosocial individuals. While it seems unlikely that selfish individuals prefer ties with other selfish individuals, they may not have a great deal of choice in the matter: they may be constrained to form ties with those who are left over once the prosocial individuals have paired up. The other is *horizontal transmission*: pairs of individuals, having formed a social tie, may learn socially from each other, influencing one another's cultural variants. Both processes may well be relevant, and there is not yet compelling evidence regarding which is the more powerful.

However, the cultural relatedness hypothesis is neutral on this question: what matters is that, for whatever reason, cultural relatedness is high enough to cause broad-scope prosocial preferences to be positively selected by CS_1. I do not think we can yet say that this claim has been empirically substantiated. The missing piece of the puzzle is compelling evidence that these prosocial dispositions have consequences for reproduction—i.e. that they impose direct fitness costs, but confer indirect fitness benefits—and that the values of r_v, b_v, and c_v are such that the $r_v b_v > c_v$ condition is satisfied. If these things were to be established, I contend that the cultural relatedness hypothesis would be in a strong empirical position. For now, it remains a speculation worthy of further investigation.

8.6 Two Objections

I want to wrap up this chapter by defending the cultural relatedness hypothesis from two possible objections. The first is that, despite being phrased in different language, it is ultimately equivalent to the 'cultural group selection' hypothesis of Richerson et al. (2016). The second is that, to the extent that broad-scope prosocial preferences are not in the interests of the genome, we should expect genetic evolution to respond to their spread by favouring genes that inhibit their acquisition or expression.

8.6.1 Cultural group selection repackaged?

Over the course of three decades, Richerson, Boyd, and collaborators have produced a great deal of the most influential work in cultural evolution theory (Boyd and Richerson, 1985, 2005; Richerson and Boyd, 2005). One of their best known ideas is that, as Richerson et al. (2016) put it in the title of a recent review article, 'cultural group selection plays an essential role in explaining human cooperation'. Let us call this the *cultural group selection hypothesis*.

Given the long history of confusion over the relationship between kin selection and group selection (the topic of Chapter 4), one might understandably wonder about the relationship between the cultural relatedness hypothesis and the cultural group selection hypothesis. Are they competing empirical hypotheses, or are they alternative perspectives on the same process? My answer, echoing the argument of Chapter 4, is that neither of these suggestions is quite right. The two hypotheses agree about the importance of horizontal transmission to the evolution of prosocial behaviour, and offer different perspectives on why it is important. In other respects, however, their empirical commitments differ.

I take the key, qualitative empirical commitments of the cultural group selection hypothesis to be the following:

1. Early human populations were divided into discrete ethnolinguistic tribes. Tribes were composed of multiple residential bands and, on average, contained approximately 500 individuals.[21]
2. The population frequencies of cultural variants were significantly influenced by inter-tribal competition.
3. A tribe's success in inter-tribal competition was significantly influenced by the cultural variants of its members.

---

[21] Richerson and Boyd's (1998) estimate of 500 for the size of the average tribe is based on Birdsell's (1953; 1968; 1973) so-called 'magic numbers' for the size of demographic units, based on data from indigenous hunter-gatherer populations in Australia.

4. Horizontal transmission mechanisms such as conformist-biased social learning suppressed variation within tribes while increasing
variance between tribes.

There is one crucial similarity here: in a tribe-structured population,
horizontal transmission mechanisms that suppress variance within tribes
are also likely to lead to positive cultural relatedness in extended social networks, and vice versa, since the members of one's extended social
network are likely to be drawn from within one's local tribe.[22] So mechanisms such as conformist-biased social learning, to the extent that they
suppress variance within tribes *and* generate positive cultural relatedness,
are important to both hypotheses. This might naturally lead to the accusation that the two hypotheses are 'formally equivalent'. This would be an
exaggeration, however, because the core empirical commitments of the
two hypotheses diverge in other respects.

On the one hand, the cultural group selection hypothesis makes
stronger assumptions than the cultural relatedness hypothesis about
population structure in the Palaeolithic. The cultural relatedness hypothesis is not committed to the claim that early human populations were
subdivided into well-defined ethnolinguistic tribes, nor is it committed
to the claim that inter-tribal conflict was a significant driver of change.
It does require that individuals have extended social networks, and that
cultural relatedness was positive in these networks, but it does not assume
that these networks were structured so as to form discrete tribal groups,
each composed of multiple bands. It allows that early human populations
may have more closely resembled 'neighbour-structured' populations in
the sense of Chapter 4: social neighbourhoods, centred on individuals,
may have blurred continuously into each other.

I see this as a virtue of the cultural relatedness hypothesis. Social
anthropologists have long been sceptical of the 'tribe' concept. There are
various reasons for this, but the one that is relevant here is that stateless
societies vary greatly in their demography (Binford, 2001), and anthropologists increasingly came to see tribal classifications as imposing sharp
boundaries that did not exist on the ground (Berndt, 1959; Southall, 1970;

---

[22] There is also a close formal relationship between a coefficient of relatedness and the
ratio of between-group variance to total variance; indeed, this ratio is often described in the
kin selection literature as the 'whole-group relatedness' (Pepper, 2000).

Fried, 1975). As Gamble (1998, 1999) has argued, by focussing on effective and extended networks, centred on individuals, we can move away from the seductive but potentially misleading assumption that, prior to the existence of well-bounded nation states, Palaeolithic networks would have carved up neatly into discrete, stable groups.[23]

On the other hand, the cultural relatedness hypothesis makes stronger assumptions than the cultural group selection hypothesis about the form of selection responsible for the cultural evolution of prosocial behaviour. For it specifically posits that CS_1—that is, individual-level differences in reproductive fitness caused by differences in cultural variants—was the main driver for most of human social evolution. For Richerson et al. (2016), by contrast, 'selection' serves as an umbrella term for a wide variety of very different processes that can cause one group to grow faster, contain fitter individuals, or beget more daughter groups than its rivals, including processes of differential migration, differential imitation, and several distinct forms of Darwinian selection on fitness differences. They avoid committing to any particular variety as the main cause of the evolution of prosociality.[24]

Thus Richerson et al. (2016) make fairly strong assumptions about the degree of group-structure in early human populations, while remaining fairly pluralistic about the processes that lead to adaptive cultural change in populations with that structure. Meanwhile, the cultural relatedness hypothesis makes a stronger assumption about the main driver of adaptive cultural change, while being more pluralistic about the sort of population structures within which that process could operate. For all that, the two approaches are in many ways closely allied attempts to apply Darwinian thinking to human cultural evolution.

---

[23] Accordingly, Gamble (1998, 1999) also urges that we rethink Birdsell's 'magic numbers' (see footnote 21) as estimates of the average sizes of social networks centred on individuals, with 500 capturing the approximate size of a typical individual's extended network.

[24] By applying the MLS1/MLS2 distinction (see Chapter 4) and the CS_1/CS_2 distinction from this chapter, we can distinguish four distinct varieties of cultural group selection. If we then add differential migration and differential imitation to the family, there are at least six distinct varieties. I leave the task of constructing a detailed taxonomy for another occasion. Morin (2016) has argued that the notion of cultural group selection as characterized by Richerson et al. (2016) is really *too* broad, and lumps together processes that should be kept distinct. I have some sympathy with this criticism.

8.6.2 *The genome strikes back?*

In Chapter 6, we noted that the encoding of costly cooperative traits on plasmids generates potential for conflict with the chromosomal part of the genome, which stands to gain by suppressing the expression of these plasmids. Horizontally transmissible cultural variants threaten to generate conflict with the genome in much the same way as horizontally transmissible plasmids. If the variant causes benefits to be conferred on recipients (e.g. members of one's extended social network) who are more likely than average to share those variants, but who are not more likely than average to share the actor's genes, a gene that suppressed the expression or acquisition of the cultural variant could in principle be selected. We should expect this to be a possibility whenever $r_v b_v > c_v > r_g b_v$, where r_g denotes the coeffient of *genetic* relatedness between actors and recipients.

However, there is a question here as to whether genetic mechanisms are able to suppress the expression or acquisition of cultural variants at a fine enough grain. For example, if a gene could selectively inhibit the social learning of the belief that one ought to contribute to public goods without *also* suppressing the social learning of other, directly advantageous beliefs, then perhaps such a gene would spread. But it is hard to see how a gene could selectively target *only* those cultural variants that conflict with the inclusive fitness interests of the organism, while leaving all the advantageous variants intact.

This leads to the thought that, provided it is beneficial *on the whole* to have powerful social learning mechanisms, genes will not evolve to suppress their development, and prosocial altruistic variants will be able to sneak in as 'hitchhikers' via these transmission mechanisms even if they promote behaviour that detracts from the organism's inclusive fitness as traditionally understood (Gintis, 2003). This parallels one of the possible solutions in the case of plasmid transfer: here too, the overall benefits of having such channels for horizontal transmission, combined with the difficulty of selectively suppressing altruism-promoting genes that enter through those channels, could allow altruism-encoding genes to avoid suppression, especially if they are carried on plasmids that also carry other, directly advantageous genes.

More research is needed in both cases before we can say with any certainty whether these proposed explanations are correct. However, it is worth emphasizing that horizontally transmissible plasmids that promote the production of public goods are an empirical reality in bacteria, so there must be some explanation for their persistence. Microbes show that it is possible—in the real world—for such traits to spread and persist without being suppressed by the rest of the genome, and this provides cultural evolution theorists with a way of responding to critics who object that it is not possible for such traits to spread or persist in humans.

So there is, I suggest, more scope than one might initially imagine for cross-disciplinary collaboration between microbiologists and anthropologists. In both cases, we would benefit from a better understanding of how horizontally transmissible cooperative traits spread and persist despite the conflict they generate with the interests of the genome. Insights as to how this is possible in one case could shed light on how it is possible in the other.

8.7 Summary of Chapter 8

Humans across cultures have a tendency to set aside their own self-interest in ways that promote cooperation and the punishment of non-cooperators, even when interacting with strangers. To explain the origin of these broad-scope prosocial preferences, we should consider the cultural-evolutionary processes that might have acted in early human populations to promote cooperation within extended social networks— networks that stretched beyond the boundaries of one's immediate residential camp.

A working hypothesis is that these cultural variants initially evolved by a process of cultural selection. Two types of cultural selection can be distinguished: CS_1, in which cultural differences between individuals lead to differences in their reproductive success; and CS_2, in which cultural differences between individuals lead to differences in their 'cultural fitness', which is to say the number of apprentices they are able to recruit. I have suggested, speculatively, that human social evolution involved a gradual transition from CS_1 to CS_2 as the most important form of cultural selection, with the latter becoming important only after widespread cooperation among non-relatives was established. This leads to a methodological proposal: to explain the origin of broad-scope prosocial preferences, we should focus on CS_1 in the first instance.

A cultural version of Hamilton's rule, in which the coefficient of genetic relatedness is replaced by a coefficient of cultural relatedness, provides a helpful organizing framework for thinking about the evolution of social behaviour by CS_1. In particular, it provides a framework within which we can articulate a 'cultural relatedness hypothesis' regarding the evolution of human prosociality.

The intuitive idea is that prosocial cultural variants spread because the benefits they produced fell differentially on other bearers of those variants. More precisely, the idea is that broad-scope prosocial behaviours conferred a benefit on recipients ($b_v > 0$) at a cost to the actor ($c_v > 0$), but were nevertheless able to spread due to positive cultural relatedness ($r_v > 0$) within extended social networks. One of the main qualitative empirical commitments of this hypothesis is that $r_v > 0$ in extended social networks in hunter-gatherer societies, due to assortative network formation and/or horizontal transmission, and a recent analysis by Apicella et al. (2012) provides support for this assumption.

This hypothesis, although related to the cultural group selection hypothesis of Richerson et al. (2016), differs from it in making fewer commitments about the degree of group-structure in Palaeolithic societies, and more commitments about the nature of the selective processes responsible for adaptive change. If the cultural relatedness hypothesis is on the right lines, it leaves us with the puzzle of why genetic evolution has been unable to suppress the expression of cultural variants that are not in the inclusive fitness interests of the genome. Gintis's (2003) 'hitchhiker' theory is one attractive possibility. Since the problem here is very similar to the problem we confront in the case of public-goods-producing plasmids, there is scope for fruitful collaboration on this issue between anthropologists and microbiologists.

. . . and Climbing Out Again

This book has covered a lot of ground. Here, in brief, are the key claims for which I have argued:

1. We should classify social behaviours as altruistic, mutually beneficial, selfish, or spiteful according to their recent selection history, not their current fitness effects. Moreover, the classification should be task-relative and strategy-relative (Chapter 1).
2. Hamilton's rule provides an organizing framework for social evolution research. It aids our understanding of causes by allowing a deliberately coarse-grained classification of more detailed explanations of change (Chapters 2 and 3).
3. Kin selection and group selection should be conceived as varieties of selection on indirect fitness differences. As Hamilton suggested, the distinction between them should be drawn in terms of differences of degree in the structural features of populations (Chapter 4).
4. Inclusive fitness and neighbour-modulated fitness are both valid ways of defining an individual's fitness on the assumption of δ-weak selection, but only inclusive fitness provides a criterion for improvement and a standard for optimality for cumulative adaptation over the evolutionary medium term (Chapter 5).
5. Gene mobility provides an intriguing and underexplored source of genetic relatedness between organisms. On a conceptual level, it should push us towards thinking of relatedness in diachronic, rather than synchronic, terms (Chapter 6).
6. Multicellular organisms can be usefully viewed as social groups of cells whose interests are aligned by high relatedness. The size and complexity of a social group are related in a feedback loop mediated by a transition in the source of robustness—from functional versatility to redundancy—that becomes possible as a group becomes larger,

and this may help explain the relationship between the size of an organism and its number of cell types (Chapter 7).

7. Cultural relatedness is a well-defined concept, and cultural relatedness in extended social networks might help explain the origin of broad-scope prosocial preferences in early human populations (Chapter 8).

I will not summarize the key arguments for these claims here; readers should consult the end-of-chapter summaries for a review of the arguments of each chapter. Instead, I want to conclude by relating some of the book's recurring themes to other debates in the philosophy of biology, and by setting out some directions for future work.

Statistics and Causality

The relationship between statistics and causality is an important recurring theme, and one particularly central to the discussions of Chapters 2, 3, and 4. Here, I want to relate some of the arguments of this book to a family of longrunning debates in the philosophy of biology concerning the relationship between statistics and causality in evolutionary theory—debates in which the rival camps have come to be known as 'statisticalists' and 'causalists'.

These debates were initiated in the early 2000s by Mohan Matthen and André Ariew (2002), and Denis M. Walsh and colleagues (2002), who argued that evolutionary theory should be interpreted as a statistical theory rather than a dynamical theory. I say 'debates' because this literature has tended to run together a variety of issues that, while not unrelated, can be usefully distinguished (Otsuka, 2016). These include the relationship between selection and drift; the question of whether natural selection should be regarded as a force, a cause, or merely as a statistical trend; the question of whether fitness is a causal property of organisms or merely a mathematical predictor of change; and the question of whether evolutionary models provide causal or non-causal explanations.[1]

---

[1] Some notable contributions to the debates include Rosenberg and Bouchard (2005); Millstein (2006); Shapiro and Sober (2007); Brandon and Ramsey (2007); Walsh (2007, 2010); Matthen and Ariew (2009); Lewens (2010b); Otsuka et al. (2011), and Ariew et al. (2015).

I have not explicitly weighed into these debates in this book, but it should be clear enough that the arguments of this book are relevant to at least some of these questions.[2] On the question of whether fitness should be interpreted as a causal property of individual organisms, the arguments of Chapter 5 provide support for the causalist view. Inclusive fitness is, after all, an inherently causal property: a weighted sum of the *effects* a focal individual has on the reproduction of itself and others. As such, it is a property constituted in part by causal relations between organisms.[3] I would argue that neighbour-modulated fitness is also inherently causal, although in a less obvious way: it too is defined as a sum of effects, but they are the effects of a set of neighbours on the reproductive output of a single focal individual. So those who would resist a causal interpretation of fitness must contend with the fact that social evolution theorists have long worked with fitness concepts that seem to demand a causal interpretation.

Other parts of the book, however, might offer some solace to the statisticalist. Robert N. Brandon and Grant Ramsey (2007), in a critique of the statisticalist interpretation of evolutionary theory advanced by Ariew, Matthen, Walsh, and colleagues, correctly point out that many models of the evolution of altruism rely on explicitly causal decompositions of fitness. Hamilton's (1970) model is a good example of this (see Chapter 5). Note, however, that Queller's (1992a) 'general model' relies on a decomposition of fitness that is explicitly statistical. In HRG, b and c are population statistics: they are coefficients in a regression model in which the predictors are the breeding value of the focal individual and the average breeding value of its social partners (see Chapter 2).

This is a deliberate choice on Queller's part. Indeed, it is the source of the rule's generality. The causal structure of individual fitness will typically be far more complicated than the structure of a two-predictor regression model. So, in many cases, when we apply the model to a set of population

---

[2] I have said nothing in particular about the relationship between selection and drift, since this book has mainly been concerned with frameworks, such as Queller's 'general model', that neglect drift in order to analyse the effects of selection (although see Grafen 2000; Okasha 2006, and Rice 2008 for discussion of how to capture the effects of drift using the Price equation).

[3] A qualification: the weights are population statistics—relatedness coefficients—so an organism's inclusive fitness is constituted by causal relations in which it stands to other organisms *and* statistical properties of the population. In this sense, inclusive fitness has a dual nature: it is a complex property that has both causal and statistical properties as its constituents (hence my conciliatory comments at the end of this subsection).

data, the residuals will be large. But the residuals make no difference to the resultant decomposition of change unless they co-vary with the focal individual's breeding value, and it is a mathematical property of ordinary least-squares regression that the residuals cannot co-vary with the predictors. The decomposition of change afforded by Queller's regression model is therefore achieved without making any assumptions about the causal paths linking genes to fitness. This is an ingenious move, because the compatibility of HRG with a wide-range of underlying causal structures is what enables it to serve as an organizing framework for a large and diverse class of models.

A statisticalist might therefore cite Queller's general model as a case in which a purely statistical decomposition of fitness is preferred, with good reason, to a causal one. There is, however, a sting in the tail for the statisticalist. For the explanatory value of HRG consists in its ability to provide an organizing framework for more detailed, dynamically richer models; and these more detailed models, which tend to explicitly represent the payoff structures and population structures that shape patterns of social interaction, are most naturally interpreted as attempts to represent causes and to construct causal explanations of evolution. Thus I maintain that HRG, although clearly a statistical result, does 'explain causally' in a liberal sense of the term: it aids our understanding of causes, by facilitating an illuminating and intentionally coarse-grained classification of more detailed causal explanations of change (Chapters 2 and 3).

Often in philosophy of science, one finds alleged dichotomies that are better treated as gradated distinctions, and one finds issues that are best handled not in a wholesale 'one size fits all' fashion but in a piecemeal way more sensitive to the details of particular cases. I suspect these things are true of the clash between statisticalists and causalists. The use of statistical concepts in formulating fundamental principles of evolutionary theory has a long history—exemplified by Fisher's (1930) fundamental theorem of natural selection—and, as principles like HRG make plain, this tradition has been influential in the study of social evolution.[4] At the same time, social evolution theory has, in other respects, been a thoroughly causal enterprise from the beginning.

[4] On Fisher's fundamental theorem and its significance, see Edwards (1994, 2014); Plutynski (2006); Okasha (2008); Ewens (2011); Birch (2016b).

We see the pull in both directions very clearly in Hamilton's (1964) paper. On the one hand, his goal in the paper is to derive a statistical maximization result for social evolution, akin to the 'mean fitness increase theorem' of Scheuer and Mandel (1959), and Mulholland and Smith (1959). On the other hand, he invokes explicitly causal concepts in the characterization of the maximized quantity, inclusive fitness.[5] In inclusive fitness, Hamilton found a way of weighting individual-level effects by population statistics (i.e. relatedness coefficients) to produce a fitness concept that yielded a mean fitness increase theorem. Social evolution theory today follows Hamilton's lead, combining a causal view of fitness with a statistical approach to the weighting of fitness components. Neither a purely statisticalist interpretation nor a purely causalist interpretation would do justice to the explanations provided by social evolution theory.

Organisms, genes, and memes

Inclusive fitness is often portrayed as gene's eye thinking repackaged for whole-organism biologists. Dawkins (1978, p. 128), for example, famously described inclusive fitness as 'that property of an organism which will appear to be maximized when what is really being maximized is gene survival'. Hamilton himself took a similar view. In his very first article, he wrote that 'the ultimate criterion that determines whether [a gene] G will spread is not whether the behaviour is to the benefit of the behaver but whether it is to the benefit of the gene G; and this will be the case if the average net result of the behaviour is to add to the gene pool a handful of genes containing G in higher concentration than does the gene pool itself' (Hamilton, 1963, pp. 354–5). In Hamilton's rule, he found a way of capturing in organism-level terms the circumstances under which this 'ultimate criterion' would be satisfied. In inclusive fitness, he found a property of whole organisms that could serve as a criterion for improvement and a standard for optimality in the context of social adaptation.

---

[5] For discussion of 'mean fitness increase theorems', see Edwards (2000) and Ewens (2004); for discussion of inclusive fitness maximization, see Chapter 5; and for discussion of fitness maximization in general, see Edwards (2007) and Birch (2016b). I regard mean fitness increase theorems as a form of maximization result, broadly construed, but I should note that others, such as Ewens, think such theorems should be distinguished from true maximization principles, which should demonstrate not simply that mean fitness reliably increases but that it does so at a maximal rate.

Gardner (2011) has recently challenged the received wisdom about the relation between Hamilton's rule and the gene's eye view. He points out, correctly, that nothing in the derivation of HRG formally requires particulate inheritance. What matters is that we can identify a transmissible basis underlying the behaviour of interest, and that we can attribute to each organism a breeding value that quantitatively captures its inherited predisposition to express the behaviour. In a world where inheritance is particulate and the particles are genes, the breeding value as defined by quantitative genetics—a sum of alleles weighted by their average effects on the phenotype—is the property we need. But HRG would still apply in a world of blending inheritance, provided we could still attribute to each organism a breeding value defined in some other appropriate way.

The arguments of Chapter 8 of this book might be seen as providing further support to Gardner's position. Cultural inheritance is not generally particulate—blending probably happens all the time—and, although I have argued that talk of cultural variants is innocuous, we should not mistake cultural variants for replicators (Richerson and Boyd, 2005). Yet the non-particulate nature of cultural transmission is no obstacle to the derivation of a Hamilton's rule-like result. On this picture, Hamilton's rule and the gene's eye view, although closely associated for historical reasons, are conceptually independent of each other.

I was attracted to this picture for some time. However, I have come to see that it leaves out something important. As I now see it, the association between Hamilton's rule and the gene's eye view, while perhaps not as close as Hamilton or Dawkins supposed, is no mere historical accident either. As explained in Chapter 2, the derivation of HRG involves setting aside the '$E(w_i \Delta p_i)$' part of the change in order to focus on the '$\text{Cov}(w_i, p_i)$' part, and this move is justified on the grounds that $\text{Cov}(w_i, p_i)$ captures the part of the change attributable to natural selection acting in a constant environment. When p_i is a breeding value, this interpretation of $\text{Cov}(w_i, p_i)$ relies on the idea that a 'constant environment' is one in which the average effects of alleles on the phenotype do not change, so that any changes in these average effects are properly counted as a form of environmental change, not as part of the response to selection.

Sometimes, though, the average effect of an allele changes not because of any change to the ecological environment, but simply due to a change in the frequencies of the various genomic contexts in which the allele may find itself. For example, in a model of heterozygote advantage, the average effects of an allele will depend on the relative frequency of the heterozygote and homozygote. To interpret $Cov(w_i, p_i)$ as the action of natural selection in a constant environment, we must regard the genomic context of an allele as part of the environment, and we must regard changes in the frequency of these genomic contexts as a form of environmental change.

From an organism-level perspective, this makes little sense, since genes at other loci and on other chromosomes are parts of the organism, not parts of its 'environment'. From a gene's eye perspective, however, it does make sense to think of the rest of the genome as part of the environment. It therefore makes sense, from this perspective, to regard a change in the frequencies of the various genomic contexts a gene might experience as a form of environmental change. Indeed, conceptualizing the rest of the genome as part of the environment has always been a core element of the gene's eye perspective on evolution, from Fisher (1930) to the present (Sterelny and Kitcher, 1988; Okasha, 2008; Edwards, 2014). Thus a form of gene's eye thinking does feature, albeit very subtly, in the derivation of HRG.

A parallel argument suggests a role for 'meme's eye' thinking in a Hamiltonian approach to culture. In principle, one can pursue a Hamiltonian approach to cultural change without invoking the meme concept, as I showed in Chapter 8. However, the discussion in Chapter 8 focussed on the simple case of a prosocial behaviour determined by a single cultural variant. This is not a particularly realistic case: a behavioural phenotype will tend to be influenced by many cultural variants, suggesting a sum of cultural variants weighted by their average effects on the phenotype, or 'cultural breeding value', might be a useful quantity to work with for the purpose of formulating a more general model, comparable to Queller's general model in the genetic case.

However, a cultural analogue of Queller's general model would bring with it an analogous problem: how to justify the interpretation of the covariance between fitness and cultural breeding value as the effect of cultural selection acting in a constant environment. This interpretation would be justified only if the average effects of cultural variants on the phenotype could be regarded as part of the environment. As in the genetic case, this makes little sense if the environment begins where the organism ends, but it does make sense if we adopt a 'cultural variant's eye view' on the cultural evolutionary process. But this in turn is hard to make intelligible unless cultural variants are discrete, well-bounded entities, allowing a clear distinction between the variant itself and the environment it experiences in the brain of its bearer.

We are therefore pushed towards a conception of cultural variants that is still quite meme-like in some respects, despite the need to accommodate the possibility of blending inheritance. So, although I argued in Chapter 8 that Hamilton's ideas could be applied to culture without invoking memes, and this is true, there is also a sense in which the Hamiltonian approach dovetails particularly well with a meme-like conception of the units of cultural transmission. Just as Queller's general model relies on a subtle form of gene's eye thinking, I suspect an attempt to construct a cultural model of similar generality would rely on a subtle form of 'meme's eye' thinking.

In any case, there is much still to be done to develop a Hamiltonian theory of cultural evolution. Chapter 8 should be seen as a tentative, initial attempt to apply Hamilton's ideas to cultural change. Extending these ideas to cases of many cultural variants, many cultural 'loci', and more realistic life cycles remains a task for the future. When this project has reached a more advanced stage, as I hope it eventually will, we will be in a better position to say how meme-like cultural variants must be in order to satisfy the assumptions of the models.

It is, in my view, a project well worth pursuing. In a recent paper, De Block and Ramsey (2016) distinguish 'organism-centred' and 'meme-centred' approaches to cultural change, and they identify this as a 'central divide' in cultural evolution theory. One important lesson of Hamilton's work is that it is possible to move beyond such divisions. His work intentionally blurs the boundaries between 'organism-centred' and 'gene-centred' approaches to the evolution of social behaviour to provide a novel synthesis of both. One of the attractions of applying ideas such as Hamilton's rule and inclusive fitness to cultural change is that it may ultimately offer a way to synthesize the organism-centred and meme-centred viewpoints—in other words, to repackage 'meme's eye' thinking for whole-agent social scientists.[6]

---

[6] For further discussion of memes, see Blackmore (1999); Atran (2001); Sterelny (2006), and Gers (2008).

Humans and Microbes

One especially promising avenue for future work emerges very clearly from the discussions of Chapter 6 and Chapter 8. In recent decades, biologists have discovered a hidden social world that exists all around us: the social world of microbes. This is an exciting development in its own right, and these remarkable phenomena are worth understanding for their own sake, and for their possible biomedical applications. But in working on this book, I have come to appreciate a less obvious reason to study the evolution of cooperation in microbes: we should do it to help us understand the evolution of cooperation in *humans*.

There are, of course, obvious differences between human evolution and microbial evolution. Microbes don't have institutions such as religions, states, and legal systems. We don't split in half every twenty minutes. But behind the obvious differences there is a crucial similarity: the importance of horizontal transmission. The mechanisms of horizontal transmission are, plainly, very different in the two cases. The transfer of mobile genetic elements via processes such as conjugation is very different, mechanistically speaking, from the acquisition of beliefs, desires, values, skills, habits, and other cultural variants through social learning. Yet, to the extent that there are abstract similarities in the population-level effects of these processes, we must confront similar questions in both contexts. Questions such as: When is it advantageous for the genome to permit horizontal transmission? Under what conditions can a horizontally transmissible trait be selected even though it harms the organism that expresses it? When is it appropriate to think of horizontal transmission as creating a new form of fitness, as opposed to simply a new source of relatedness? What does relatedness even mean in the presence of horizontal transmission?

I do not claim to have definitively answered any of these questions. I have made some tentative suggestions, which I hope will stimulate further work from philosophers of biology on these issues. One thing of which I am convinced is that we should change the way we think about the relationship between relatedness and time. We tend to think that whether or not two organisms count as 'genetically related' depends on their *past*— on whether or not they have parents or other ancestors in common. Hamilton's (1964) emphasis on Wright's coefficient of relationship as a measure of relatedness arguably encourages this way of thinking. But, as

Hamilton's (1963) 'ultimate criterion' indicates, what matters in evolution is the *future*. To assess whether a social behaviour satisfies the criterion, the fundamental question is not 'Does the actor share ancestors with the recipient?' but rather, 'Does the behaviour increase the representation in future populations of the genes it expresses?'

The possibility of genes that help their potential future hosts, discussed in Chapter 6, makes this point quite vividly. The idea is that a plasmid, when producing a public good, makes nearby organisms fitter. These organisms, by virtue of being nearby, are also likely candidates for future infection by the plasmid. This correlation, whereby the benefits of the public good fall differentially on potential future bearers of the gene that produces it, might just be enough to lead to the selection of the gene under the right conditions. This could help explain how public-goods-producing plasmids are able to invade populations when rare, despite harming their hosts.

This observation led me to suggest that, when thinking about the evolution of cooperation in microbes, we should think of relatedness in terms of correlations between the genotype of the actor and the *future* genotype of the recipient. In principle, they need not have a recent common ancestor, and they need not share the gene at the moment they interact. What matters, fundamentally, are the net consequences of expressing a gene for the representation of that gene in future populations. Hamilton's 'ultimate criterion' is correct, but a traditional, synchronic concept of relatedness no longer captures that criterion in the presence of horizontal transmission. We need a diachronic concept of relatedness instead.

These points carry over to the case of cultural evolution. Here we have something analogous to plasmid transfer: people influence the beliefs, desires, values, and other cultural variants of other members of their generation, and they have differential influence over nearby agents. This leads to the possibility of a cultural analogue of helping potential future hosts, whereby a belief (such as the belief that one should contribute to a public good) benefits individuals who are more likely than average to acquire that variant in the future.

It would be wonderful to see some of the conjectures of Part II of this book subjected to experimental test. Does gene mobility promote the evolution of cooperation even when it occurs after the expression of social traits? Does greater redundancy in task structures predict greater social complexity, controlling for group size? Does greater cultural relatedness in extended social networks predict greater cooperation in public goods games? All these questions require empirical work to settle. I have proposed some hypotheses, and argued for their plausibility, but cannot claim to have established them empirically.

More broadly, it would be exciting to see more coordinated work on the evolution of cooperation in humans and microbes: projects that address, in an integrated way, the effects of horizontal transmission on social evolution at different scales of biological organization. It seems to me that philosophers of science have a lot to contribute to projects of this sort. Microbes and humans, in different but related ways, challenge us to examine and rethink the conceptual foundations of social evolution theory, and philosophers of science should rise to that challenge. Yet the overarching message of this book is that, although new conceptual innovations will be needed along the way, the basic organizing framework we owe to Hamilton still provides a powerful way of thinking about these issues.

Appendix: The Price Equation

Ingredients

The Price equation (Price, 1970, 1972a) is an abstract description of the change in aggregate properties between two sets. It is a piece of mathematics: its biological interpretation and application to evolution are optional. To derive the equation, all we need is two sets of countable entities. In biology, the entities will often be organisms, but the derivation of the Price equation does not assume this. We label one population the ancestral set (A) and the other population the descendant set (D). In biology, the sets will usually be earlier and later census points of the same population, or simply consecutive generations, so the labels are usually apt. But the derivation does not assume this either.

The sets A and D must satisfy two conditions. First, the members of the two sets must be related by a mapping relation. In the abstract, we can represent this mapping relation as R. We need to be able to say, for each member of A, to which descendants it is connected by R; and, for each member of D, to which ancestors it is connected by R. In biology, the most common choice of R is the relation of direct lineal descent; that is, R will connect each member of A to all and only those members of D of which it is a direct, genealogical ancestor. Again, however, the derivation of the equation does not assume any particular biological interpretation of the R relation.

Second, we must be able to attribute to each member of A and D a property, p; and we need to be able to attribute to each member of A two additional properties, w and p'. Let us consider each of these properties in turn.

The first property, p, is the property we are interested in studying, perhaps because its mean changes between the two sets, or perhaps because its mean stays the same. In biology, this will usually be a phenotypic or genotypic property of some kind, such as an individual gene frequency or a breeding value (as in the main text). The only formal constraint on the nature of p is that we must be able to assign to each member of A and D a number representing its value for that property (if the property is qualitative, we can define a dummy variable that takes the value 1 if an individual has the property and 0 otherwise, and then study the change in this dummy variable).

The second property, w, represents, for any particular ancestor, the number of entities in D to which it is connected by R. In biology, this will usually be the number of organisms to which it is connected by direct lineal descent. This quantity is often called fitness (or realized fitness, when it is important to distinguish realized from expected fitness). I adopt this terminology here, but with an important caveat: an entity's fitness in this sense may come apart significantly from the intuitive notion of fitness as a measure of an organism's number of offspring, for two main reasons. First, w in the Price formalism can, in principle, be ascribed to any countable entity, whenever we have two sets of these entities connected by an appropriate mapping relation. The entities need not be organisms. Second, even when the w-bearers are organisms, and even when the mapping relation R is direct lineal descent, an organism's number of offspring is only the best measure of its value for w in special cases. An organism's fitness, in the sense of the Price formalism, will align with its number of offspring when generations do not overlap and when the A and D populations are separated by a single generation. But if generations do overlap (so that organisms of different ages coexist in the same population), or if A and D are separated by multiple generations, an organism's number of offspring may not be a good indicator of the number of descendants it contributes to D.

The third property, p', represents, for any particular member of A, the average value of p in the members of the descendant-set to which it is related by R. To calculate p' for the ith individual, we look at the value of p in its descendants, and take the average of these values. Importantly, although we may calculate p' by looking at D, it is still a property of a member of A. It is a relational property of an ancestor, a piece of information about the way it transmits its p-value to its descendants.

Derivation

We begin by writing the change in the mean value of p between A and D as its mean value in D $(\overline{p}_D)$, minus its mean value in $\overline{p}_A$:

$$\Delta\overline{p} = \overline{p}_D - \overline{p}_A \tag{A1.1}$$

We then express each of these averages as a sum over properties of members of A. To calculate the average p-value in A, we simply sum over the p-values of each of the n members of that set, and divide by n:

$$\overline{p}_A = \frac{1}{n}\sum_i^n p_i \tag{A1.2}$$

To calculate the average p-value in D, we do *not* sum over the p-values of the members of D. Instead, we sum over the p'-values of individuals in A, weighting each ancestor by its relative value for w_i (i.e. by the number of members of D to which it is connected by R, divided by the population mean, $\overline{w}$):

$$\bar{p}_D = \frac{1}{n} \sum_i^n \frac{w_i}{\bar{w}} p_i' \qquad (A1.3)$$

At first sight, expressing the average p-value in D as a fitness-weighted sum of p'-values in A may seem an odd move. However, it is critical to the derivation. By expressing the average p-value in D as a sum over properties of members of A, we lay the foundations for a result that describes how the properties of the two sets relate to one another. This is also the only point at which the derivation makes a substantive assumption about the sets it describes. It is assumed here that all descendants have the same number of ancestors, since it is only on this assumption that $\bar{p}_D$ is equal to a fitness-weighted average of p' in A. Since there are possible pairs of ancestral and descendant sets in which the R-mapping violates this assumption, there are possible pairs of sets for which the standard Price equation does not hold (Kerr and Godfrey-Smith, 2009).

Combining A1.1, A1.2, and A1.3, we obtain:

$$\Delta\bar{p} = \frac{1}{n} \sum_i^n \frac{w_i}{\bar{w}} p_i' - \frac{1}{n} \sum_i^n p_i \qquad (A1.4)$$

The rest is an exercise in rearrangement and re-labelling. First, we rewrite A1.4 as:

$$\Delta\bar{z} = \frac{1}{n} \sum_i^n \frac{w_i}{\bar{w}} (p_i' - p_i) + \frac{1}{n} \sum_i^n \frac{w_i}{\bar{w}} p_i - \frac{1}{n} \sum_i^n p_i \qquad (A1.5)$$

By merging the second and third summations, and re-labelling $p_i' - p_i$ as Δp_i, we obtain:

$$\Delta\bar{z} = \frac{1}{n} \sum_i^n \frac{w_i}{\bar{w}} (\Delta p_i) + \frac{1}{n} \sum_i^n p_i \left(\frac{w_i}{\bar{w}} - 1 \right) \qquad (A1.6)$$

This is the Price equation in algebraic form. To put it in Price's preferred statistical notation, we need to introduce Price's slightly unorthodox conceptions of 'expectation' and 'covariance'. Here are the usual definitions of these notions. For a discrete random variable X, the expectation of the variable, $E(X)$, is $\sum q_i x_i$, where x_i is the ith possible state of X, and q_i is the probability of that state. The covariance of two random variables is the expected product of their deviations from expectation, that is, $\text{Cov}(X, Y) = E[(X - E[X])(Y - E[Y])]$ or, equivalently, $\text{Cov}(X, Y) = E(XY) - E(X)E(Y)$.

In statistics, covariances and expectations are normally understood either as properties of the probability distributions of random variables, or as properties of a sample drawn at random from a larger population. Price, however, makes no assumption that p_i is a random variable, or that A and D are samples from a larger population. In Price's notation, $E[p_i]$ is simply the population mean of p_i (for this reason, he sometimes preferred to write it as Ave.$[p_i]$). The covariance of p_i with w_i is simply the population mean of $(w_i - E[w_i])(p_i - E[p_i])$. So Price's notation does generate scope for confusion. However, provided we are clear that in talking of 'expectations' we are talking about population means, it is innocuous enough (see Marshall, 2015 for a stronger defence of the use of statistical notation in this context).

Introducing this statistical notation, we can rewrite A1.6 as:

$$\Delta \bar{p} = \frac{E(w_i \Delta p_i)}{\bar{w}} + \frac{\text{Cov}(w_i, p_i)}{\bar{w}} \tag{A1.7}$$

By reversing the order of the terms, we arrive at the equation in its most commonly seen form:

$$\Delta \bar{p} = \frac{1}{\bar{w}} \left[\text{Cov}(w_i, p_i) + E(w_i \Delta p_i) \right] \tag{A1.8}$$

It is important to appreciate that A1.8 is fundamentally the same equation as A1.6: the switch from algebraic to statistical notion makes no mathematical difference. It is also possible to rewrite the Price equation in vector notation, or even in information-theoretic notation (Frank, 2012). Since these variants are all equivalent statements of the same theorem, the notational preferences of theorists no doubt reflect prior views as to how the evolutionary process ought to be represented. Price's statistical formulation is in keeping with Fisher's (1930) conviction that natural selection, like the behaviour of gases, is a phenomenon properly described in the language of statistics.

Causal Interpretation

The Price equation is often said to separate the overall evolutionary change in some gene, breeding value, or other property into a component attributable to natural selection and a component attributable to biased transmission (Frank, 1995, 1997b, 1998; Gardner et al., 2007, 2011; Gardner, 2008; Gardner and Foster, 2008; Wenseleers et al., 2010; Gardner et al., 2011; Birch, 2014b). The covariance term is taken to quantify the former, while the expectation term is taken to quantify the latter. However, as Okasha (2006) notes, matters are not so simple. The problem with this interpretation is that both terms are affected by fitness differences. For recall that the second term is an average of $w_i \Delta p_i$, not simply Δp_i. This means that the personal transmission biases of fitter individuals make a bigger difference to the value of this term than those of less fit individuals.

Frank (1997a, 1998) derives a modified Price equation with an expectation term that is independent of fitness differences:

$$\bar{w} \Delta \bar{p} = \text{Cov}(w_i, p_i') + \bar{w} E(\Delta p_i) \tag{A1.9}$$

Frank's equation differs from the standard Price equation in two important respects. First, the covariance term replaces p_i, the ith individual's personal p-value, with p'_i, the average p-value of its descendants. Second, the expectation term is no longer weighted by fitness. In effect, the two versions differ in how they account for any covariance between an individual's fitness (w_i) and its individual transmission bias (Δp_i) (Godfrey-Smith, 2007a; Okasha, 2011). In the standard Price equation $\text{Cov}(w_i, \Delta p_i)$ is implicitly included in the expectation term. In the modified version, it is implicitly included in the covariance term.

Okasha (2006) suggests that the modified Price equation succeeds where the standard Price equation fails: that is, it does provide a clean separation of the effects of selection and biased transmission. In response to Okasha, Godfrey-Smith (2007a) and Waters (2011) have separately argued that this is not quite right. For, although taking w_i out of the expectation term makes it independent of variation in fitness, replacing p_i with p'_i in the covariance term has the effect of making it sensitive to variation in transmission biases. In cases in which $\text{Cov}(w_i, \Delta p_i) \neq 0$, there is simply no way to separate the effects of selection and biased transmission completely cleanly, because some of the change is causally attributable to both processes: the $\text{Cov}(w_i, \Delta p_i)$ component is attributable selection on variation in individual transmission biases (Okasha, 2011).

There is also one important technical advantage that the standard Price equation has over the modified Price equation. Δp_i is undefined for ancestors with no descendants. This means that, in cases where some ancestors have no descendants, $E(\Delta p_i)$ will be an undefined quantity. By contrast, the standard Price equation cleverly avoids this problem by weighting Δp_i by fitness, so that individuals with zero fitness contribute nothing to this term. This suggests that, if our aim is to compare the effects of selection and transmission bias in models in which $\text{Cov}(w_i, \Delta p_i) = 0$, we are better off using the standard formulation.

I agree with Frank (1998, 2012) that both versions have their uses. One must choose the appropriate version for the task at hand. If the aim is to compare the effects of selection and transmission, and if we can reasonably assume that $\text{Cov}(w_i, \Delta p_i) = 0$, the standard Price equation is best. But if our aim is to understand the response to selection in cases in which it may be that $\text{Cov}(w_i, \Delta p_i) \neq 0$, we should use the modified version.

This is why I use the modified version in my analyses of the effects of gene mobility on social evolution in microbes and of the effects of horizontal cultural transmission on human social evolution. These are scenarios in which it may well be the case that $\text{Cov}(w_i, \Delta p_i) \neq 0$. For example, bacteria that interact with bearers of altruism-encoding plasmids may be both fitter than average and more likely than average to have their genotype changed by plasmid transfer.

To apply the modified Price equation, one must invoke additional assumptions in order to avoid the problem of ancestors with no descendants. There are three straightforward solutions. One is to assume that all ancestors leave at least one descendant, but this is usually biologically unrealistic. Another is to replace p'_i with a regression prediction based on the parental genotype and the fidelity of transmission (see Chapter 6, equation 6.3). The third is to stipulatively set $E(\Delta p_i) = 0$ (see Chapter 6, equation 6.4) in order to focus specifically on the part of the change that depends on fitness differences. I make use of the second and third assumptions in the main text.

Bibliography

Abbot, P. and 136 others (2011). Inclusive fitness theory and eusociality. *Nature*, 471(7339):E1–E2.

Alexander, J. M. (2007). *The Structural Evolution of Morality*. Cambridge University Press, Cambridge.

Alexander, R. D. (1987). *The Biology of Moral Systems*. Foundations of Human Behavior. Aldine de Gruyter, New York.

Allen, B. and Nowak, M. A. (2015). Games among relatives revisited. *Journal of Theoretical Biology*, 378:103–16.

Allen, B., Nowak, M. A., and Wilson, E. O. (2013). Limitations of inclusive fitness. *Proceedings of the National Academy of Sciences of the United States of America*, 110(50):20135–9.

Allen, C., Bekoff, M., and Lauder, G. V., editors (1998). *Nature's Purposes: Analyses of Function and Design in Biology*. Bradford Books, Cambridge MA.

Allison, P. D. (1992a). The cultural evolution of beneficent norms. *Social Forces*, 71(2):279–301.

Allison, P. D. (1992b). Cultural relatedness under oblique and horizontal transmission rules. *Ethology and Sociobiology*, 13(3):153–69.

Anderson, C. and Franks, N. (2001). Teams in animal societies. *Behavioral Ecology*, 12(5):534–40.

Anderson, C., Franks, N. R., and McShea, D. W. (2001). The complexity and hierarchical structure of tasks in insect societies. *Animal Behaviour*, 62(4):643–51.

Anderson, C. and McShea, D. W. (2001). Individual *versus* social complexity, with particular reference to ant colonies. *Biological Reviews*, 76(2):211–37.

Apicella, C. L., Marlowe, F. W., Fowler, J. H., and Christakis, N. A. (2012). Social networks and cooperation in hunter-gatherers. *Nature*, 481(7382):497–501.

Ariew, A., Rice, C., and Rohwer, Y. (2015). Autonomous-statistical explanations and natural selection. *British Journal for the Philosophy of Science*, 66(3):635–58.

Arnold, S. J. and Wade, M. J. (1984a). On the measurement of natural and sexual selection: Applications. *Evolution*, 38(4):720–34.

Arnold, S. J. and Wade, M. J. (1984b). On the measurement of natural and sexual selection: Theory. *Evolution*, 38(4):709–19.

Atran, S. (2001). The trouble with memes: Inference versus imitation in cultural creation. *Human Nature*, 12(4):351–81.

Avital, E. and Jablonka, E. (2000). *Animal Traditions: Behavioural Inheritance in Evolution*. Cambridge University Press, Cambridge.

Axelrod, R. (1984). *The Evolution of Cooperation*. Basic Books, New York.

Axelrod, R. and Hamilton, W. D. (1981). The evolution of cooperation. *Science*, 211(4489):1390–6.

Bayne, C. J. (1990). Phagocytosis and non-self recognition in invertebrates. *BioScience*, 40(10):723–31.

Bell, G. and Mooers, A. O. (1997). Size and complexity among multicellular organisms. *Biological Journal of the Linnean Society*, 60(3):345–63.

Berleman, J. E. and Kirby, J. R. (2009). Deciphering the hunting strategy of a bacterial wolfpack. *FEMS Microbiology Reviews*, 33(5):942–57.

Berndt, R. M. (1959). The concept of 'the tribe' in the Western Desert of Australia. *Oceania*, 30(2):81–107.

Binford, L. R. (2001). *Constructing Frames of Reference: An Analytical Method for Archaeological Theory Building Using Ethnographic and Environmental Data Sets*. University of California Press, Berkeley and Los Angeles, CA.

Binmore, K., Shaked, A., and Sutton, J. (1985). Testing noncooperative bargaining theory: A preliminary study. *American Economic Review*, 75(5):1178–80.

Birch, J. (2012). Collective action in the fraternal transitions. *Biology and Philosophy*, 27(3):363–80.

Birch, J. (2013a). Explaining the human syndrome. *Metascience*, 22(2):347–50.

Birch, J. (2013b). *Kin selection: a philosophical analysis*. PhD thesis, University of Cambridge.

Birch, J. (2014a). Gene mobility and the concept of relatedness. *Biology and Philosophy*, 29(4):445–76.

Birch, J. (2014b). Hamilton's rule and its discontents. *British Journal for the Philosophy of Science*, 65(2):381–411.

Birch, J. (2014c). Has Grafen formalized Darwin? *Biology and Philosophy*, 29(2):175–80.

Birch, J. (2014d). How cooperation became the norm. *Biology and Philosophy*, 29(3):433–44.

Birch, J. (2016a). Hamilton's two conceptions of social fitness. *Philosophy of Science*, 83(5):848–60.

Birch, J. (2016b). Natural selection and the maximization of fitness. *Biological Reviews*, 91(3):712–27.

Birch, J. and Marshall, J. A. R. (2014). Queller's separation condition explained and defended. *American Naturalist*, 184(4):531–40.

Birch, J. and Okasha, S. (2015). Kin selection and its critics. *BioScience*, 65(1): 22–32.

Birdsell, J. B. (1953). Some environmental and cultural factors influencing the structuring of Australian Aboriginal populations. *American Naturalist*, 87(834):171–207.

Birdsell, J. B. (1968). Some predictions for the Pleistocene based on equilibrium systems of recent hunter-gatherers. In Lee, R. B. and DeVore, I., editors, *Man the Hunter*, pages 229–40. Aldine, Chicago.

Birdsell, J. B. (1973). A basic demographic unit. *Current Anthropology*, 14(4): 337–56.

Blackmore, S. (1999). *The Meme Machine*. Oxford University Press, New York.

Boehm, C. (2012). *Moral Origins: The Evolution of Virtue, Altruism, and Shame*. Basic Books, New York.

Bonner, J. T. (1959). *The Cellular Slime Molds*. Princeton University Press, Princeton, NJ.

Bonner, J. T. (1988). *The Evolution of Complexity by Means of Natural Selection*. Princeton University Press, Princeton, NJ.

Bouchard, F. and Huneman, P., editors (2013). *From Groups to Individuals: Evolution and Emerging Individuality*. MIT Press, Cambridge, MA.

Bourke, A. F. G. (1999). Colony size, social complexity and reproductive conflict in social insects. *Journal of Evolutionary Biology*, 12(2):245–57.

Bourke, A. F. G. (2011). *Principles of Social Evolution*. Oxford University Press, Oxford.

Bourke, A. F. G. and Franks, N. R. (1995). *Social Evolution in Ants*. Princeton University Press, Princeton, NJ.

Bowles, S. and Gintis, H. (2011). *A Cooperative Species: Human Reciprocity and its Evolution*. Princeton University Press, Princeton.

Boyd, R., Gintis, H., Bowles, S., and Richerson, P. J. (2003). The evolution of altruistic punishment. *Proceedings of the National Academy of Sciences of the United States of America*, 100(6):3531–5.

Boyd, R. and Lorberbaum, J. (1987). No pure strategy is evolutionarily stable in the repeated prisoner's dilemma game. *Nature*, 327(6117):58–9.

Boyd, R. and Richerson, P. J. (1985). *Culture and the Evolutionary Process*. University of Chicago Press, Chicago, IL.

Boyd, R. and Richerson, P. J. (2005). *The Origin and Evolution of Cultures*. Oxford University Press, New York.

Braddon-Mitchell, D. and Jackson, F. (2007). *The Philosophy of Mind and Cognition*. Blackwell, Oxford, 2nd edition.

Brandon, R. N. (1990). *Adaptation and Environment*. Princeton University Press, Princeton, NJ.

Brandon, R. N. and Ramsey, G. (2007). What's wrong with the emergentist statistical interpretation of natural selection and random drift? In Hull, D. L. and Ruse, M., editors, *The Cambridge Companion to the Philosophy of Biology*, pages 66–84. Cambridge University Press, Cambridge.

Buller, D. J., editor (1999). *Function, Selection and Design*. SUNY Press, Albany, NY.

Bushman, F. (2002). *Lateral DNA Transfer: Mechanisms and Consequences*. Cold Spring Harbor Laboratory Press, Coldspring Spring Harbor, NY.

Buss, L. W. (1987). *The Evolution of Individuality*. Princeton University Press, Princeton, NJ.

Calcott, B. (2006). *Transitions in biological organization*. PhD thesis, Australian National University.

Calcott, B. (2008). The other cooperation problem: Generating benefit. *Biology and Philosophy*, 23(2):173–203.

Calcott, B. (2013). Why how and why aren't enough: More problems with Mayr's proximate-ultimate distinction. *Biology and Philosophy*, 28(5):767–80.

Calcott, B. and Sterelny, K., editors (2011). *The Major Transitions in Evolution Revisited*. MIT Press, Cambridge, MA.

Camerer, C. F. (2003). *Behavioral Game Theory: Experiments in Strategic Interaction*. Princeton University Press, Princeton, NJ.

Cao, R. (2014). Signaling in the brain: In search of functional units. *Philosophy of Science*, 81(5):891–901.

Carroll, S. B. (2001). Chance and necessity: The evolution of morphological complexity and diversity. *Nature*, 409(6823):1102–09.

Carroll, S. B. (2005). *Endless Forms Most Beautiful: The New Science of Evo Devo*. W. W. Norton and Company, New York.

Carter, G. G. and Wilkinson, G. S. (2013). Food sharing in vampire bats: Reciprocal help predicts donations more than relatedness or harassment. *Proceedings of the Royal Society of London B: Biological Sciences*, 280(1753):20122573.

Cavalli-Sforza, L. L. and Feldman, M. W. (1978). Darwinian selection and 'altruism'. *Theoretical Population Biology*, 12(2):268–80.

Cavalli-Sforza, L. L. and Feldman, M. W. (1981). *Cultural Transmission and Evolution: A Quantitative Approach*. Princeton University Press, Princeton, NJ.

Chapuisat, M., Goudet, J., and Keller, L. (1997). Microsatellites reveal high population viscosity and limited dispersal in the ant *Formica paralugubris*. *Evolution*, 51(2):475–82.

Clarke, E. (2011). Plant individuality and multilevel selection theory. In Calcott, B. and Sterelny, K., editors, *The Major Transitions in Evolution Revisited*, pages 227–50. MIT Press, Cambridge, MA.

Clarke, E. (2012). Plant individuality: A solution to the demographer's dilemma. *Biology and Philosophy*, 27(3):321–61.

Clarke, E. (2013). The multiple realizability of biological individuals. *Journal of Philosophy*, (8):413–35.

Clutton-Brock, T. (2009). Cooperation between non-kin in animal societies. *Nature*, 462(7269):51–7.

Clutton-Brock, T. H., Brotherton, P. N. M., Oriain, M. J., Griffin, A. S., Gaynor, D., Sharpe, L., R. Kansky, M. B. M., and McIlrath, G. M. (2000). Individual contributions to babysitting in a cooperative mongoose, Suricata suricatta. *Proceedings of the Royal Society of London B: Biological Sciences*, 267(1440): 301–05.

Clutton-Brock, T. H. and Parker, G. A. (1995). Punishment in animal societies. *Nature*, 373(6511):209–16.

Cornforth, D. M., Sumpter, D. J., Brown, S. P., and Brännström, Å. (2012). Synergy and group size in microbial cooperation. *American Naturalist*, 180(3): 296–305.

Crespi, B. J. (2001). The evolution of social behavior in microorganisms. *Trends in Ecology and Evolution*, 16(4):178–83.

Damuth, J. and Heisler, I. L. (1988). Alternative formulations of multilevel selection. *Biology and Philosophy*, 3(4):407–30.

Darwin, C. R. (1859). *On the Origin of Species by Means of Natural Selection, or the Preservation of Favoured Races in the Struggle for Life*. John Murray, London, 1st edition.

Dawkins, R. (1976). *The Selfish Gene*. W. W. Norton and Company, New York.

Dawkins, R. (1978). Replicator selection and the extended phenotype. *Zeitschrift für Tierpsychologie*, 47(1):61–76.

Dawkins, R. (1979). Twelve misunderstandings of kin selection. *Zietschrift für Tierpsychologie*, 51:184–200.

Dawkins, R. (1982). *The Extended Phenotype: The Gene as the Unit of Selection*. W. W. Norton and Company, New York.

Dawkins, R. (1996). *Climbing Mount Improbable*. W. W. Norton and Company, New York.

De Block, A. and Ramsey, G. (2016). The organism-centered approach to cultural evolution. *Topoi*, 35(1):283–90.

De Regt, H. W. and Dieks, D. (2005). A contextual approach to scientific understanding. *Synthese*, 144(1):137–70.

Dennett, D. C. (1991). Real patterns. *Journal of Philosophy*, 88(1):27–51.

Dennett, D. C. (1995). *Darwin's Dangerous Idea: Evolution and the Meanings of Life*. Simon and Schuster, New York.

Detrain, C. and Pasteels, J. M. (1992). Caste polyethism and collective defense in the ant Pheidole pallidula: The outcome of quantitative differences in recruitment. *Behavioral Ecology and Sociobiology*, 29(6):405–12.

Dickins, T. E. and Barton, R. A. (2013). Reciprocal causation and the proximate–ultimate distinction. *Biology and Philosophy*, 28(5):747–56.

Dimitriu, T., Lotton, C., Bénard-Capelle, J., Misevic, D., Brown, S. P., Lindner, A. B., and Taddei, F. (2014). Genetic information transfer promotes cooperation in bacteria. *Proceedings of the National Academy of Sciences of the United States of America*, 111(30):11103–8.

Dimitriu, T., Misevic, D., Lindner, A. B., and Taddei, F. (2015). Mobile genetic elements are involved in bacterial sociality. *Mobile Genetic Elements*, 5(1): 7–11.

Duarte, A., Pen, I., Keller, L., and Weissing, F. J. (2012). Evolution of self-organized division of labor in a response threshold model. *Behavioral Ecology and Sociobiology*, 66(6):947–57.

Duarte, A., Weissing, F. J., Pen, I., and Keller, L. (2011). An evolutionary perspective on self-organized division of labor in social insects. *Annual Review of Ecology, Evolution, and Systematics*, 42(1):91–110.

Dunbar, R. I. M. (1992). Neocortex size as a constraint on group size in primates. *Journal of Human Evolution*, 22(6):469–493.

Dunbar, R. I. M. (1998). *Grooming, Gossip, and the Evolution of Language*. Harvard University Press, Cambridge, MA.

Dupré, J. (2012). *Processes of Life: Essays in the Philosophy of Biology*. Oxford University Press, New York.

Ebberink, R. H. M., Smit, A. B., and Minnen, J. V. (1989). The insulin family: evolution of structure and function in vertebrates and invertebrates. *Biological Bulletin*, 177(2):176–82.

Edwards, A. W. F. (1994). The fundamental theorem of natural selection. *Biological Reviews*, 69(4):443–74.

Edwards, A. W. F. (2000). *Foundations of Mathematical Genetics*. Cambridge University Press, Cambridge, 2nd edition.

Edwards, A. W. F. (2007). Maximisation principles in evolutionary biology. In Matthen, M. and Stephens, C., editors, *Handbook of the Philosophy of Science: Philosophy of Biology*, pages 335–47. North-Holland, Amsterdam.

Edwards, A. W. F. (2014). R.A. Fisher's gene-centred view of evolution and the fundamental theorem of natural selection. *Biological Reviews*, 89(1):135–47.

El Mouden, C., André, J.-B., Morin, O., and Nettle, D. (2014). Cultural transmission and the evolution of human behaviour: A general approach based on the Price equation. *Journal of Evolutionary Biology*, 27(2):231–41.

Ereshefsky, M. and Pedroso, M. (2013). Biological individuality: The case of biofilms. *Biology and Philosophy*, 28(2):331–49.

Erwin, D. and Davidson, E. (2002). The last common bilaterian ancestor. *Development*, 129(13):3021–32.

Eshel, I. and Feldman, M. W. (1984). Initial increase of new mutants and some continuity properties of ESS in two locus systems. *American Naturalist*, 124(5): 631–40.

Eshel, I. and Feldman, M. W. (2001). Optimality and evolutionary stability under short- and long-term selection. In Orzack, S. H. and Sober, E., editors, *Adaptationism and Optimality*, pages 161–90. Cambridge University Press, Cambridge.

Eshel, I., Feldman, M. W., and Bergman, A. (1998). Long-term evolution, short-term evolution and population genetic theory. *Journal of Theoretical Biology*, 191(4):391–6.

Ewens, W. J. (2004). *Mathematical Population Genetics*. Springer, New York, 2nd edition.

Ewens, W. J. (2011). What is the gene trying to do? *British Journal for the Philosophy of Science*, 62(1):155–76.

Fagerström, T., Briscoe, D. A., and Sunnucks, P. (1998). Evolution of mitotic cell-lineages in multicellular organisms. *Trends in Ecology & Evolution*, 13(3):117–20.

Falconer, D. S. and Mackay, T. F. C. (1996). *Introduction to Quantitative Genetics*. Longman, London, 4th edition.

Fehr, E. and Fischbacher, U. (2003). The nature of human altruism. *Nature*, 425(6960):785–91.

Fehr, E., Fischbacher, U., and Gächter, S. (2002). Strong reciprocity, human cooperation, and the enforcement of social norms. *Human Nature*, 13(1):1–25.

Fehr, E. and Gächter, S. (2000). Fairness and retaliation: The economics of reciprocity. *Journal of Economic Perspectives*, 14(3):159–81.

Ferguson-Gow, H., Sumner, S., Bourke, A. F. G., and Jones, K. E. (2014). Colony size predicts division of labour in attine ants. *Proceedings of the Royal Society of London B: Biological Sciences*, 281(1793):20141411.

Fischbacher, U., Gächter, S., and Fehr, E. (2001). Are people conditionally co-operative? Evidence from a public goods experiment. *Economics Letters*, 71(3): 397–404.

Fisher, D. C. (1985). Evolutionary morphology: Beyond the analogous, the anec-dotal and the ad hoc. *Paleobiology*, 11(1):120–38.

Fisher, R. A. (1930). *The Genetical Theory of Natural Selection*. Clarendon Press, Oxford, 1st edition.

Fisher, R. A. (1941). Average excess and average effect of a gene substitution. *Annals of Human Genetics*, 11(1):53–63.

Fisher, R. M., Cornwallis, C. K., and West, S. A. (2013). Group formation, related-ness, and the evolution of multicellularity. *Current Biology*, 23(12):1120–5.

Fletcher, J. A. and Doebeli, M. (2006). How altruism evolves: Assortment and synergy. *Journal of Evolutionary Biology*, 18(5):1389–93.

Fletcher, J. A. and Doebeli, M. (2009). A simple and general explanation for the evolution of altruism. *Proceedings of the Royal Society of London B: Biological Sciences*, 276(1654):13–19.

Fletcher, J. A. and Doebeli, M. (2010). Assortment is a more fundamental explan-ation for the evolution of altruism than inclusive fitness or multilevel selection. *Proceedings of the Royal Society of London B: Biological Sciences*, 277(1682): 677–8.

Forber, P. and Smead, R. (2015). Evolution and the classification of social behavior. *Biology and Philosophy*, 30(3):405–21.

Fortunato, S. (2010). Community detection in graphs. *Physics Reports*, 486 (3–5):75–174.

Foster, K. R., Shaulsky, G., Strassmann, J. E., Queller, D. C., and Thompson, C. R. L. (2004). Pleiotropy as a mechanism to stabilize cooperation. *Nature*, 431(7009):693–6.

Foster, K. R., Wenseleers, T., and Ratnieks, F. L. W. (2006). Kin selection is the key to altruism. *Trends in Ecology and Evolution*, 21(2):57–60.

Frank, S. A. (1985). Hierarchical selection theory and sex ratios. II. On applying the theory, and a test with fig wasps. *Evolution*, 39(5):949–64.

Frank, S. A. (1995). George Price's contributions to evolutionary genetics. *Journal of Theoretical Biology*, 175(3):373–88.

Frank, S. A. (1997a). Multivariate analysis of correlated selection and kin selection, with an ESS maximization method. *Journal of Theoretical Biology*, 189(3): 307–16.

Frank, S. A. (1997b). The Price equation, Fisher's fundamental theorem, kin selection, and causal analysis. *Evolution*, 51(6):1712–29.

Frank, S. A. (1998). *Foundations of Social Evolution*. Princeton University Press, Princeton, NJ.

Frank, S. A. (2012). Natural selection. IV. The Price equation. *Journal of Evolutionary Biology*, 25(6):1002–19.

Frank, S. A. (2013). Natural selection. VII. History and interpretation of kin selection theory. *Journal of Evolutionary Biology*, 26(6):1151–84.

Franks, N. R. (1986). Teams in insect societies: Group retrieval of prey by army ants (Eciton burchelli, Hymenoptera: Formicidae). *Behavioral Ecology and Sociobiology*, 18(6):425–9.

Franks, N. R. (1987). The organization of working teams in insect societies. *Trends in Ecology and Evolution*, 2(6):72–5.

Fried, M. H. (1975). *The Notion of Tribe*. Cummings Publishing Company, Menlo Park, CA.

Frost, L. S., Leplae, R., Summers, A. O., and Toussaint, A. (2005). Mobile genetic elements: The agents of open source evolution. *Nature Reviews Microbiology*, 3(9):722–32.

Gamble, C. (1998). Palaeolithic society and the release from proximity: A network approach to intimate relations. *World Archaeology*, 29(3):426–49.

Gamble, C. (1999). *The Palaeolithic Societies of Europe*. Cambridge World Archaeology. Cambridge University Press, Cambridge.

Gamble, C., Gowlett, J., and Dunbar, R. (2014). *Thinking Big: How the Evolution of Social Life Shaped the Human Mind*. Thames & Hudson, London.

Gardner, A. (2008). The Price equation. *Current Biology*, 18(5):R198–R202.

Gardner, A. (2009). Adaptation as organism design. *Biology Letters*, 5(6):861–4.

Gardner, A. (2011). Kin selection under blending inheritance. *Journal of Evolutionary Biology*, 284(1):125–9.

Gardner, A. (2013). Ultimate explanations concern the adaptive rationale for organism design. *Biology and Philosophy*, 28(5):787–91.

Gardner, A. (2015). The genetical theory of multilevel selection. *Journal of Evolutionary Biology*, 28(2):305–19.

Gardner, A. and Foster, K. R. (2008). The evolution and ecology of cooperation— history and concepts. In Korb, J. and Heinze, J., editors, *Ecology of Social Evolution*, pages 1–36. Springer-Verlag, Heidelberg.

Gardner, A. and Grafen, A. (2009). Capturing the superorganism: A formal theory of group adaptation. *Journal of Evolutionary Biology*, 22(4):659–71.

Gardner, A. and West, S. A. (2004a). Spite among siblings. *Science*, 305(5689): 1413–14.

Gardner, A. and West, S. A. (2004b). Spite and the scale of competition. *Journal of Evolutionary Biology*, 17(2):1195–203.

Gardner, A. and West, S. A. (2006). Spite. *Current Biology*, 16(17):R662–4.

Gardner, A. and West, S. A. (2010). Greenbeards. *Evolution*, 64(1):25–38.

Gardner, A., West, S. A., and Barton, N. H. (2007). The relation between multilocus population genetics and social evolution theory. *American Naturalist*, 169(2):207–26.

Gardner, A., West, S. A., and Wild, G. (2011). The genetical theory of kin selection. *Journal of Evolutionary Biology*, 24(5):1020–43.

Gers, M. (2008). The case for memes. *Biological Theory*, 3(4):305–15.

Gintis, H. (2000). Strong reciprocity and human sociality. *Journal of Theoretical Biology*, 206(2):169–79.

Gintis, H. (2003). The hitchhiker's guide to altruism: Gene-culture coevolution, and the internalization of norms. *Journal of Theoretical Biology*, 220(4):407–18.

Giraud, T. and Shykoff, J. A. (2011). Bacteria controlled by mobile elements: Kin selection versus infectivity. *Heredity*, 107(3):277–8.

Godfrey-Smith, P. (1994). A modern history theory of functions. *Nôus*, 28(3): 344–62.

Godfrey-Smith, P. (2000). Information, arbitrariness and selection: Comments on Maynard Smith. *Philosophy of Science*, 67(2):202–7.

Godfrey-Smith, P. (2006). Local interaction, multilevel selection, and evolutionary transitions. *Biological Theory*, 1(4):372–80.

Godfrey-Smith, P. (2007a). Conditions for evolution by natural selection. *Journal of Philosophy*, 104(10):489–516.

Godfrey-Smith, P. (2007b). Information in biology. In Hull, D. L. and Ruse, M., editors, *The Cambridge Companion to the Philosophy of Biology*, pages 103–13. Cambridge University Press, Cambridge.

Godfrey-Smith, P. (2008). Varieties of population structure and the levels of selection. *British Journal for the Philosophy of Science*, 59(1):25–50.

Godfrey-Smith, P. (2009a). Abstraction, idealizations, and evolutionary biology. In Barberousse, A., Morange, M., and Pradeu, T., editors, *Mapping the Future of Biology: Evolving Concepts and Theories*, pages 47–56. Springer, Dordrecht.

Godfrey-Smith, P. (2009b). *Darwinian Populations and Natural Selection*. Oxford University Press, Oxford.

Godfrey-Smith, P. (2011). Darwinian populations and transitions in individuality. In Calcott, B. and Sterelny, K., editors, *The Major Transitions in Evolution Revisited*, pages 65–81. MIT Press, Cambridge, MA.

Godfrey-Smith, P. (2012). Darwinism and cultural change. *Philosophical Transactions of the Royal Society of London B: Biological Sciences*, 367(1599):2160–70.

Godfrey-Smith, P. (2016a). Complex life cycles and the evolutionary process. *Philosophy of Science*, 83(5):816–27.

Godfrey-Smith, P. (2016b). Individuality and life cycles. In Guay, A. and Pradeu, T., editors, *Individuals Across the Sciences*, pages 85–102. Oxford University Press, Oxford.

Godfrey-Smith, P. and Kerr, B. (2002). Individualist and multi-level perspectives on selection in structured populations. *Biology and Philosophy*, 17(4):477–517.

Godfrey-Smith, P. and Wilkins, J. F. (2009). Adaptationism and the adaptive landscape. *Biology and Philosophy*, 24(2):199–214.

Goodnight, C. J. (2013). On multilevel selection and kin selection: Contextual analysis meets direct fitness. *Evolution*, 67(6):1539–48.

Goodnight, C. J. (2015). Multilevel selection theory and evidence: A critique of Gardner, 2015. *Journal of Evolutionary Biology*, 28(9):1734–46.

Goodnight, C. J., Schwartz, J. M., and Stevens, L. (1992). Contextual analysis of models of group selection, soft selection, hard selection, and the evolution of altruism. *American Naturalist*, 140(5):743–61.

Goodnight, C. J. and Stevens, L. (1997). Experimental studies of group selection: What do they tell us about group selection in nature? *American Naturalist*, 150(S1):s59–s79.

Gould, S. J. (2002). *The Structure of Evolutionary Theory*. Harvard University Press, Cambridge, MA.

Gould, S. J. and Vrba, E. (1982). Exaptation – a missing term in the science of form. *Paleobiology*, 8(1):4–15.

Grafen, A. (1979). The hawk-dove game played between relatives. *Animal Behaviour*, 27(3):905–7.

Grafen, A. (1982). How not to measure inclusive fitness. *Nature*, 298(5873):425–6.

Grafen, A. (1984). Natural selection, kin selection and group selection. In Krebs, J. R. and Davies, N. B., editors, *Behavioural Ecology*, pages 62–84. Blackwell, Oxford, 2nd edition.

Grafen, A. (1985). A geometrical view of relatedness. *Oxford Surveys in Evolutionary Biology*, 2:28-89.

Grafen, A. (2000). Developments of the Price equation and natural selection under uncertainty. *Proceedings of the Royal Society of London B: Biological Sciences*, 267(1449):1223-7.

Grafen, A. (2002). A first formal link between the Price equation and an optimization program. *Journal of Theoretical Biology*, 217(1):75-91.

Grafen, A. (2006a). Optimization of inclusive fitness. *Journal of Theoretical Biology*, 238(3):541-63.

Grafen, A. (2006b). A theory of Fisher's reproductive value. *Journal of Mathematical Biology*, 53(1):15-60.

Grafen, A. (2006c). Various remarks on Lehmann and Keller's article. *Journal of Evolutionary Biology*, 19(5):1397-9.

Grafen, A. (2014). The formal Darwinism project in outline. *Biology and Philosophy*, 29(2):155-74.

Griffiths, P. E. (1993). Functional analysis and proper functions. *British Journal for the Philosophy of Science*, 44(3):409-22.

Griffiths, P. E. (2001). Genetic information: A metaphor in search of a theory. *Philosophy of Science*, 68(3):394-412.

Grosberg, R. K. and Strathmann, R. R. (2007). The evolution of multicellularity: A minor major transition? *Annual Review of Ecology, Evolution and Systematics*, 38:621-54.

Güth, W., Schmittberger, R., and Schwarze, B. (1982). An experimental analysis of ultimatum bargaining. *Journal of Economic Behavior and Organization*, 3(4):367-88.

Haeckel, E. (1904). *Die Lebenswunder*. Alfred Kröner Verlag, Stuttgart.

Haig, D. (2013). Proximate and ultimate causes: How come? And what for? *Biology and Philosophy*, 28(5):781-6.

Haldane, J. B. S. (1955). Population genetics. In Johnson, M. L., Abercrombie, M., and Fogg, G. E., editors, *New Biology 18*, pages 34-51. Penguin, London.

Hamilton, W. D. (1963). The evolution of altruistic behaviour. *American Naturalist*, 97(896):354-6.

Hamilton, W. D. (1964). The genetical evolution of social behaviour I and II. *Journal of Theoretical Biology*, 7(1):1-52.

Hamilton, W. D. (1967). Extraordinary sex ratios. *Science*, 156(3774):477-88.

Hamilton, W. D. (1970). Selfish and spiteful behaviour in an evolutionary model. *Nature*, 228(5277):1218-20.

Hamilton, W. D. (1971). Selection of selfish and altruistic behaviour in some extreme models. In Eisenberg, J. F. and Dillon, W. S., editors, *Man and Beast: Comparative Social Behavior*, pages 57-91. Smithsonian press, Washington, DC.

Hamilton, W. D. (1975). Innate social aptitudes of man: An approach from evolutionary genetics. In Fox, R., editor, *Biosocial Anthropology*, pages 133–55. Wiley, New York.

Hamilton, W. D. (1996). *Narrow Roads of Gene Land: The Collected Papers of W. D. Hamilton*, volume 1: The Evolution of Social Behaviour. W. H. Freeman and Company, New York.

Hammerstein, P. (1996). Darwinian adaptation, population genetics and the streetcar theory of evolution. *Journal of Mathematical Biology*, 34(5–6):511–32.

Hardin, R. (1982). *Collective Action*. Johns Hopkins University Press, Baltimore, MD.

Harman, O. (2010). *The Price of Altruism: George Price and the Search for the Origins of Kindness*. The Bodley Head, London.

Harper, J. L. (1977). *Population Biology of Plants*. Academic Press, New York.

Hauert, C. (2010). Replicator dynamics of reward & reputation in public goods games. *Journal of Theoretical Biology*, 267(1):22–8.

Heisler, I. L. and Damuth, J. (1987). A method for analyzing selection in hierarchically structured populations. *American Naturalist*, 130(4):582–602.

Helanterä, H. and Uller, T. (2010). The Price equation and extended inheritance. *Philosophy and Theory in Biology* 2:e101.

Henrich, J. (2000). Does culture matter in economic behavior? Ultimatum game bargaining among the Machiguenga of the Peruvian Amazon. *The American Economic Review*, 90(4):973–9.

Henrich, J. (2004). Cultural group selection, coevolutionary processes and large-scale cooperation. *Journal of Economic Behavior and Organization*, 53(1):3–35.

Henrich, J., Boyd, R., Bowles, S., Camerer, C., Fehr, E., and Gintis, H. (2004). *Foundations of Human Sociality: Economic Experiments and Ethnographic Evidence from Fifteen Small-Scale Societies*. Oxford University Press, Oxford.

Henrich, J., Boyd, R., McElreath, R., Gurven, M., Richerson, P. J., Ensminger, J., Alvard, M., Barr, A., Barrett, C., Bolyanatz, A., Camerer, C. F., Cardenas, J.-C., Fehr, E., Gintis, H. M., Gil-White, F., Gwako, E. L., Henrich, N., Hill, K., Lesorogol, C., Patton, J. Q., Marlowe, F. W., Tracer, D. P., and Ziker, J. (2012). Culture does account for variation in game behavior. *Proceedings of the National Academy of Sciences of the United States of America*, 109(2):E32–3.

Henrich, J., Ensminger, J., McElreath, R., Barr, A., Barrett, C., Bolyanatz, A., Cardenas, J. C., Gurven, M., Gwako, E., Henrich, N., Lesorogol, C., Marlowe, F., Tracer, D., and Ziker, J. (2010a). Markets, religion, community size, and the evolution of fairness and punishment. *Science*, 327(5972):1480–4.

Henrich, J., Heine, S. J., and Norenzayan, A. (2010b). The weirdest people in the world? *Behavioral and Brain Sciences*, 33(2–3):61–135.

Herbers, J. M. (1981). Reliability theory and foraging by ants. *Journal of Theoretical Biology*, 89(1):175–90.

Heyes, C. M. and Galef, Jr, B. G., editors (1996). *Social Learning in Animals: The Roots of Culture*. Academic Press, San Diego, CA.

Hill, K. R., Walker, R. S., Božičević, M., Eder, J., Headland, T., Hewlett, B., Hurtado, A. M., Marlowe, F., Wiessner, P., and Wood, B. (2011). Co-residence patterns in hunter-gatherer societies show unique human social structure. *Science*, 331(6022):1286–9.

Hölldobler, B. and Wilson, E. O. (1990). *The Ants*. Harvard University Press, Cambridge, MA.

Hölldobler, B. and Wilson, E. O. (2009). *The Superorganism: The Beauty, Elegance and Strangeness of Insect Societies*. W. W. Norton and Company, New York.

Hölldobler, B. and Wilson, E. O. (2011). *The Leafcutter Ants: Civilization by Instinct*. W. W. Norton and Company, New York.

Holzhaider, J. C., Hunt, G. R., and Gray, R. D. (2010). Social learning in New Caledonian crows. *Learning & Behavior*, 38(3):206–19.

Imhof, L. A., Fudenberg, D., and Nowak, M. A. (2007). Tit-for-tat or win-stay, lose-shift? *Journal of Theoretical Biology*, 247(3):574–80.

Immler, S., Moore, H. D. M., Breed, W. G., and Birkhead, T. R. (2007). By hook or by crook? Morphometry, cooperation and competition in rodent sperm. *PLoS ONE*, 2:e170.

Ingold, T. (2007). The trouble with 'evolutionary biology'. *Anthropology Today*, 23(2):13–17.

Jablonka, E. and Lamb, M. J. (2005). *Evolution in Four Dimensions: Genetic, Epigenetic, Behavioral, and Symbolic Variation in the History of Life*. MIT Press, Cambridge, MA.

Janzen, D. H. (1977). What are dandelions and aphids? *American Naturalist*, 111(979):586–9.

Jeanson, R., Fewell, J. H., Gorelick, R., and Bertram, S. M. (2007). Emergence of increased division of labor as a function of group size. *Behavioral Ecology and Sociobiology*, 62(2):289–98.

Jensen, K., Call, J., and Tomasello, M. (2007). Chimpanzees are rational maximizers in an ultimatum game. *Science*, 318(5847):107–9.

Joyce, R. (2006). *The Evolution of Morality*. MIT Press, Cambridge, MA.

Kagel, J. H. and Roth, A. E. (1995). *The Handbook of Experimental Economics*. Princeton University Press, Princeton, NJ.

Kahneman, D., Knetsch, J. L., and Thaler, R. H. (1986). Fairness and the assumptions of economics. *Journal of Business*, 59(4):S285–S300.

Keller, L. and Ross, K. G. (1998). Selfish genes: A green beard in the red fire ant. *Nature*, 394(6693):573–5.

Kennedy, P., Uller, T., and Helanterä, H. (2014). Are ant supercolonies crucibles of a new major transition in evolution? *Journal of Evolutionary Biology*, 27(9):1784–96.

Kerr, B. and Godfrey-Smith, P. (2009). Generalization of the Price equation for evolutionary change. *Evolution*, 63(2):531–6.

Kim, J. (1998). *Mind in a Physical World: An Essay on the Mind-Body Problem and Mental Causation*. MIT Press, Cambridge, MA.

Kim, J. (2005). *Physicalism, or Something Near Enough*. Princeton University Press, Princeton, NJ.

Kimura, M. (1983). *The Neutral Theory of Molecular Evolution*. Cambridge University Press, Cambridge.

Kitcher, P. (1981). Explanatory unification. *Philosophy of Science*, 48(4):507–31.

Kitcher, P. (1989). Explanatory unification and the causal structure of the world. In Kitcher, P. and Salmon, W. C., editors, *Scientific Explanation*, pages 410–505. University of Minnesota Press, Minneapolis.

Kitcher, P. (2011). *The Ethical Project*. Harvard University Press, Cambridge, MA.

Kramer, P. J. (1984). Misuse of the term strategy. *BioScience*, 34(7):405.

Krützen, M., Mann, J., Heithaus, M. R., Connor, R. C., Bejder, L., and Sherwin, W. B. (2005). Cultural transmission of tool use in bottlenose dolphins. *Proceedings of the National Academy of Sciences of the United States of America*, 102(25):8939–43.

Laland, K. N. and Brown, G. (2011). *Sense and Nonsense: Evolutionary Perspectives on Human Behaviour*. Oxford University Press, Oxford, 2nd edition.

Laland, K. N., Odling-Smee, J., Hoppitt, W., and Uller, T. (2013). More on how and why: Cause and effect in biology revisited. *Biology and Philosophy*, 28(5): 719–45.

Laland, K. N., Sterelny, K., Odling-Smee, J., Hoppitt, W., and Uller, T. (2011). Cause and effect in biology revisited: Is Mayr's proximate-ultimate dichotomy still useful? *Science*, 334(6062):1512–16.

Lamba, S. and Mace, R. (2011). Demography and ecology drive variation in cooperation across human populations. *Proceedings of the National Academy of Sciences of the United States of America*, 108(35):14426–30.

Lamba, S. and Mace, R. (2012). Reply to Henrich et al.: Behavioral variation needs to be quantified at multiple levels. *Proceedings of the National Academy of Sciences of the United States of America*, 109(2):E34.

Lande, R. and Arnold, S. J. (1983). The measurement of selection on correlated characters. *Evolution*, 37(6):1210–26.

Lederberg, N. D. and Tatum, J. (1946). Genetic exchange in salmonella. *Journal of Bacteriology*, 64(5):679–99.

Ledyard, J. O. (1995). Public goods: A survey of experimental research. In Kagel, J. H. and Roth, A. E., editors, *The Handbook of Experimental Economics*, pages 111–94. Princeton University Press, Princeton, NJ.

Lehmann, L. and Feldman, M. W. (2008). The co-evolution of culturally inherited altruistic helping and cultural transmission under random group formation. *Theoretical Population Biology*, 73(4):506–16.

Lehmann, L., Feldman, M. W., and Foster, K. R. (2008). Cultural transmission can inhibit the evolution of altruistic helping. *American Naturalist*, 172(1): 12–24.

Lehmann, L. and Keller, L. (2006). The evolution of cooperation and altruism—a general framework and a classification of models. *Journal of Evolutionary Biology*, 19(5):1365–76.

Lehmann, L., Keller, L., West, S., and Roze, D. (2007). Group selection and kin selection: Two concepts but one process. *Proceedings of the National Academy of the Sciences of the United States of America*, 104(16):6736–9.

Lehmann, L. and Rousset, F. (2014a). Fitness, inclusive fitness, and optimization. *Biology and Philosophy*, 29(2):181–95.

Lehmann, L. and Rousset, F. (2014b). The genetical theory of social behaviour. *Philosophical Transactions of the Royal Society of London B: Biological Sciences*, 369(1642):20130357.

Lehtonen, J. (2016). Multilevel selection in kin selection language. *Trends in Ecology and Evolution*, 31(10):752–62.

Lerner, D., editor (1965). *Cause and Effect*. Free Press, New York.

Levy, N. (2017). Embodied savoir-faire: Knowledge-how requires motor representations. *Synthese*, 194(2):511–30.

Lewens, T. (2007a). Adaptation. In Hull, D. L. and Ruse, M., editors, *The Cambridge Companion to the Philosophy of Biology*, pages 1–21. Cambridge University Press, Cambridge.

Lewens, T. (2007b). Functions. In Matthen, M. and Stephens, C., editors, *Handbook of the Philosophy of Science: Philosophy of Biology*, pages 525–49. North Holland, Amsterdam.

Lewens, T. (2010a). Natural selection then and now. *Biological Reviews*, 85(4): 829–35.

Lewens, T. (2010b). The natures of selection. *British Journal for the Philosophy of Science*, 61(2):313–33.

Lewens, T. (2013). Cultural evolution. In Zalta, E. N., editor, *The Stanford Encyclopedia of Philosophy* Spring 2013 Edition.

Lewens, T. (2015). *Cultural Evolution: Conceptual Challenges*. Oxford University Press, Oxford.

Lewis, D. K. (1973). Causation. *Journal of Philosophy*, 70(17):556–67.

Lewontin, R. C. (1969). The bases of conflict in biological explanation. *Journal of the History of Biology*, 2(1):35–45.

Lloyd, E. A. (1988). *The Structure and Confirmation of Evolutionary Theory*. Greenwood Press, Westport, CT.

Lycett, S. J. (2008). Acheulean variation and selection: Does handaxe symmetry fit neutral expectations? *Journal of Archaeological Science*, 35(9):2640–8.

Machamer, P., Darden, L., and Craver, C. F. (2000). Thinking about mechanisms. *Philosophy of Science*, 67(1):1–25.

Mameli, M. (2004). Nongenetic selection and nongenetic inheritance. *British Journal for the Philosophy of Science*, 55(1):35–71.

Mameli, M. (2008). Understanding culture: A commentary on Richerson and Boyd's *Not By Genes Alone*. *Biology and Philosophy*, 23(2):269–81.

Marlowe, F. W. (2005). Hunter-gatherers and human evolution. *Evolutionary Anthropology*, 14(2):54–67.

Marshall, J. A. R. (2011a). Group selection and kin selection: Formally equivalent approaches. *Trends in Ecology and Evolution*, 26(7):325–32.

Marshall, J. A. R. (2011b). Queller's rule OK: Comment on van Veelen, 'When inclusive fitness is right and when it can be wrong'. *Journal of Theoretical Biology*, 270(1):185–8.

Marshall, J. A. R. (2011c). Ultimate causes and the evolution of altruism. *Behavioral Ecology and Sociobiology*, 65(3):503–12.

Marshall, J. A. R. (2015). *Social Evolution and Inclusive Fitness Theory: An Introduction*. Princeton University Press, Princeton, NJ.

Matthen, M. and Ariew, A. (2002). Two ways of thinking about fitness and natural selection. *Journal of Philosophy*, 99(2):55–83.

Matthen, M. and Ariew, A. (2009). Selection and causation. *Philosophy of Science*, 76(2):201–24.

Maynard Smith, J. (1964). Group selection and kin selection. *Nature*, 200(4294):1145–7.

Maynard Smith, J. (1975). Survival through suicide. *New Scientist*, 67(964): 496–7.

Maynard Smith, J. (1976). Group selection. *Quarterly Review of Biology*, 21(2): 20–9.

Maynard Smith, J. (1982). *Evolution and the Theory of Games*. Cambridge University Press, Cambridge.

Maynard Smith, J. (1983). Models of evolution. *Proceedings of the Royal Society of London B: Biological Sciences*, 219(1216):315–25.

Maynard Smith, J. and Harper, D. G. C. (2003). *Animal Signals*. Oxford University Press, Oxford.

Maynard Smith, J. and Szathmáry, E. (1995). *The Major Transitions in Evolution*. Oxford University Press, Oxford.

Mayr, E. (1961). Cause and effect in biology. *Science*, 134(3489):1501–6.

Mayr, E. (1964). The evolution of living systems. *Proceedings of the National Academy of Sciences of the United States of America*, 51(5):934–41.

Mayr, E. (1974). Behavior programs and evolutionary strategies: Natural selection sometimes favors a genetically 'closed' behavior program, sometimes an 'open' one. *American Scientist*, 62(6): 650–9.

Mayr, E. (1993). Proximate and ultimate causations. *Biology and Philosophy*, 8(1):93–4.

Mc Ginty, S. E., Lehmann, L., Brown, S. P., and Rankin, D. J. (2013). The interplay between relatedness and horizontal gene transfer drives the evolution of plasmid-carried public goods. *Proceedings of the Royal Society of London B: Biological Sciences*, 280(1761):20130400.

Mc Ginty, S. E. and Rankin, D. J. (2012). The evolution of conflict resolution between plasmids and their bacterial hosts. *Evolution*, 66(5):1662–70.

Mc Ginty, S. E., Rankin, D. J., and Brown, S. P. (2011). Horizontal gene transfer and the evolution of bacterial cooperation. *Evolution*, 65(1):21–32.

McElreath, R. and Boyd, R. (2007). *Mathematical Models of Social Evolution: A Guide for the Perplexed*. University of Chicago Press, Chicago, IL.

McGlothlin, J. W., Wolf, J. B., Brodie, E. D., and Moore, A. J. (2014). Quantitative genetic versions of Hamilton's rule with empirical applications. *Philosophical Transactions of the Royal Society of London B: Biological Sciences*, 369(1642):20130358.

McShea, D. W. (2002). A complexity drain on cells in the evolution of multicellularity. *Evolution*, 56(3):441–52.

Martin, G. and Lenormand, T. (2006). A general multivariate extension of Fisher's geometrical model and the distribution of mutation fitness effects across species. *Evolution* 60(5):893–907.

Melis, A. P. and Semmann, D. (2010). How is human cooperation different? *Philosophical Transactions of the Royal Society of London B: Biological Sciences*, 365(1553):2663–74.

Mesoudi, A. (2011). *Cultural Evolution: How Darwinian Theory Can Explain Human Culture and Synthesize the Social Sciences*. University of Chicago Press, Chicago, IL.

Metz, J. A. J. (2011). Thoughts on the geometry of meso-evolution: Collecting mathematical elements for a postmodern synthesis. In Chalub, F. A. C. C. and Rodrigues, J. F., editors, *The Mathematics of Darwin's Legacy*, pages 193–232. Birkhäuser, Basel.

Michod, R. E. (1999). *Darwinian Dynamics: Evolutionary Transitions in Fitness and Individuality*. Princeton University Press, Princeton, NJ.

Michod, R. E. (2005). On the transfer of fitness from the cell to the multicellular organism. *Biology and Philosophy*, 20(5):967–87.

Michod, R. E. (2006). The group covariance effect and fitness trade-offs during evolutionary transitions in individuality. *Proceedings of the National Academy of Science of the United States of America*, 103(24):9113–17.

Michod, R. E. (2011). Evolutionary transitions in individuality: Multicellularity and sex. In Calcott, B. and Sterelny, K., editors, *The Major Transitions in Evolution Revisited*, pages 169–98. MIT Press, Cambridge, MA.

Mills, S. K. and Beatty, J. H. (1979). The propensity interpretation of fitness. *Philosophy of Science*, 46(2):263–86.

Millstein, R. L. (2006). Natural selection as a population-level causal process. *British Journal for the Philosophy of Science*, 57(4):627–53.

Moore, H. D. M., Dvoráková, K., Jenkins, N., and Breed, W. (2002). Exceptional sperm cooperation in the wood mouse. *Nature*, 418(6894):174–7.

Moore, H. D. M. and Taggart, D. A. (1995). Sperm pairing in the opossum increases the efficiency of sperm movement in a viscous environment. *Biology of Reproduction*, 52(4):947–53.

Moore, T. and Moore, H. D. (2002). Marsupial sperm pairing: A case of 'sticky' green beards? *Trends in Ecology and Evolution*, 17(3):112–13.

Morin, O. (2016). The disunity of cultural group selection. *Behavioral and Brain Sciences*, 39:e46 (2 pages).

Morrison, M. (2000). *Unifying Scientific Theories: Physical Concepts and Mathematical Structures*. Cambridge University Press, Cambridge.

Mulholland, H. P. and Smith, C. A. B. (1959). An inequality arising in genetical theory. *American Mathematical Monthly*, 66(8):673–83.

Neander, K. (1995). Explaining complex adaptations: A reply to Sober's reply to Neander. *British Journal for the Philosophy of Science*, 46(4):583–7.

Neander, K. (1996). Swampman meets swampcow. *Mind and Language*, 11(1):118–29.

Nogueira, T., Rankin, D. J., Touchon, M., Taddei, F., Brown, S. P., and Rocha, E. P. C. (2009). Horizontal gene transfer of the secretome drives the evolution of bacterial cooperation and virulence. *Current Biology*, 19(20):1683–91.

Nowak, M. A. (2006). *Evolutionary Dynamics: Exploring the Equations of Life*. Harvard University Press, Cambridge, MA.

Nowak, M. A. and Sigmund, K. (1993). A strategy of win-stay, lose-shift that outperforms tit for tat in prisoner's dilemma. *Nature*, 364(6432):56–8.

Nowak, M. A. and Sigmund, K. (2005). Evolution of indirect reciprocity. *Nature*, 437(7063):1291–8.

Nowak, M. A., Tarnita, C. E., and Wilson, E. O. (2010). The evolution of eusociality. *Nature*, 466(7310):1057–62.

Nowak, M. A., Tarnita, C. E., and Wilson, E. O. (2011). Nowak et al. reply. *Nature*, 471(7339):E9–E10.

Nunney, L. (1985). Group selection, altruism, and structured-deme models. *American Naturalist*, 126(2):212–30.

Ochs, J. and Roth, A. E. (1989). An experimental study of sequential bargaining. *American Economic Review*, 79(3):355–84.

Odling-Smee, F. J., Laland, K. N., and Feldman, M. W. (2003). *Niche Construction: The Neglected Process in Evolution*. Princeton University Press, Princeton, NJ.

Okasha, S. (2002). Genetic relatedness and the evolution of altruism. *Philosophy of Science*, 69(1):139–49.

Okasha, S. (2006). *Evolution and the Levels of Selection*. Oxford University Press, Oxford.

Okasha, S. (2008). Fisher's fundamental theorem of natural selection—a philosophical analysis. *British Journal for the Philosophy of Science*, 59(3): 319–51.

Okasha, S. (2011). Reply to Sober and Waters. *Philosophy and Phenomenological Research*, 82(1):241–8.

Okasha, S. (2016). The relation between kin and multi-level selection: An approach using causal graphs. *British Journal for the Philosophy of Science*, 67(2):435–70.

Okasha, S. and Martens, J. (2016a). The causal meaning of Hamilton's rule. *Royal Society Open Science*, 3(3):160037.

Okasha, S. and Martens, J. (2016b). Hamilton's rule, inclusive fitness maximization, and the goal of individual behaviour in symmetric two-player games. *Journal of Evolutionary Biology*, 29(3):473–82.

Okasha, S. and Paternotte, C. (2014a). Adaptation, fitness and the selection-optimality links. *Biology and Philosophy*, 29(2):225–32.

Okasha, S. and Paternotte, C., editors (2014b). The Formal Darwinism Project [special issue]. *Biology and Philosophy* 29(2).

Olson, M. (1965). *The Logic of Collective Action: Public Goods and the Theory of Groups*. Harvard University Press, Cambridge, MA.

O'Malley, M., editor (2010). The Tree of Life [special issue]. *Biology and Philosophy* 25(4).

O'Malley, M., editor (2013). Philosophy and the Microbe [special issue]. *Biology and Philosophy* 28(2).

O'Malley, M. (2014). *Philosophy of Microbiology*. Cambridge University Press, Cambridge.

O'Malley, M. and Boucher, Y., editors (2011). Beyond the tree of life [online special issue]. *Biology Direct* 25(4).

Oosterbeek, H., Sloof, R., and van de Kuilen, G. (2004). Cultural differences in ultimatum game experiments: Evidence from a meta-analysis. *Experimental Economics*, 7(2):171–88.

Orlove, M. J. (1975). A model of kin selection not invoking coefficients of relationship. *Journal of Theoretical Biology*, 49(2):289–310.

Orlove, M. J. (1979). A reconciliation of inclusive fitness and personal fitness approaches: A proposed correcting term for the inclusive fitness formula. *Journal of Theoretical Biology*, 81(3):577–86.

Orr, H. A. (1998). The population genetics of adaptation: The distribution of factors fixed during adaptive evolution. *Evolution*, 52(4):935–49.

Orzack, S. H. (2014). A commentary on 'the Formal Darwinism project': There is no grandeur in this view of life. *Biology and Philosophy*, 29(2):259–70.

Orzack, S. H. and Sober, E. (1994). Optimality models and the test of adaptationism. *American Naturalist*, 143(3):361–80.

Orzack, S. H. and Sober, E., editors (2001). *Adaptationism and Optimality*. Cambridge University Press, Cambridge.

Oster, G. F. and Wilson, E. O. (1978). *Caste and Ecology in the Social Insects*. Princeton University Press, Princeton, NJ.

Otsuka, J. (2015). Using causal models to integrate proximate and ultimate causation. *Biology and Philosophy*, 30(1):19–37.

Otsuka, J. (2016). A critical review of the statisticalist debate. *Biology and Philosophy*, 31(4):459–82.

Otsuka, J., Turner, T., Allen, C., and Lloyd, E. (2011). Why the causal view of fitness survives. *Philosophy of Science*, 78(2):209–24.

Pan, J. J. and Price, J. S. (2001). Fitness and evolution in clonal plants: The impact of clonal growth. *Evolutionary Ecology*, 15(4):583–600.

Panchanathan, K. and Boyd, R. (2004). Indirect reciprocity can stabilize cooperation without the second-order free rider problem. *Nature*, 432(7016): 499–502.

Papineau, D. (2001). The status of teleosemantics, or how to stop worrying about swampman. *Australasian Journal of Philosophy*, 79(2):279–89.

Parsek, M. R. and Greenberg, E. P. (2005). Sociomicrobiology: The connections between quorum sensing and biofilms. *Trends in Microbiology*, 13(1):27–33.

Paul, L. A. and Hall, N. (2013). *Causation: A User's Guide*. Oxford University Press, Oxford.

Pearl, J. (2009). *Causality: Models, Reasoning and Inference*. Cambridge University Press, Cambridge, 2nd edition.

Pepper, J. W. (2000). Relatedness in trait-group models of social evolution. *Journal of Theoretical Biology*, 206(3):355–68.

Peterson, K. and Davidson, E. (2000). Regulatory evolution and the origin of bilaterians. *Proceedings of the National Academy of Sciences of the United States of America*, 97(9):4430–3.

Pizzari, T. and Foster, K. R. (2008). Sperm sociality: Cooperation, altruism and spite. *PLoS Biology*, 6(5):e130.

Plutynski, A. (2006). What was Fisher's fundamental theorem of natural selection and what was it for? *Studies in History and Philosophy of Biological and Biomedical Sciences*, 37(1):59–82.

Potochnik, A. (2009). Optimality modeling in a suboptimal world. *Biology and Philosophy*, 24(2):183–97.

Powers, S. T., Penn, A. S., and Watson, R. A. (2011). The concurrent evolution of cooperation and the population structures that support it. *Evolution*, 65(6):1527–43.

Price, G. R. (1970). Selection and covariance. *Nature*, 227(5257):520–1.

Price, G. R. (1972a). Extension of covariance selection mathematics. *Annals of Human Genetics*, 35(4):485–90.

Price, G. R. (1972b). Fisher's 'fundamental theorem' made clear. *Annals of Human Genetics*, 36(2):129–40.

Price, G. R. (1995). The nature of selection. *Journal of Theoretical Biology*, 175(3):389–96.

Queller, D. C. (1984). Kin selection and frequency dependence: A game-theoretic approach. *Biological Journal of the Linnaean Society*, 23(2–3):133–43.

Queller, D. C. (1985). Kinship, reciprocity, and synergism in the evolution of social behaviour. *Nature*, 318(6044):366–7.

Queller, D. C. (1992a). A general model for kin selection. *Evolution*, 46(2):376–80.

Queller, D. C. (1992b). Quantitative genetics, inclusive fitness and group selection. *American Naturalist*, 139(3):540–58.

Queller, D. C. (1994). Genetic relatedness in viscous populations. *Evolutionary Ecology*, 8(1):70–3.

Queller, D. C. (1997). Cooperators since life began. *Quarterly Review of Biology*, 72(2):184–8.

Queller, D. C. (2000). Relatedness and the fraternal major transitions. *Philosophical Transactions of the Royal Society of London B: Biological Sciences*, 355(1403):1647–55.

Queller, D. C. (2011). Expanded social fitness and Hamilton's rule for kin, kith and kind. *Proceedings of the National Academy of Sciences of the United States of America*, 108(Supplement 2):10792–9.

Queller, D. C. and Strassmann, J. E. (2009). Beyond society: The evolution of organismality. *Philosophical Transactions of the Royal Society of London B: Biological Sciences*, 355(1533):1647–55.

Ramsey, G. and Brandon, R. (2011). Why reciprocal altruism is not a kind of group selection. *Biology and Philosophy*, 26(3):385–400.

Ramsey, G. and de Block, A. (2017). Is cultural fitness hopelessly confused? *British Journal for the Philosophy of Science*, 68(2):305–28.

Rankin, D. J., Mc Ginty, S. E., Nogueira, T., Touchon, M., Taddei, F., Rocha, E. P. C., and Brown, S. P. (2011a). Bacterial cooperation controlled by mobile genetic elements: Kin selection and infectivity are part of the same process. *Heredity*, 107(3):279–81.

Rankin, D. J., Rocha, E. P. C., and Brown, S. P. (2011b). What traits are carried on mobile genetic elements, and why? *Heredity*, 106(1):1–10.

Ratcliff, W. C., Denison, R. F., Borrello, M., and Travisano, M. (2012). Experimental evolution of multicellularity. *Proceedings of the National Academy of Sciences of the United States of America*, 109(5):1595–600.

Ratnieks, F. L. W. (1988). Reproductive harmony via mutual policing by workers in eusocial Hymenoptera. *American Naturalist*, 132(2):217–36.

Ratnieks, F. L. W., Foster, K. R., and Wenseleers, T. (2011). Darwin's special difficulty: The evolution of 'neuter insects' and current theory. *Behavioral Ecology and Sociobiology*, 65(3):481–92.

Ratnieks, F. L. W. and Helanterä, H. (2009). The evolution of extreme altruism and inequality in insect societies. *Philosophical Transactions of the Royal Society of London B: Biological Sciences*, 364(1533):3169–79.

Ratnieks, F. L. W. and Wenseleers, T. (2008). Altruism in insect societies: Voluntary or enforced? *Trends in Ecology and Evolution*, 23(1):45–52.

Reinecke, M. and Collet, C. (1998). The phylogeny of the insulin-like growth factors. *International Review of Cytology*, 183:1–94.

Rendell, L. and Whitehead, H. (2001). Culture in whales and dolphins. *Behavioral and Brain Sciences*, 24(2):309–82.

Reynolds, A. (2007a). The cell's journey: From metaphorical to literal factory. *Endeavour*, 31(2):65–70.

Reynolds, A. (2007b). The theory of the cell state and the question of cell autonomy in nineteenth- and early twentieth-century biology. *Science in Context*, 20(1):71–95.

Reynolds, A. (2008). Ernst Haeckel and the theory of the cell state: Remarks on the history of a bio-political metaphor. *History of Science*, 46(152):123–52.

Reynolds, A. (2010). The redoubtable cell. *Studies in History and Philosophy of Biological and Biomedical Sciences*, 41(3):194–201.

Rice, S. H. (2004). *Evolutionary Theory: Mathematical and Conceptual Foundations*. Sinauer, Sunderland, MA.

Rice, S. H. (2008). A stochastic version of the price equation reveals the interplay of deterministic and stochastic processes in evolution. *BMC Evolutionary Biology*, 8:262.

Richerson, P., Baldini, R., Bell, A. V., Demps, K., Frost, K., Hillis, V., Mathew, S., Newton, E. K., Naar, N., Newson, L., Ross, C., Smaldino, P. E., Waring, T. M., and Zefferman, M. (2016). Cultural group selection plays an essential role in explaining human cooperation: A sketch of the evidence. *Behavioral and Brain Sciences*, 39:e30 (19 pages).

Richerson, P. J. and Boyd, R. (1998). The evolution of human ultra-sociality. In Eibl-Eibesfeldt, I. and Salter, F. K., editors, *Indoctrinability, Ideology, and Warfare: Evolutionary Perspectives*, pages 71–96. Berghahn Books, New York.

Richerson, P. J. and Boyd, R. (2005). *Not by Genes Alone: How Culture Transformed Human Evolution*. University of Chicago Press, Chicago, IL.

Ridley, M. and Grafen, A. (1981). Are green beard genes outlaws? *Animal Behaviour*, 29(3):944–55.

Robb, D. and Heil, J. (2014). Mental causation. In Zalta, E. N., editor, *The Stanford Encyclopedia of Philosophy*, Spring 2014 edition. https://plato.stanford.edu/archives/spr2014/entries/mental-causation/. Metaphysics Research Laboratory, Stanford.

Robertson, A. (1966). A mathematical model of the culling process in dairy cattle. *Animal Production*, 8(1):95–108.

Rose, M. R. and Lauder, G. V., editors (1996). *Adaptation*. Academic Press, San Diego, CA.

Rosenberg, A. and Bouchard, F. (2005). Matthen and Ariew's obituary for fitness: Reports of its death have been greatly exaggerated. *Biology and Philosophy*, 20(2–3):343–53.

Ross, C. N., French, J. A., and Ortí, G. (2007). Germ-line chimerism and parental care in marmosets (*Callithrix kuhlii*). *Proceedings of the National Academy of Sciences of the United States of America*, 104(15):6278–82.

Rousset, F. (2004). *Genetic Structure and Selection in Subdivided Populations*. Princeton University Press, Princeton, NJ.

Russell, A. F. and Hatchwell, B. J. (2001). Experimental evidence for kin-biased helping in a cooperatively breeding vertebrate. *Proceedings of the Royal Society of London B: Biological Sciences*, 268(1481):2169–74.

Salmon, W. C. (1984). *Scientific Explanation and the Causal Structure of the World*. Princeton University Press, Princeton, NJ.

Sanfey, A. G., Rilling, J. K., Aronson, J. A., Nystrom, L. E., and Cohen, J. D. (2003). The neural basis of economic decision-making in the ultimatum game. *Science*, 300(5626):1755–8.

Sasaki, T. and Unemi, T. (2011). Replicator dynamics in public goods games with reward funds. *Journal of Theoretical Biology*, 287:109–14.

Scheuer, P. A. G. and Mandel, S. P. H. (1959). An inequality in population genetics. *Heredity*, 13(4):519–24.

Schreuders, P., Lewisohn, M., and Smith, A. (2008). *The Beatles' London: A Guide to 467 Beatles Sites in and around London*. Anova Books, London.

Seeley, T. D. (1989). The honey bee colony as a superorganism. *American Scientist*, 77(6):546–53.

Segerstrale, U. (2013). *Nature's Oracle: The Life and Work of W. D. Hamilton*. Oxford University Press, Oxford.

Shapiro, J. A. (1998). Thinking about bacterial populations as multicellular organisms. *Annual Review of Microbiology*, 52(1):81–104. PMID: 9891794.

Shapiro, J. A. and Dworkin, M., editors (1997). *Bacteria as Multicellular Organisms*. Oxford University Press, New York.

Shapiro, L. A. and Sober, E. (2007). Epiphenomenalism: The do's and the don'ts. In Wolters, G. and Machamer, P. K., editors, *Thinking About Causes: From Greek Philosophy to Modern Physics*, pages 235–64. University of Pittsburgh Press, PA.

Sharpe, F. A. and Dill, L. M. (1997). The behavior of Pacific herring schools in response to artificial humpback whale bubbles. *Canadian Journal of Zoology*, 75(5):725–30.

Shea, N. (2014). Neural signalling of probabilistic vectors. *Philosophy of Science*, 81(5):902–13.

Sigmund, K. (2012). Moral assessment in indirect reciprocity. *Journal of Theoretical Biology*, 299:25–30.

Sigmund, K., Hauert, C., and Nowak, M. A. (2001). Reward and punishment. *Proceedings of the National Academy of Sciences of the United States of America*, 98(19):10757–62.

Skloot, R. (2010). *The Immortal Life of Henrietta Lacks*. Crown Publishers, New York.

Skyrms, B. (2004). *The Stag Hunt and the Evolution of Social Structure*. Cambridge University Press, Cambridge.

Smead, R. and Forber, P. (2013). The evolutionary dynamics of spite in finite populations. *Evolution*, 67(3):698–707.

Smith, J. (2001). The social evolution of bacterial pathogenesis. *Proceedings of the Royal Society of London B: Biological Sciences*, 268(1462):61–9.

Smith, J., van Dyken, J. D., and Zee, P. C. (2010). A generalization of Hamilton's rule for the evolution of microbial cooperation. *Science*, 328(5986):1700–3.

Sober, E. (1984). *The Nature of Selection: Evolutionary Theory in Philosophical Focus*. University of Chicago Press, Chicago, IL.

Sober, E. (1993). *Philosophy of Biology*. Oxford University Press, Oxford.

Sober, E. (2011). Realism, conventionalism, and causal decomposition in units of selection: Reflections on Samir Okasha's Evolution and the Levels of Selection. *Philosophy and Phenomenological Research*, 82(1):221–31.

Sober, E. and Wilson, D. S. (1998). *Unto Others: The Evolution and Psychology of Unselfish Behaviour*. Harvard University Press, Cambridge, MA.

Southall, A. W. (1970). The illusion of tribe. In Gutkind, P. C. W., editor, *The Passing of Tribal Man in Africa*, pages 28–50. E. J. Brill, Leiden.

Spencer, H. (1851). *Social Statics; or, the Conditions Essential to Human Happiness Specified, and the First of Them Developed*. John Chapman, London, 1st edition.

Spirtes, P., Glymour, C., and Scheines, R. (2000). *Causation, Prediction and Search*. MIT Press, Cambridge, MA, 2nd edition.

Stanley, J. (2011). *Know-How*. Oxford University Press, Oxford.

Sterelny, K. (2006). Memes revisited. *British Journal for the Philosophy of Science*, 57(1):145–65.

Sterelny, K. (2007). Macroevolution, minimalism, and the radiation of the animals. In Hull, D. L. and Ruse, M., editors, *The Cambridge Companion to the Philosophy of Biology*, pages 182–210. Cambridge University Press, Cambridge.

Sterelny, K. (2012a). *The Evolved Apprentice: How Evolution Made Humans Unique*. MIT Press, Cambridge, MA.

Sterelny, K. (2012b). Morality's dark past. *Analyse & Kritik*, 34(1):91–115.

Sterelny, K. (2013a). Cooperation in a complex world: The role of proximate factors in ultimate explanations. *Biological Theory*, 7(4):358–67.

Sterelny, K. (2013b). Life in interesting times: Cooperation and collective action in the Holocene. In Sterelny, K., Joyce, R., Calcott, B., and Fraser, B., editors, *Cooperation and Its Evolution*, pages 89–108. MIT Press, Cambridge, MA.

Sterelny, K. (2016). Cooperation, culture, and conflict. *British Journal for the Philosophy of Science*, 67(1):31–58.

Sterelny, K. and Kitcher, P. (1988). The return of the gene. *Journal of Philosophy*, 85(7):339–61.

Sterelny, K., Smith, K. C., and Dickison, M. (1996). The extended replicator. *Biology and Philosophy*, 11(3):377–403.

Strassmann, J. E. and Queller, D. C. (2010). The social organism: Congresses, parties and committees. *Evolution*, 64(3):605–16.

Strassmann, J. E. and Queller, D. C. (2011). Evolution of cooperation and control of cheating in a social microbe. *Proceedings of the National Academy of Sciences of the United States of America*, 108(Supplement 2):10855–62.

Strassmann, J. E., Zhu, Y., and Queller, D. C. (2000). Altruism and social cheating in the social amoeba Dictyostelium discoideum. *Nature*, 408(6815):965–7.

Szathmáry, E. (1986). The eukaryotic cell as an information integrator. *Endocyto-biological Cell Research*, 3:113–32.

Szathmáry, E. and Demeter, L. (1987). Group selection of early replicators and the origin of life. *Journal of Theoretical Biology*, 128(4):463–86.

Szathmáry, E. and Wolpert, L. (2003). The transition from single cells to multicellularity. In Hammerstein, P., editor, *Genetic and Cultural Evolution of Cooperation*, pages 285–304. MIT Press, Cambridge, MA.

Taylor, P. (2013). Inclusive and personal fitness in synergistic evolutionary games on graphs. *Journal of Theoretical Biology*, 325:76–82.

Taylor, P. (2016). Hamilton's rule in finite populations with synergistic interactions. *Journal of Theoretical Biology*, 397:151–57.

Taylor, P. and Maciejewski, W. (2012). An inclusive fitness analysis of synergistic interactions in structured populations. *Proceedings of the Royal Society of London B: Biological Sciences*, 279(1747):4596–603.

Taylor, P. D. (1990). Allele frequency change in a class-structured population. *American Naturalist*, 135(1):95–106.

Taylor, P. D. (1992). Altruism in viscous populations—an inclusive fitness model. *Evolution and Ecology*, 6(4):352–6.

Taylor, P. D. and Frank, S. A. (1996). How to make a kin selection model. *Journal of Theoretical Biology*, 180(1):27–37.

Taylor, P. D., Wild, G., and Gardner, A. (2007). Direct fitness or inclusive fitness: How shall we model kin selection? *Journal of Evolutionary Biology*, 20(1):301–9.

Thomas, C. M. and Nielsen, K. M. (2005). Mechanisms of, and barriers to, horizontal gene transfer between bacteria. *Nature Reviews Microbiology*, 3(9): 711–21.

Thomson-Jones, M. (2005). Abstraction and idealization: A framework. In Thomson-Jones, M. and Cartwright, N., editors, *Idealization XII: Correcting the Model*, pages 173–217. Rodopi, Amsterdam.

Tomasello, M. (2014). *A Natural History of Human Thinking*. Princeton University Press, Princeton, NJ.

Tomasello, M., Melis, A. P., Tennie, C., Wyman, E., and Herrmann, E. (2012). Two key steps in the evolution of human cooperation: The interdependence hypothesis. *Current Anthropology*, 53(6):673–92.

Traulsen, A. (2010). Mathematics of kin- and group-selection: Formally equivalent? *Evolution*, 64(2):316–23.

Trivers, R. (1971). The evolution of reciprocal altruism. *Quarterly Review of Biology*, 46(1):35–57.

Trivers, R. L. (1985). *Social Evolution*. Benjamin/Cummings, Menlo Park, CA.

Úbeda, F. and Gardner, A. (2012). Genomic imprinting in the social brain: Elders. *Evolution*, 66(5):1567–81.

van Veelen, M. (2009). Group selection, kin selection, altruism, and cooperation: When inclusive fitness is right and when it can be wrong. *Journal of Theoretical Biology*, 259(3):589–600.

van Veelen, M., Garcia, J., Sabelin, M. W., and Egas, M. (2012). Group selection and inclusive fitness are not equivalent; the Price equation vs. models and statistics. *Journal of Theoretical Biology*, 299:64–80.

Velicer, G. J. and Vos, M. (2009). Sociobiology of the myxobacteria. *Annual Review of Microbiology*, 63:599–623.

Virchow, R. (1859). Atoms and individuals. In Rather, L. J., editor, *Disease, Life, and Man: Selected Essays by Rudolf Virchow*, pages 120–41. Stanford University Press, Stanford, CA.

Wagner, A. (1999). Redundant gene functions and natural selection. *Journal of Evolutionary Biology*, 12:1–16.

Wagner, A. (2005a). Distributed robustness versus redundancy as causes of mutational robustness. *Bioessays*, 27(2):176–88.

Wagner, A. (2005b). *Robustness and Evolvability in Living Systems*. Princeton University Press, Princeton, NJ.

Walsh, D. M. (2007). The pomp of superfluous causes: The interpretation of evolutionary theory. *Philosophy of Science*, 74(3):281–303.

Walsh, D. M. (2010). Not a sure thing: Fitness, probability, and causation. *Philosophy of Science*, 77(2):147–71.

Walsh, D. M., Ariew, A., and Lewens, T. (2002). The trials of life: Natural selection and random drift. *Philosophy of Science*, 69(3):452–73.

Waters, C. K. (1986). Natural selection without survival of the fittest. *Biology and Philosophy*, 1(2):207–25.

Waters, C. K. (2011). Okasha's unintended argument for toolbox theorizing. *Philosophy and Phenomenological Research*, 82(1):232–40.

Wates, N. (1976). *The Battle for Tolmers Square*. Routledge and Kegan Paul, London.

Watt, W. B. (2013). Causal mechanisms of evolution and the capacity for niche construction. *Biology and Philosophy*, 28(5):757–66.

Watts, D. J. and Strogatz, S. H. (1998). Collective dynamics of 'small-world' networks. *Nature*, 393(6684):440–2.

Waxman, D. and Welch, J. J. (2005). Fisher's microscope and Haldane's ellipse. *American Naturalist* 166(4):447–57.

Wenseleers, T., Gardner, A., and Foster, K. R. (2010). Social evolution theory: A review of methods and approaches. In Székely, T., Moore, A. J., and Komdeur, J., editors, *Social Behaviour: Genes, Ecology and Evolution*, pages 132–58. Cambridge University Press, Cambridge.

Wenseleers, T., Hart, A. G., and Ratnieks, F. L. W. (2004a). When resistance is useless: Policing and the evolution of reproductive acquiescence in insect societies. *American Naturalist*, 164(6):E154–67.

Wenseleers, T., Helanterä, H., Hart, A. G., and Ratnieks, F. L. W. (2004b). Worker reproduction and policing in insect societies: An ESS analysis. *Journal of Evolutionary Biology*, 17(5):1035–47.

Wenseleers, T. and Ratnieks, F. L. W. (2006). Enforced altruism in insect societies. *Nature*, 444(7115):50.

West, S. A., Diggle, S. P., Buckling, A., Gardner, A., and Griffin, A. S. (2007a). The social lives of microbes. *Annual Review of Ecology, Evolution and Systematics*, 38:53–77.

West, S. A., El Mouden, C., and Gardner, A. (2011). Sixteen common misconceptions about the evolution of cooperation in humans. *Evolution and Human Behavior*, 32(4):231–262.

West, S. A. and Gardner, A. (2010). Altruism, spite and greenbeards. *Science*, 327(5971):1341–4.

West, S. A. and Gardner, A. (2013). Adaptation and inclusive fitness. *Current Biology*, 23(13):R577–84.

West, S. A., Griffin, A. S., and Gardner, A. (2007b). Evolutionary explanations for cooperation. *Current Biology*, 17(16):R661–72.

West, S. A., Griffin, A. S., and Gardner, A. (2007c). Social semantics: Altruism, cooperation, mutualism, strong reciprocity and group selection. *Journal of Evolutionary Biology*, 20(2):415–32.

West, S. A., Griffin, A. S., and Gardner, A. (2008). Social semantics: How useful has group selection been? *Journal of Evolutionary Biology*, 21(2):374–83.

West, S. A., Griffin, A. S., Gardner, A., and Diggle, S. P. (2006). Social evolution theory for microbes. *Nature Reviews Microbiology*, 4(8):597–607.

West, S. A., Pen, I., and Griffin, A. S. (2002). Cooperation and competition between relatives. *Science*, 296(5565):72–5.

West-Eberhard, M. J. (2003). *Developmental Plasticity and Evolution*. Oxford University Press, New York.

Wheeler, W. M. (1911). The ant colony as organism. *Journal of Morphology*, 22(2):307–25.

Whiten, A., Goodall, J., McGrew, W. C., Nishida, T., Reynolds, V., Sugiyama, Y., Tutin, C. E. G., Wrangham, R. W., and Boesch, C. (1999). Cultures in chimpanzees. *Nature*, 399(6737):682–5.

Wild, G. and Traulsen, A. (2007). The different limits of weak selection and the evolutionary dynamics of finite populations. *Journal of Theoretical Biology*, 247(2):382–90.

Wilkinson, G. S. (1984). Reciprocal food sharing in the vampire bat. *Nature*, 308(5955):181–4.

Williams, G. C. (1966). *Adaptation and Natural Selection: A Critique of Some Current Evolutionary Thought*. Princeton University Press, Princeton, NJ.

Wilson, D. S. (1975). A theory of group selection. *Proceedings of the National Academy of Sciences of the United States of America*, 72(1):143–6.

Wilson, D. S. (1977). Structured demes and the evolution of group-advantageous traits. *American Naturalist*, 111(977):157–85.

Wilson, D. S. (1980). *The Natural Selection of Populations and Communities*. Benjamin Cummings, Menlo Park, CA.

Wilson, D. S. (1990). Weak altruism, strong group selection. *Oikos*, 59(1):135–48.

Wilson, D. S., Pollock, G. B., and Dugatkin, L. A. (1992). Can altruism evolve in purely viscous populations? *Evolutionary Ecology*, 6(4):331–41.

Wilson, D. S. and Sober, E. (1989). Reviving the superorganism. *Journal of Theoretical Biology*, 136(3):337–356.

Wilson, D. S. and Wilson, E. O. (2007). Rethinking the theoretical foundation of sociobiology. *The Quarterly Review of Biology*, 82(4):327–48.

Wilson, E. O. (2012). *The Social Conquest of Earth*. W. W. Norton and Company, New York.

Wilson, E. O. and Hölldobler, B. (2005). Eusociality: Origin and consequences. *Proceedings of the National Academy of Sciences of the United States of America*, 102(38):13367–71.

Wilson, J. (2002). The accidental altruist. *Biology and Philosophy* 17(1):71–91.

Woodward, J. (2003). *Making Things Happen: A Theory of Causal Explanation*. Oxford University Press, New York.

Woodward, J. (2014). Scientific explanation. In Zalta, E. N., editor, *The Stanford Encyclopedia of Philosophy*, Winter 2014 edition. https://plato.stanford.edu/archives/win2014/entries/scientific-explanation/. Metaphysics Research Laboratory, Stanford, CA.

Zinder, N. D. and Lederberg, J. (1952). Genetic exchange in salmonella. *Journal of Bacteriology*, 64(5):679–99.

Index

Footnotes are indicated by *n* following the page number.

Made in the USA
Middletown, DE
26 February 2023

25697609R00156